W9-BNE-813

LETTERS AND DRAWINGS OF BRUNO SCHULZ

WITH SELECTED PROSE

LETTERS AND DRAWINGS OF BRUNO SCHULZ

WITH SELECTED PROSE

EDITED BY JERZY FICOWSKI

TRANSLATED BY WALTER ARNDT

WITH VICTORIA NELSON

PREFACE BY ADAM ZAGAJEWSKI

COLD SPRING HARBOR LIBRARY
The Community Center
Goose Hill Road
COLD SPRING HARBOR, NEW YORK 11724

HARPER & ROW / PUBLISHERS / NEW YORK

CAMBRIDGE, PHILADELPHIA, SAN FRANCISCO, LONDON, MEXICO CITY, SÃO PAULO, SINGAPORE, SYDNEY

33583

Frontispiece: self-portrait, pencil.

The editor gratefully acknowledges Lucjan Dobroszycki, Joanna Dobroszycki, and Jacob Schulz for their help with this book, and to Madame Rita Gombrowicz for permission to include Witold Gombrowicz's open letter to Bruno Schulz. Gombrowicz's letter and Schulz's review of *Ferdydurke,* translated by Victoria Nelson and Aleksander Fiut, appeared in slightly different form in *Antaeus,* no. 58, Spring 1987.

LETTERS AND DRAWINGS OF BRUNO SCHULZ. Copyright © 1988 by Jacob Schulz. Notes and editorial content copyright © 1988 by Jerzy Ficowski. English translation copyright © 1988 by Harper & Row. All rights reserved. Printed in the United States of America. No part of this book may be used or reproduced in any manner whatsoever without written permission except in the case of brief quotations embodied in critical articles and reviews. For information address Harper & Row, Publishers, Inc., 10 East 53rd Street, New York, N.Y. 10022. Published simultaneously in Canada by Fitzhenry & Whiteside Limited, Toronto.

FIRST EDITION

DESIGNER: JOEL AVIROM

LIBRARY OF CONGRESS CATALOGUE CARD NUMBER: 88-45056

ISBN: 0-06-015896-4

88 89 90 91 92 DT/MP 10 9 8 7 6 5 4 3 2 1

FICTION BY BRUNO SCHULZ

Cinnamon Shops

(United States edition *The Street of Crocodiles*)

Sanatorium Under the Sign of the Hourglass

CONTENTS

ILLUSTRATIONS

Unless otherwise noted, the photos and drawings are from the collection of Jerzy Ficowski.

TRANSLATOR'S NOTE

During the grueling decades of Stalinism, Russian writers of talent and independence were silenced, harassed, and ground down in penal servitude but seldom killed outright or subjected to a policy of extermination as a group or class. To the Soviet regime, the first three treatments seemed enough for writers, even for Jewish writers. But no scruples hampered German programs for rapid extermination of all Polish Jews and—hardly less desirable, but slower in accomplishment—the destruction of Polish intellectual leadership in the years 1939 to 1945. The author of the letters and fragments in this book, Bruno Schulz, was a trilingual Polish writer of original and unsurpassed gifts, Jewish by milieu and upbringing, all-European in his literary culture, as shy and unworldly as his idol, Rilke, but less lucky than he in attracting patronesses who would not only admire but also finance him. He lived in a Jewish-Polish-Ukrainian *shtetl*, Drohobycz, off the north slope of the Carpathians, in the Polish province the Austro-Hungarian occupants called Galicia, "Celtic land," for reasons, unknown to most of them, that go back some two millennia. As a gentle, lonely, oversensitive man and a compulsively unorthodox artist, his auspices in a European society that was losing its humane bearings or had already plunged into savagery were grim. He was sickly, he was destitute, he was unresourceful at a time when to be what one was could become a capital crime, and even the robust and canny failed. He was in the wrong place—Jewish southeastern Poland between Nazi Germany and Soviet Russia, in a country town where everyone knew everyone else; at the wrong time—the mid-thirties, when the rapacious dictatorships were preparing Eastern Europe for slaughter; in the wrong political climate—where, as Yeats put it, "*The best lack all conviction, while the worst/Are full of passionate intensity.*"

The present book is the third one by or about Bruno Schulz to come before the American public. Thanks to the writer's indefatigable disciple and posthumous sponsor, the poet Jerzy Ficowski, these materials (here newly arranged) were collected over the last forty years, expertly edited, and published in Poland. Earlier, thanks in part to the sponsorship of Philip Roth, Schulz's two collections of extant prose pieces appeared in the United States: *Cinnamon Shops* (known in English as *The Street of Crocodiles*) and *Sanatorium Under the Sign of the Hourglass,* published by Walker and Co., New York, and Penguin Books. It is a striking fact that Jerzy Ficowski has played a role in relation to Schulz very similar to that played by Max Brod in relation to another genius of the same culture and era, Franz Kafka. Their works might have been lost to the world but for two gifted men sacrificing much of their own careers for these artists.

—W. A.

Photo portrait of Schulz as a young man.

PREFACE TO THE AMERICAN EDITION

The small, shy drawing and crafts teacher at the secondary school in Drohobycz had tasted a few sweet moments of literary renown before he died in November of 1942, gunned down on a street in his native town by a member of the SS. His career—if we forget for a moment about his tragic death—resembles writing careers in other countries or continents. A provincial autodidact begins to write and draw for himself and a handful of close friends. He corresponds with unknown, beginning artists like himself, sharing with them his dreams, thoughts, and projects. Whenever he meets anyone who has access to the real artistic world, to real publishing houses and known writers, he is awestruck and ingratiating—as in his letters to the psychologist Professor Szuman (whom I would occasionally see in Kraków in the sixties: an old man forced, for political reasons, into a premature and complete break with the university).

Then, mainly thanks to the influence of the eminent writer Zofia Nałkowska, the talented drawing teacher becomes the literary sensation of the season and suddenly the names of the most significant figures of the prewar Polish cultural scene appear among his correspondents: Stanisław Ignacy Witkiewicz (Witkacy), Julian Tuwim, Witold Gombrowicz. Schulz comes to know Bolesław Leśmian, a poet whom he admires. He has a brief love affair with Nałkowska. He visits Warsaw where, unassuming and quiet as always, he is introduced into its literary salons. Here he has a look at the literary theater of pre–World War II Warsaw: coffeehouses and elegant apartments where, for the time being and on equal terms, the future victims of two totalitarianisms, and the future postwar functionaries of a nationalized literature, meet. Witkacy will commit suicide in September 1939 after the invasion of Poland's eastern territories by the Red Army. Gombrowicz will leave for Argentina, Tuwim for the United States. Nałkowska and Tadeusz Breza will become representatives of the Communist literary establishment.

Yet the known and recognized Schulz will not cast off his less illustrious correspondents, especially if they are women. He will write long letters to Debora Vogel, Romana Halpern, and Anna Płockier. All of them will perish in various episodes of the Holocaust.

Schulz published his works with the best publishers and in the more prominent weekly, *Wiadomości Literackie (The Literary News)*. He was, to be sure, attacked by critics on both sides of the political spectrum: by aggressive Marxist critics for not being realistic and by publicists of the extreme right for being too Jewish; yet his position was not weakened by these sallies. Schulz, who as an artist was a poet and bard of the provinces, was, paradoxically, supported and protected in the literary world by those in the political and literary mainstream. His trips to Hegelian Warsaw (aren't all capitals Hegelian?) became another source of tension in his life and thought. Of course, the luminaries of the capital had their appeal. In one of his letters, for example, he does not omit noting that he has made the acquaintance of the famous director Ryszard Ordyński, yet he returns to his little Drohobycz with relief. He considers moving to Warsaw, but always returns to his native city.

The lesser known of Schulz's correspondents are often people with deep-seated identity conflicts, people who were sometimes suspended between illness and health, who vacillated between two languages—Yiddish and Polish, were uncertain of their artistic choices, and were drawn by music and painting as strongly as by literature. They were close to Schulz because he too was uncertain of his choice between graphic art and prose, between family life and creative solitude, between Polish and German literature (he adored Rilke and Mann), between Drohobycz and Warsaw. Nevertheless, he was able to create his own sovereign and evocative vision from these contradictions and irresolutions. Even in the late thirties, when awarded the Golden Laurel by the Polish Literary Academy, Schulz still understood his unfulfilled, hybrid, lacerated correspondents. He acquired fame, made the ritual pilgrimage to Paris, sought to have his stories translated into foreign languages; yet throughout he remained in willing contact with these letter writers, for their dilemmas and conflicts were an emblem of the peripheral, of everything that was borderline and provincial—and Schulz needed to be bound to the provinces the way he needed air to breathe.

There was only one thing he defended with great ferocity and ruthlessness: the meaning and stature of the spiritual world. When in an ornery letter written at the request of a literary journal, his old ally, Witold Gombrowicz, attacked him—saying that for the proverbial middle-class "doctor's wife from Wilcza Street" the artistic world of Schulz's stories can have no reality, that for this hyper-sober personage the author of *Cinnamon Shops* is "merely pretending"—Schulz replied sharply and resolutely. The value of the spiritual world can be undermined by depression, despair, doubt, the attack of a malicious critic, but not by a mythical "doctor's wife from Wilcza Street." Here the paths of two friends parted. Gombrowicz was fascinated by the question of the value of art as seen by Philistines, simpletons, idiots; he was capable of looking at literature from the outside and inquiring into its sociological status. Schulz, on the other hand, lived inside a frail ivory (cinnamon?) tower, and he was reluctant to leave it even for a moment.

Schulz's letters frequently take up the classic theme of the struggle to maintain the tension of an inner life, which is incessantly threatened by trivial, external circumstances and melancholy. A universal theme. Schulz, like many artists, confided to his correspondents the doubts he had about the destiny of his own work. Today we look at Bruno Schulz's destiny from the perspective of his absurd death in the ghetto of Drohobycz; the shadow of this death falls across his entire life. Yet there were many normal and ordinary things in his biography. The most extraordinary was undoubtedly his talent: the wondrous ability to transmute the commonplace into the bewitching. And it is exactly here—as in the case of many writers—that Schulz's anxiety is located, in the fear that he would lack the time, the inspiration, that the agony of daily teaching would devour him.

Who was Bruno Schulz, "sociologically speaking"? In his prose, provincial Drohobycz was transformed into some sort of eastern Baghdad, into an exotic city out of a *A Thousand and One Nights.* His life, touched by the same magical wand, also eludes classification. If he had not written and not drawn, he would have been only a melancholy, Jewish, middle-class crafts teacher, the hapless scion of a merchant family, a dreamer writing long letters to other dreamers. But because he wrote and drew so fluently, he left sociology behind; he even left behind that peculiar social stratum typical of interwar Poland, the intelligentsia, or that part of the intelligentsia which could not and did not wish to join in the life of the country, was not accepted by—and did not accept—the temporary reality of the Second Republic, and sometimes longed for the fulfillment of a political, leftist utopia.

Schulz's utopia did not oblige one to wait for it; it lived in his imagination, in his pen, in his epithets and synecdoches. There is no key to Schulz's work. Almost everything is said in his stories, including the erotic obsession which he treats as familiarly and intimately as others treat their hay fever or migraines. Most frequently Schulz's prose reacts to stimuli of a purely poetic nature; if one were to write down the questions he wanted to "answer" artistically, they would be the questions of a metaphysical poet who wants to know what the essence of spring, a tree, or a house is. His is a breathtaking directness of attack, a driving passion for ultimate answers. In his philosophical-poetic curiosity, we can discern Schulz's spiritual ancestry. His writing derives from the neoromantic, antipositivistic and antinaturalistic strain of literature, inspired in part by Bergson and Nietzsche, but which in fact was a response to the real, increasingly visible supremacy of the hard sciences.

In Central Europe this neoromantic strain, which wanted some sort of undefined religion in spite of the fact that God had "died," gave birth to many poets and writers touched by a metaphysical fever; they were authors of mystical treatises and novels who threw themselves at the mystery of being on the very first page of their works. Needless to say, many who took part in this metaphysical movement suffered artistic defeat. Those who were belated, slower and more patient than the rest sometimes succeeded, sometimes achieved their own language, their own method, their own private metaphysics. Veterans of the neoromantic crisis—which reached its apogee at the turn of the century—included outstanding European writers such as Robert Musil and even Rilke, who completed his *Duino Elegies* in quite another epoch—when that emissary of the spirit of jazz, sport, and the laconic, Ernest Hemingway, was making his appearance in Paris.

Being late can be a virtue, and it certainly was in Schulz's case, just as Witkacy and Leśmian were fortunate in appearing after their time in Polish literature. Schulz's case, however, is distinct: In his work the metaphysical, imaginative tendency finds a real counterweight in the form of a specific geographic and familial reality, which the author of *Sanatorium Under the Sign of the Hourglass* draws from hand over fist, as if recalling that literature is made of body and soul and that the neoromantic longing for the final, absolute elements of the world must be confronted with a hard, merciless, provincial, and idiomatic being.

This hard partner in Schulz's mysticism is Drohobycz (a small town in the vicinity of Lwów), which Schulz did not choose just as one does not choose one's body, freckles, or genes. Schulz was born in Drohobycz, a town as modest as his own person. His imagination lived in Drohobycz, and the imagination is unbelievably sly. It is capable of praising a real, corporeal object in a manner that is highly ambivalent. It is capable of praising, augmenting, glorifying, embellishing; yet, at the same time, the embellishment and praise are the most sophisticated escape, the most elegant trick in the world, allowing us to leave our adored city! In transforming the cramped and dirty Drohobycz—in which probably only the half-wild gardens, orchards, cherry trees, sunflowers, and moldering fences were really beautiful—into an extraordinary, divine place, Schulz could say good-bye to it, he could leave it.

He could escape into the world of the imagination without offending the little town, but rather by elevating it to rare heights. Now even New York knows a bit about Drohobycz, about the Drohobycz which no longer exists; all because of the mad subterfuges of the imagination of a little arts and crafts teacher.

And only the Drohobycz created by Schulz has survived; the old, historic town, full of Jewish shops and twisting lanes, has vanished from the face of the earth. Now only Soviet Drohobycz exists, in all likelihood a masterpiece of socialist realism.

Among Schulz's favorite objects of contemplation are the seasons of the year, especially as they sweep across drowsy, provincial towns. The capital lives its own nervous, narcissistic life, while the province is a place where civilization, diluted in the peripheries, takes up a dialogue with the cosmos, with nature. In the story "Autumn," Schulz characterizes summer as the season of utopia, a lush, opulent time of the year, which

Drohobycz, from a 1910 postcard.

promises much but is incapable of keeping its promises because at its edges lurks a stingy and severe autumn, which has no respect for summer's oaths.

The sequence of utopian summer and cruel, cynical fall is a tempting metaphor both for Schulz's life—passing from the creative tension of his work to his tragic death in the Drohobycz ghetto—and for the fate of European literature, which first delights in the pleasures of the imagination and immediately afterward is doubly warned by history: the First World War and the coup de grace of World War II with its associates, genocide and vile totalitarianism. Schulz's life and work succumb to the summer/autumn schema as if the spirit of European literature needed someone who, through his fate, confirmed the development of things: the passing of the epoch of the imagination, the arrival of the epoch of devastation.

Schulz's language, its poetic and profligate riches, is characterized by great precision. The language reverberates with the same joining of oxymoronic qualities that is present in Schulz's overall artistic profile: the uniting of metaphysical passion with love of detail, of specific, absolutely individual things.

The German poet Gottfried Benn, born six years earlier than Schulz, often used the term *die Ausdrückswelt,* the world of expression. This term does not refer to any separate group or artistic direction; rather, it characterizes the work of writers who, with a greater or lesser degree of awareness, survived the tempestuous years of the neoromantic eruption and emerged dazzled once and for all by the linguistic and expressive possibilities of literature. The writers under the sign of *Ausdrückswelt* are enamored of the aesthetic force of the language, and at the same time depend on its ability to sing the melody of the inner life. Let us not expect these writers to participate in discussions on the state of society.

In Schulz's writing there appear—built into the masterly structure of the poetic linguistic fabric—the warnings connected with the inevitable approach of autumn/annihilation. Sober Adela reminds one of the character of Teresa in Elias Canetti's *Auto-da-Fé;* imagination is encircled by enemies. So, too, in these letters there is an inner tension—creative moods surrounded by enemies, by the boredom of class lessons, by life's sad exigencies. There are evil demons and good demons; the world is full of mysteries; the tramp hidden in the garden may be the pagan god Pan. But Schulz is no prophet. He does not foresee the war; he does not foresee his own death. His message is delicate and reveals itself only to trusting readers in the act of reading. It is inaccessible to critics. Schulz was reticent; he proclaimed nothing. He was even more restrained than Kafka. For him, art was the supreme pleasure, an act of expression, the amplification of seeing, speaking, the primary act of binding things that were once remote from one another. His statement was neither political nor even philosophical. That which we call Schulz's philosophy is a bird that can live in only one cage, in the captivating sentences of his downy prose.

—Adam Zagajewski
translated by Lillian Vallee

EDITOR'S INTRODUCTION

This book about Bruno Schulz is not merely a collection of letters and prose pieces; it is also a partial account of the writer's life. Relatively few tangible facts can be found here. Schulz was born in Drohobycz in 1892, and spent most of his life there. Remarkably bare as it was of external incident, his life was made up for the most part of inner events, spiritual and aesthetic quests, and writing (which in the general Slavic tradition is called, simply and boldly, *Twórczość,* "creation"), which to him is the only worthwhile concern, the exclusive purpose of best effort, and the whole meaning of existence. There is almost nothing else in his life but the daily chores and trivialities he so often complains of, which chop up his time and stand in the way of literary and graphic creation. Life in its everyday aspects and dimensions was synonymous with frustration—the source of debilitating depressions and writer's block for an artist who, like Rilke, was inept in practical matters and able to function only in his art. If at times he pursued personal contacts without distaste and even with some zeal, showing (not always sincerely) an approving interest in subjects and problems seemingly alien to his real concerns, it was ultimately for the sake of his work. He was, in a word, an extreme egoist, but with the qualification that he never strove for advantages other than those which in his judgment might benefit his art.

Schulz's extant letters reflect at most a meager remnant of an enormously copious correspondence. Had it not been for the war, which spared neither the letters nor the majority of their addressees, one could have assembled a multivolume collection of great artistic consequence and many times larger than his extant strictly literary oeuvre. As it is, we have to take our stand on the relatively modest number of preserved letters located over the years and gathered for this volume.

Contemporary witnesses and Schulz's own accounts categorize the letters according to two different periods, though this classification puts not a few of the later letters into the wrong camp.

The first category comprises letters antedating his literary debut, i.e., written before 1933. Only four of these have survived. We have two 1933 letters that predate publication of his first book; one letter to Ostap Ortwin of 1921 and one to Stefan Szuman of 1931. Only in the letter to Szuman can one discern the series of microessays, as one may call them, which were characteristic of the letters of that vintage.

What are the distinguishing marks of these early letters that set them apart from the later ones, those no longer written by a mere teacher of drawing and crafts with a secret drawer full of manuscripts, but by the author of the published and much-noticed *Cinnamon Shops*?

Schulz himself, appraising in retrospect his earliest epistolary output, writes to Romana Halpern in1936: "It is a pity we didn't know each other a few years ago; I was still able to write beautiful letters then. It was out of my letters that *Cinnamon Shops* gradually grew. Most of these letters were addressed to Debora Vogel, the author of *The Acacias Are Blooming*." A year later in a letter to the same correspondent, he remarks, "Back then I felt no responsibility weighing on my shoulders, no burden, I wrote for myself. That makes it much easier." He strikes the same note in a letter to the literary critic Andrzej Pleśniewicz: "There was a time when I put everything I had into letter writing, then my only creative outlet. It's a shame we can't carry on our correspondence retroactively. Nowadays I can't write like that any more. . . ."

Letter writing, like diary keeping (Schulz intermittently kept a diary, which has disappeared), has been on the decline for many generations and now may be considered a dead branch of literature; having lost their raison d'être, letters occur more often as an anachronistic formal device than as a creative medium.

But in the "sticks," in the godforsaken provinces, the tradition held out. Drohobycz threatened to consign the writer, far from close friends and kindred souls as he was, to intellectual and artistic isolation; letters were to combat it and break its hold. They permitted him to share reflections, to hold conversations over a distance; they reached out for a recipient. With the aid of letters, Schulz was able to share his creative reflections and ideas, sometimes developing them in the process to full-fledged works of art, as he did in his correspondence with Debora Vogel. Through the agency of letters he lamented, over and over, the bouts of depression and barrenness that tormented him and sought to enlist confessors, counselors, companions, people to communicate with. Letters enabled him to populate the wasteland of his life without exposing himself to the personal contact that never failed to abash him.

At times he gave direct expression to this need, most clearly in a letter to Tadeusz Breza: "I need a friend. I need the closeness of a kindred spirit. I want some affirmation of the inner world whose existence I postulate. To cling to it by sheer faith alone, to lug it along with me in defiance of everything, is the toil and anguish of Atlas."

He was able to find friendly correspondents, numbers of them who, fascinated by his extraordinary work, did not spare him their recognition—or, on occasion, their active support. But only a few of the numerous addressees of his letters deserve to be called genuine partners of epistolary conversations; only a few became catalyzers of his writing. Of these, two were of particular importance to the beginning of his career, and not a single letter from Schulz to either of them has been preserved.

It is not known precisely when Schulz's first efforts at writing began, or how to date those first works, which were destined only some twelve to fifteen years later to emerge from the drawer and, in part, go into the makeup of his second volume of prose, *Sanatorium Under the Sign of the Hourglass,* published in 1937. It is possible that the prehistory of his writing dates farther back, but the earliest hazy evidence points to the years 1924–25, when he began teaching. His earliest attempts at writing were spurred by his friendship with Władysław Riff, his junior by almost ten years. Riff proved the ideal "comrade on quests of discovery" for Schulz. He was a student of Polish philology at Kraków's Jagiellonian University, but had moved permanently to Zakopane for treatment of a rapidly advancing case of tuberculosis. Schulz visited him there on leaves and started a correspondence with him, which continued almost to his young friend's death, on December 25, 1927, at the age of twenty-six.

Riff was writing poetry as well as an ambitious avant-gardist piece of prose, which he himself described as "a novel of psychic adventures." He and Schulz exchanged letters taken up with the concerns of literary art, with the theory of "mythologization" they both professed; these offered little in the way of the usual exchange of news. Linked by a shared passion, both had a single interest and "matter to attend to": literary creation and its nature, a new vision and interpretation of the world by way of certain heretical aesthetic programs and processes just then taking shape in their minds.

Adam Ważyk was to recall decades later in his *Kwestia gustu* (*A Question of Taste*), Warsaw, 1966: "Bruno Schulz sent me some letters written to him by Riff from Zakopane to Drohobycz. [Riff's] boarding-house had been transformed into a ship in these letters, and a crew recruited from among the boarders under the command of a fictitious captain. The ship was bizarre, the prose supple and thickly sown with metaphors. . . ."

Although Riff was the younger of the correspondents, he had early made up his mind to be a writer and had already accumulated finished, though unpublished, manuscripts, whereas Schulz at this point devoted what spare time his teaching duties left him chiefly, if not exclusively, to drawing, painting, and graphics. With all their discussion of literary aesthetics Schulz was evidently just trying his hand at writing in his letters to his friend. Who owed more to whom in this correspondence? Did both benefit from the exchange of thoughts and creative experiences? Answers to these questions went up in smoke when the zealous orderlies who disinfected the TB victim's room at Zakopane incinerated all Riff's unpublished manuscripts and all his letters from Schulz.

Nevertheless it's reasonable to assume that Schulz's literary creativity not only began at the time of his contacts with Riff but ripened to active exercise through their correspondence. According to Schulz "A Night in July," the story published in 1934 in *Sygnały*, was "an old piece, dating back to 1928"—within a year after his literary relationship with Riff had come to its premature end.

It was at Zakopane in 1929 or 1930 that Schulz became acquainted with Debora Vogel , who had come to the resort from her native Lwów for a rest. She was to have an even greater impact on his career. Vogel was a Ph.D. in philosophy, an enthusiast of modernist painting, the author of *The Acacias Are Blooming* and two volumes of verse. A fortuitous introduction to Schulz, made through their mutual friend Stanisław Witkiewicz, turned into a lasting friendship. Within a year after they started writing to each other there began to appear, piece by piece, the brilliant stories which would become the stuff of Schulz's first book—couched in extensive postscripts which gradually took over the whole substance of the letters. As one would a serialized tale, Debora would take in, with a delight that grew with each letter, the magical recital of Drohobycz sunken in a mythical era, the stories of Jakob the father and Josef the son, steeped in equal measure in retail mercery and cosmogony. *Cinnamon Shops* thus evolved from letters meant for a single person's eyes.

There followed Schulz's official debut as a writer. His work became public property, various literati entered his ken, he was promoted into the company of recognized and valued creators of Polish avant-garde fiction. Characteristically, though he appreciated the recognition, the attention afflicted him with a tremulous sense of responsibility, a fear that his ensuing efforts would not live up to expectations. It tended to impede his work, and it also interfered with that correspondence which had so catalyzed his imagination and intellect.

Of the Vogel correspondence, too, nothing now remains but a few fragments of her letters to Schulz, written years later in a different season of their relationship, and containing only a handful of references to the fruitful exchange that, sealed piece by piece in envelopes and dropped into a mailbox, produced a masterpiece.

All but four of the letters in the present collection were written after *Cinnamon Shops* was accepted for publication. They constitute only a fraction of the great volume of letters Schulz wrote between 1934 and 1941. The selection was made by indifferent fortune, which preserved items of importance along with the odd trifle, but consigned much that is priceless and irreplaceable to destruction under the boot of a barbarism which unleashed a war and then used it to justify atrocities against men and books.

In the present book of letters were brought together, besides fairly trivial letters to editors, items of substance and consequence, among them virtually complete correspondences with Tadeusz Breza and Romana Halpern, plus selections from a lengthy correspondence with Zenon Waśniewski. Unlike isolated letters to other addressees, they constitute solid contributions to the study of Schulz's life and work, containing matters large and small of lively interest bearing on both.

The preserved letters are noticeably less rich in clues to major creative designs than in discursive passages often shot through with shrewd percepts about literary art, such as the one about imaginative literature and realism written a year before the Nazi *Kopfschuss* in the Drohobycz ghetto. But in this edition a collection of Schulz's literary essays and prose pieces, previously uncollected in an English translation, bring Schulz's larger aesthetic concerns into focus, and "The Republic of Dreams," "Autumn," and "Fatherland" are fresh examples of his luminous narrative prose.

And throughout the letters themselves there occur fragments so "Schulzian" they seem like excerpts from, or pieces destined for, published writings. Even though Schulz was neither able nor willing to expend all his literary creativity in letters to friends after 1933, his need to open his world to others finds expression in letters which remain peculiarly essential sidelights to his literary output. The form of the letter, the communication aimed at a specific recipient, always held a special fascination for Schulz, as evidenced by his use of it in various disquisitions on literary theory—such as the polemical letter to Witold Gombrowicz, which was designed as an open letter and so published.

Despite his excursions to Warsaw, which became more frequent in the thirties, and his broadening acquaintanceship with prominent men of letters, which he valued, Schulz remained an outsider and anchorite in the provincial backwater of Drohobycz—at a remove from the mainstream of ideas and events in the cultural centers of Warsaw, Kraków, and Lwów. Any sign of reader appreciation was helpful to him in lightening the burden of his isolation—an isolation which, by the paradox of his nature, was also a necessary condition of his existence. "Is it not an arbitrary and undeserved boon," he writes in one of his letters acknowledging a message of praise for his work, "that a book brings one friends on top of its other gifts?"

Schulz regarded his letter writing as an art-craft, a component of his creative endeavor which eventually became marginal, just as his letters to Debora Vogel were overtaken by their literary postscipts. Almost invariably he would make an outline of letters he regarded as important, would amend, elaborate, and polish the draft, and send out a fair copy. He did this even when writing to his fiancée.

The letters to his betrothed . . . They were not to know the fate of Franz Kafka's *Letters to Milena.* We are never going to read them; war and genocide have ensured complete and permanent privacy for this

Debora Vogel, about 1932.

intimate communication between Schulz and Józefina Szelińska. These particular letters of Schulz's must have totaled nearly 150, and they all perished together, not gradually mislaid or scattered by their addressee. Like everything Schulz left behind at Drohobycz, her answers to him perished also.

It is not by inadvertence but for a conscious purpose that the introduction to this collection of Schulz letters features many listings and discussions of what the reader will not find in this book or anywhere else.

The relics which this writer was able to locate and assemble over decades of searching have allowed us to reconstruct, however sketchily, Schulz's biography. It remains incomplete, the map of his life strewn with blank spots and lacunae. We don't even know how many blanks there are or where to try to fill them in with conjectures. For the ruin that overtook the letters did not occur as it generally does when the passage of time depletes a hoard of documents but spares a great many—gradually, without erasing the tracks of the persons involved or vaporizing whole archives. Schulz's letters were destroyed as violently as their author and his correspondents, but we can retrieve at least a few more strands of this lost network through accounts, notes, and the testimony of witnesses.

In addition to Riff and Vogel there was Maria Chazen (or Chasin), an eminent pianist who mobilized her connections abroad to aid Schulz in his attempts to make contact with foreign publishing houses. My search for Schulz's letters to her, which she had buried in the yard of her house just before her flight from Łódź at the beginning of the war, proved unsuccessful. Maria Chazen was, like Nałkowska, one of those "muses"

Czacki and Mickiewicz Streets, where Schulz was killed by the Gestapo agent Karl Güenther.

to whom Schulz paid the somewhat idolatrous homage peculiar to his susceptible nature, which combined subservience in the emotional sphere with equality in matters intellectual and aesthetic. Letters to her were doubtless of high literary quality, as they were an opportunity for discourse with a distinguished woman whose rank and virtues, real and supposed, were greatly admired by Schulz.

Schulz corresponded for several years with Zofia Nałkowska, Maria Kuncewicz, Stanisław Ignacy Witkiewicz, and Witold Gombrowicz, to cite some of the more prominent names from the literary world. And during the last 18 months before the war he exchanged letters with Thomas Mann.

Mann, next to Rilke the foremost deity in Schulz's Parnassus, received from Schulz in 1938 the typescript of the only fiction ever written by Schulz in German, titled *Die Heimkehr* ("The Homecoming"), with a covering letter. This started a correspondence, which was still in progress in 1939. Mann's letters, of course, were lost with the rest of Schulz's belongings, but Schulz's letters to Mann may yet appear, although their whereabouts are still uncertain after decades of searching.

Zofia Nałkowska, the distinguished patroness and friend of the author of *Cinnamon Shops,* promised in 1954 to send me some fragments of Schulz's letters to her, explaining that she had to copy them out and stipulating that if they were to be published she would prefer "in view of their private character" that their addressee not be identified. Nałkowska died the following December, however, with her promise unfulfilled. Later, a thorough search of Nałkowska's papers among the archival materials deposited in the National Library in Warsaw turned up no letters from Schulz.

As it turns out the evidence suggests that all letters to Nałkowska from Schulz were reduced to ashes in 1944 in Warsaw. Nałkowska herself affirmed this in her *Dzienniki czasu wajny (Wartime Diaries),* published posthumously in 1970. But in passages of a diary pre-dating the war, there are two small handwritten insertions representing two sentences from Schulz's letters. Perhaps it was these quotations that Nałkowska had in mind.

In the *Diaries* we find, besides those textual relics, much interesting material relating to the letters and their appraisal by Nałkowska, as well as to Schulz's person and the bonds between the two friends. In this regard, the *Diaries* are a revelatory source which adds to Schulz's biography a previously unknown chapter, and to the gallery of women in his life still another remarkable figure.

The extant remnant of Schulz's letters contains almost nothing about Nałkowska except for references to her help in getting him published. One exception occurs in a letter to Zenon Waśniewski, where he permits himself the following discreet mention: "It was very nice in Warsaw. I was there six days, which I spent mainly with Nałkowska, my patroness and, I may say, friend."

Her diaries also confirm what one may deduce from examining the variety of his letters. He tried to give each correspondent a piece of himself (glad to shape it to the assumed needs or wishes of the person concerned) which he felt would be congenial and expected. Without ceasing to be himself—he was too strong a creative personality for that—he clearly "fraternized" with his correspondents, with each in a different manner, sharing with them only that portion of his own resources which his view of their personal or artistic styles suggested. It was part of his attempt, perhaps, to shepherd his creative and literary reserves.

But Schulz was, as he himself put it at one point, a "reactive character," and on those grounds alone it is not surprising that his letters to Waśniewski were somewhat "Waśniewskian," those to Nałkowska, "Nałkowskian"—if one may judge from two snippets singled out by the novelist precisely for the trenchancy and beauty *she* found in them. There are no formulations to be found in any of the letters available to us that come as close to being a blend of their respective manners, a "Nałkowsko-Schulzian style," as the first quotation excerpted by the lady of the *Diaries:* "When God uttered you, he already uttered me in you as well. Why did I utter myself once more, why did I commit such a pleonasm?"

Nałkowska's reaction to Schulz's letters, to the quality of their content and form, was unequivocal. She stated in the *Diaries* that they were of exceptional power and beauty, and ranked them as works of art. Adding this to the evidence of the Riff and Vogel correspondence, one might wonder if Schulz was an artist in the medium of letters whom a combination of circumstances—fortunately for us—turned into a writer of fiction, but also if, in a conflict between ambition and a need for privacy, this metamorphosis contributed something to the tormenting paralysis of his powers he experienced in the late thirties.

One may still hope that more of Schulz's legacy of letters will yet be found, and that manuscripts which the war did not devour may still emerge from whatever nooks and corners now hide them. Although the present collection, with its necessarily fortuitous range of "selections by survival," falls short of representing Schulz's full epistolary oeuvre, there emerges from it a portrait of the author of such power, and, at times, involuntary detachment, as it would be idle to seek in the letters or autobiographies of writers absorbed in externals, in the flow of surrounding affairs and events—writers who capture and register these in the raw, so to speak, and mine them for personal meanings. Here we find a portrayal of the inner self, and accordingly we find very little of the world of facts, the surface of daily life, the "chaff of time." Schulz's mind was remote from the chronicling urge in even the broadest and most metaphorical sense; he neglected everything that wasn't grist for his mill, that he could not "use creatively," as he put it. There are enough references to the everyday routine of his Drohobycz existence and its usually chafing realia to give the reader an idea of his small-scale curriculum vitae, but it is his "spiritual biography" that emerges more fully: the psychic likeness of a man to whom writing meant life.

—Jerzy Ficowski
Warsaw

Schulz on the front steps of his house, about 1933.

LETTERS AND ESSAYS

1921–1941

TO OSTAP ORTWIN

Ostap Ortwin, pseudonym for Oskar Katzenellenbogan (1876–1942), was a respected literary and drama critic, though eclectic in his approach and not in the mainstream of critical analysis in his country. He took little part in controversies and rarely promulgated his work. The collection of his essays and critical treatises covering a number of years, Proby Przekrojów *(approximately* Cross-Sections*), appeared only in 1935, with no apparent effort by the author to get them published. For many years, until the outbreak of World War II, he was on the board of the Związek Literatów (Society of Literati or Literary Society) of Lwów, and later served as its president, but after that he published little or no criticism. This retirement permitted private expression of his views and judgments within a small circle, however, and a close friend of Ortwin's, Herman Sternbach, told Schulz of Ortwin's "positive reaction" to* Cinnamon Shops.[1]

Warsaw, May 20, 1921
Plac G[2]

I

Dear Sir:

Though I have been in Warsaw a few days, only yesterday did I have the opportunity to call on Mr. Horzyca[3], to whom by your kind suggestion I was to turn for advice and support of my aspirations.

It came as a pleasant surprise to learn that I was not unknown to Wilam Horzyca, that he had been advised of my coming and received me with such cordial affability that I am genuinely happy to have made the aquaintance of so worthy a man and one so well disposed toward me.

It was not hard for me to guess to whom I owed so friendly a disposition toward me on Mr. Horzyca's part. As a matter of fact in the end he disclosed to me that you, dear sir, had written warmly on my behalf of your own accord and asked him to take me under his wing, though there had been no thought of a letter of recommendation at the time.

I am truly grateful to you, dear sir, for the goodwill and interest you show in furthering my artistic aspirations, although I do not know how I could have deserved this and can only hope that one day I shall be able to prove your confidence well placed.

As a result of many new things I have seen, I labor under an oppressive consciousness of my own shortcomings and general backwardness.

Mr. Horzyca has recommended me to Skoczylas,[4] whom I am going to see tomorrow and in whose school I may start working. Mr. Horzyca will also introduce me to Kramsztyk.[5]

I took the liberty of enclosing with this letter one pencil sketch as well as some graphics[6]—I have been struggling with this temptation ever since I got back from Lwów—in the hope that you, dear sir, will not deny me the very real pleasure your acceptance of this trifle will give me.

With renewed heartfelt thanks and assurances of my high esteem, I am

Sincerely yours
Bruno Schulz

2

Dear Sir:

I have long sought a pretext to recall myself to your mind after so many years.[7] It was a great pleasure to hear from Ludwik[8] Lille and simultaneously from H. Sternbach[9] that you had read *Cinnamon Shops* and responded very favorably.

I felt I should express to you what profound satisfaction your endorsement gives me. For some considerable time the prospect of my book's coming before the bar of your judgment has given me pause.

Do you recall, my dear sir, that it was yourself, fifteen years ago, who discovered me as a painter? It happened at the home of Dr. Roman Aleksandrowicz.[10] Thanks to your recommendation I

Ostap Ortwin, about 1900.

made the acquaintance of Karol Irzykowski,[11] whom I had long hoped to meet. I was unable, though, to make use of this acquaintanceship later because of the formidable inhibitions I suffered at the time. Even now, years later, this feeling of constraint is revived in me upon contact with Irzykowski, leaving me in no condition to talk with him about anything. Please forgive me, dear sir, if I have perhaps written to you without adequate purpose.

I am, with profound respect,

Yours
Bruno Schulz

Drohobycz [now Drogobych, U.S.S.R],
10 Floriańska Street
May 15, 1935

TO STEFAN SZUMAN

The first of Schulz's extant letters to Professor Szuman was written in 1932, when Schulz was trying to get his recently completed manuscript (Cinnamon Shops) *published. At that point his work was known only to a few friends and acquaintances, Szuman among them. Stefan Szuman (1889–1972) was a psychologist and author of numerous treatises on psychology and its points of connection with pedagogy and aesthetics. Szuman became acquainted with Schulz at Żywiec, when Schulz participated in a vacation workshop for teachers of drawing. "One evening," writes Szuman in a letter dated January 25, 1968, "he came up to my table in the hotel lobby, where I was relaxing by myself. He declared that my lectures had won his trust, and that this motivated his request to me to read the typescript of his narratives." The professor read both the pieces—sections of a quasi-novel which, according to him, were to be named "Reminiscences of Father" or something like it—in a few hours that night. "I was dazzled," he said. He persuaded Schulz to give the whole book the title of one of its stories, "Cinnamon Shops," promised to lend his support to its publication and draw it to the attention of Kazimierz Czachowski, which he did after his return to Kraków. As it turned out it was not so much his influence as that of Zofia Nałkowska [see editor's note p. 46] that decided the matter. Szuman for his part gave Schulz typescripts of his poems, which were published the following year in the volume titled* Drzwi uchylone (Door Ajar)*, under the pseudonym Łukasz Flis.*

Schulz's first letter to Szuman consists largely of flattery and only ostensibly of real judgments of Szuman's verses; but the marginal digressions are interesting. One may wonder why Schulz should have made even glancing comparisons to the Rilke he worshipped, much less have devoted panegyrics to the unexceptional poetry of an otherwise worthy scholar. Unknown as Schulz was, he must have been hungry for praise and seen in Szuman an access to the publishing world.

Apart from the self-serving aspect of the letter, it is fascinating for its substantive content, constituting as it does a little cycle of microessays against the backdrop of the main thematic burden Schulz had shouldered. One of these is the description of the dream he remembered from his childhood. It is a startling example of the self-reflexive nature of Schulz's imagination, which finds expression also in the reviews he writes—a tendency to search for links to the complex layers of his own world in the work of others.

Żywiec, July 24, 1932

3

My dear Professor:

A letter to you has been waiting on my desk—a letter in which I felt compelled to justify what was thought by some a piratical raid into your territory, by which I obtruded myself and my work upon your notice. I raised a claim in that letter to be a part of that world, that atmosphere which the creators of spiritual universes partake of. My concern was to be accepted into the family of creative spirits, to feel that my world borders on other worlds, that at those borders these worlds cross and interpenetrate, exchanging currents and ripples. In this letter I attempted to explain why I am not satisfied with crystallizations of the spirit or intellect, objectivized intellectual constructs contained in systems, in books. What accounts for the strange fascination exerted by the living individuality, for the amazing charm of communicating with it? It's as if a certain concentration of thought took place around the heads of creative people, whirlpools and upheavals in the mental atmosphere, some sort of ill-defined but creative plasma, into which we plunge as into a spring storm, ourselves full of discharges and internal explosions. That's why I felt such excitement, such tumult, during your lectures.[1] The subject as such, the questions broached, were of secondary importance. What was important was the plane, the intellectual level on which they circulated—the class and manner of thought—certain imponderables that, separately absorbed on the subconscious plane, condensed collectively into the perception of a magnificent structure that made the heart swell, as the sight of a woman we know nothing about can pierce us with a sudden shock of certainty that she has all those qualities, hidden and unidentifiable even to ourselves, that our nature yearns for so intensely.

That letter, those justifying arguments, turned out to be unnecessary, rendered obsolete by your letter.

I found an echo, a stronger and fuller resonance than I could have dreamed of.

For this I am deeply grateful to you. And there was more still.

You made this resonance truly full, you increased its dimensions by the glimpse you gave me of your extraordinary poetic creation. I know the value of this and I am deeply grateful. I am far from any idea of appraising them critically. Those poems were a full and joyous experience for me; they were like an expansion of my own world into a new, strange, yet somehow familiar outlying region, the discovery in my town of some long-lost street. I may be wrong, but I feel we must have been on close neighborly terms somewhere, as if we had once knocked against the same wall from opposite sides. This seems a strange and happy closeness to me, and I fear I may be too rashly demolishing the distance between us. I console myself with the thought that I wasn't first to do this. For that matter, in the realm of intellect, distance loses its authority.

I have no literary education; I don't know contemporary poetry and am unable to establish the genealogy, the proper niche of these poems. The only comparison that comes readily to mind is with Rilke, godlike Rilke.[2] I am suggesting a very quiet, self-isolated world; one has to withdraw very far from the tumult and descend very deep to hear this poetry. Narcissism, solitude, seclusion inside a glass globe.

The state of spellbound suspension within a personal solitude, this cutting oneself off from life and action—the delight and tragedy of it ("Dance with Oneself"[3])—brings to mind my truest and profoundest dream, which I dreamed at age seven, a dream that foretold my fate. In my dream I am in a forest at night, in the dark; I cut off my penis with a knife, scoop out a little cavity in the earth, and bury it there. This is the antecedent, as it were, the part of the dream without emotional tone. What follows is the real dream: I come to my senses, bring my conscious mind to bear on the atrocity, the horror of the sin I have committed. I refuse to believe that I really committed it and keep finding to my despair that it is so, that what I have perpetrated is irrevocable. I seem already to be beyond time, *sub specie aeternitatis,* an eternity that cannot be anything else for me now but a dreadful consciousness of guilt, awareness of irreparable loss down through the eons. I am condemned forever, and the form this takes is public confinement in a glass retort, from which I shall never escape. That feeling of interminable torment, damnation through ages uncounted, I shall never forget. How is one to explain, at such an age, the symbolic charge, the semantic potential of this dream, which I have been unable to exhaust to this day? Here I see a point of contact with the glass house ("the prepared exhibit"[4]).

In "Death and Dream"[5] the third stanza is a marvel: "The world was lost like a silver spoon. Mother poured the whole sleep-

Old synagogue at Drohobycz.

Ancient wooden church of St. Jur at Drohobycz.

ing potion into me, and long did she watch over me."

Here you reach for umbilical archimages, for that depth where we were closest to being itself, for visions belonging to those long, incurably afflicted winter nights when we keened in an endless festering whimper over the severed end of the umbilical cord.

That poem, as well as "Dance with Oneself," I don't fully understand yet. "Colloquy"[6] is a wonderful thing, bringing to mind the finest lines of Rilke's. You have a similar way of working with internal rhyme and the leitmotif of a single rhyme sound extending over several stanzas. This is an immensely effective and creative device, unfolding the word into some new dimension, teasing it out to a new tonal-semantic reach.

The same device applied in "Diana"[7] yielded a sort of wondrous old tapestry, full of secret life, a serpentine writhing, a dense jungle of plant growth, as it reproduces and bursts forth in the mythological ages that unfold in the life of the species and the individual. This interbraiding of the pantheistic mythology of the species with the individual mythology of the child, which has to do with tapestry and furniture, seems to me legitimate, very much on target and real, since these two mythologies in a strange way interpret and complement each other. This piece has the marvelous plenitude, wealth, and perfection of Rilke's mythological legends or "histories." You can read it backward and forward and in any direction; it is all meat and live, thick growth. Each poem has its particular magic—"Crows,"[8] for instance, which I cannot read without being strangely moved. (Similar elements, or germs, occur in my introduction to "Birds."[9])

Or take "Quiet on the Table,"[10] a still life brought by its intensity to a metaphysical shimmer, a secret mutter of spellbound things wanting to speak out—a thrust analogous to the *Neue Sachlichkeit*[11] in German painting. And the splendid "Tower of Babel,"[12] whose first two stanzas are especially outstanding.

Please forgive me for picking out, discriminating, and thereby seeming to pass judgment. I am far from doing that, but it is in the nature of things that certain parts make a stronger impression on me than others.

I must quote one more lovely place: "Has opened the leafy umbrella wide,/As if rain were spattering; the gear on the table looks in my eyes/As if something were happening . . . " ("Quiet on the Table").

Maybe I haven't been with these poems long enough to understand them fully. They are the kind that develop and proliferate as one communicates with them. May I consider them my property? You would give me great joy if you were to send me more of your poems. Don't you intend to publish them? I thank you once again

Number 10 Floriańska Street.

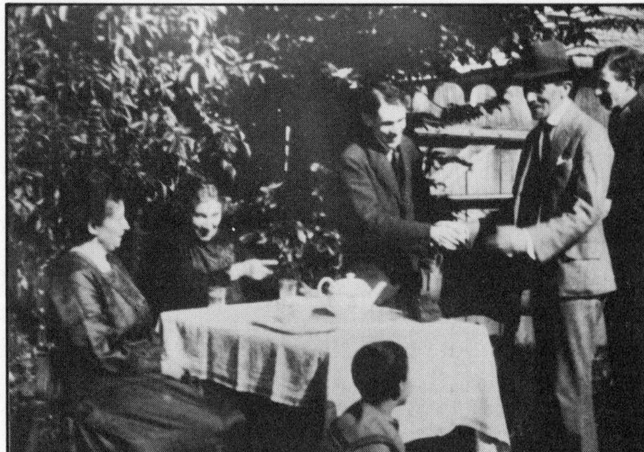

Schulz family, about 1920. From the left: Hania Hoffman, Bruno's sister; Henrietta Schulz, his mother; Bruno Schulz; Izydor, his brother; Ludwik Hoffman, his nephew; foreground, back to camera, Bruno's younger nephew Zygmunt Hoffman.

for the aesthetic experience you have granted me, one that, next to the impact of Rilke's work, is among the profoundest I have received from poetry.

The book on visions induced by mescaline aroused my curiosity; it will be a real pleasure to read it, and with your permission, dear Professor, I will share my impressions and observations with you. (I hope you will forgive me, but in the intermonadic part of our exchanges the common modes of address seemed out of place to me.)

Thank you very much for your efforts in the matter of getting my book published. I don't know what claim I have on your time and efforts. It may ease matters if I tell you, dear Professor, that my brother,[13] who is well to do, promised me he would make a financial contribution toward the publication of this work; this means he would undertake to assume half the cost, and if need be the total. Thus it would mainly be a matter of finding a reputable publishing firm, well known in the trade and able to give its titles appropriate publicity, and of arranging for a suitable dust jacket. The frontispiece I will draw myself. I have been thinking of illustrating this book with woodcuts inserted into the body of the text, like books of the early nineteenth century; but I don't know if I am going to do it.[14] I am anxious to get this book out at last, for the intellectual climate is growing more unfavorable to it with every passing day.

Once again let me thank you very warmly, dear Professor. I remain, with deep respect,

Bruno Schulz

4 Drohobycz, October 22, 1933

Dear Professor:

Thank you warmly for your thoughtful gift [typescript of Szuman's poetry collection *Drzwi uchylone (Door Ajar)*]. That book has given me genuine pleasure. I started on it at once and felt a familiar redolence, as in a house from one's past.

I am still ensconced in the opening cycles, haven't had time to delve into the depth of this work, which branches out and proliferates its detail like a forest. I close it each time with the feeling I had as a child when putting away a favorite toy: the sense of owning a treasure, a Sesame I didn't need to try to exhaust all at once.

When I have read it all, I'll write you—though I can see now that one really should deal with every poem separately, each being a self-contained microcosm.

I see the essential property of this verse in its being "occasional poetry" in the noblest sense of the term, memoranda of internal adventures, a diary of metaphysical experiences, the fact that each poem does not come into being as the result of some method or

Pencil portrait of Stanisław Weingarten, Schulz's friend from childhood, 1919.

India-ink sketch for book plate for Weingarten, 1919.

Book plate for Weingarten, about 1920.

Untitled pencil and ink-wash drawing, 1921. Schulz, Weingarten, and models.

Self-portrait, 1920s. Pencil and ink-wash drawing. (Private collection, Lvóv.)

formal stance or static disposition but is unforeseen and without premise, arising from the givens of the moment, crystallizing all at that moment, developing from its dialectic, growing from its resources. In vain do I search for traces of some manner, some formal trick common to all this body of poetry. Each poem grows out of itself, unlike any other, knowing nothing besides itself. Each turns up as if it had no predecessors, as if it were the first specimen of a new species.

I am struck by the self-sufficiency, independence, privacy, and absolute candor of this poetry. Many years ago, I remember, Irzykowski in an introduction to a book of his poems drew an ideal picture of such a lyric—completely private, depatheticized—but at the time he could find no example for it. Your volume seems to me the realization of that ideal.

I really have no business saying these things. They belong to the critic, whose comparing and appraising view I do not and cannot arrogate to myself. I ought rather to have spoken of how those worlds of yours secretly percolate into my mind, how each of them fills me with a deep joy of recognition, a kind of anamnesis, a sense of glittering treasures now becoming accessible and palpable. I am in my own trusted element here, deeply suited by this neighborhood of things near and small in which chinks open up to infinity. I feel this much more vividly than a year ago, when I experienced with some poems a certain consternation in the face of such depatheticized form, remote from convention, constantly reborn from the moment's rhythm.

This book will always be close to me. The mere awareness of its existence nourishes and cheers as a testimony of the reality and wealth of that inner world to whose existence I too am committed.

It has been a long time since I last wrote—please do not think I had forgotten. I meant my letter to accompany my book [*Cinnamon Shops*], which I have been waiting to see published since August. It will be brought out by *Rój,* which offered me better terms than Kraków did. That book has secured me a great deal of goodwill in various quarters; above all, I owe to it the friendship of Zofia Nałkowska. But I won't forget you were the first to take to it.

Please give my respects to Madame Szuman and to Grażynka [the Szumans' daughter]. With warm personal greetings, I am

Bruno Schulz

Zofia Nałkowska, about 1930.

It was thanks to Zofia Nałkowska's backing that Cinnamon Shops *was accepted for publication by* Rój*: she had become his patroness. Nałkowska (1884–1954), a prose writer, dramatist, and essayist, was considered an outstanding representative of the "psychological school" in Polish letters. During World War II she was active in the literary underground, organizing among other things the attempt to smuggle Schulz out of Drohobycz and take him to a safe hiding place in Warsaw. Although she and Schulz maintained a close correspondence after the publication of* Shops*, and her name appears frequently in this collection, his letters to her from the period 1933 to 1939 were burned during the Warsaw uprising.*

5

My dear Professor:

My heartfelt thanks for your book [the previous collection in book form]. I hadn't expected such a hefty tome; I am delighted and will sit down to it with genuine pleasure.

At Zofia Nałkowska's in Warsaw I found a volume of your poetry among the books she had set aside for priority reading. She went over some of the introductory poems in my presence and found them very intriguing. She singled out "*Cisza na stole*" ("Quiet on the Table") and "*Szlafrok*" ("Dressing Gown") in words filled with approval and sympathy. I took this to be the right moment to lift the incognito—leaving her much surprised and interested. When further reading was precluded by the visit of Ordynski,[15] she declared she would go back to it. I have the impression that she already knew something about you from Witkiewicz, who had visited her recently.

Miss Nałkowska will leave very shortly for Zakopane for the whole season. I am much intrigued by the idea of a personal meeting between the two of you and the intellectual fireworks that might result from two such minds rubbing against each other.

Any day now I expect the publication of my book, which has been dragging at *Rój* since August. But since it is already in the production stage one may hope it will come out eventually.

Warm greetings to you, with best regards to Madame Szuman and Grażynka.

Bruno Schulz

Drohobycz, November 24, 1933

Dust jacket for first edition of *Cinnamon Shops*, 1933.

TO ARNOLD SPAET

Arnold Spaet, Germanist on the faculty of the classical high school at Stryj (now Stryy, U.S.S.R.), later at Lwów, was translator of such German poets as Stefan George, Richard Dehmel, and Goethe. He maintained contacts in literary circles of the time—e.g., with S. Przybyszewski, J. Tuwim, K. Rychterówna. Schulz presented him with a cycle of his prints, Xsięga Bałwochwałcza. *Spaet died in Lwów in 1943.*[1]

6

My dear Sir:

Your letter woke the sweetest memories in me. How did you imagine I could fail to remember you and the lovely talks we had at Kudowa?[2] My warm thanks to you for writing. I am touched by your lively concern for the destinies of my book [*Cinnamon Shops*] and the obvious pleasure you take in its success. This success was a sincere and joyful surprise to me. I had considered it an almost esoteric work and was upheld in this judgment by acquaintances who knew it in manuscript. Yet the number of the "initiated" and "admitted" turned out to be considerable. My copies have long since melted away, I'm afraid; my nearest and dearest divided up my cache so I can't even give myself the pleasure of sending you an author's copy.

Have you read it? Did you like it? Of our conversations I remember only the general atmosphere—the content has slipped my mind. It will be a pleasure to respond to your kind invitation and pay a visit to you—and take up our interrupted dialogue after eleven years.

I am ashamed to say I know nothing of your literary work. I have lately heard about some unusual, masterly translation of yours, or was it an original piece? It shames me not only that I haven't read it but that I don't even know what it was. I don't dare solicit a copy from you when I have been so remiss myself.

I beg you to keep me in your kind favor and warmly clasp your hand.

Bruno Schulz

Drohobycz, March 13, 1934
10 Floriańska

7

My dear Sir:

You truly delighted me with this mark of your remembrance; it was a beautiful and unexpected gift. When did you manage to complete this excellent translation? What an imposing body of work and what resources of creative élan and inspiration! You have truly rendered a fine service to Polish literature in bestowing honorary citizenship, by your splendid translation, on such a sizable selection of Dehmel's work.[3]

I was not familiar with this poet in the original, and reading your rendering I did not have the impression of a translation at all, it is so vibrant with inspiration, naturalness, and authenticity. I haven't finished the whole volume yet, only sounded it in a few places, and everywhere I struck the genuine bedrock of poetry. I am no connoisseur of poetry; I have never written any verse, and claim no more than the judgment of a private consumer.

If I had your gift of transposing poetry, I would attempt something I have long dreamed of, as of a thing almost unattainable: translating R. M. Rilke, whom I worship above all poets. What is your attitude toward that uncommon poet? Do you know *Neue Gedichte* or *Buch der Bilder*?

Warm congratulations on this book, which I hope will find the recognition it deserves.

Your observations on my book, even though derived from a superficial contact with it, are very subtle and penetrating. Those few words from you breathed an aura of confidential intimacy and understanding. You clearly belong to the inner circle of genuine readers of this book.

I am really embarrassed to be unable to return your kindness by sending it to you, but I ran out of books a long time ago and I can't seem to make the publisher come up with a few extra copies. I'll write him again. I'm curious to know your opinion of the whole work.

Any news from you is a reminder of old times that is more welcome than I can say. Your name comes up often when I am in the company of our common friend, Józefina Szelińska, whom a coincidence brought here, and who speaks of you with real feeling.

It goes without saying that when I am in Lwów I won't deny myself the pleasure of calling on you, a visit I'm already looking forward to.

Dr. Mantel,[4] the Germanist at the local high school, has asked me to convey his respects.

Sincere thanks once more for thinking of me. I remain, in deep respect and with heartfelt greetings,

Yours
Bruno Schulz

Drohobycz, June 10, 1934

In the letter below Schulz responds to Spaet's translation of Pieśni (Songs), *by Süsskind von Trimberg, an early thirteenth-century troubadour and German court bard.*

8

My dear Sir:

Thank you so much for the beautiful, truly masterly translation you sent me. So far I've only had the chance to read a few lines, being much preoccupied just now with my forthcoming trip to Warsaw. As for reviewing this book—I must confess I have very little expertise in poetry and it would be rather presumptuous of me to write about it. In any case, it would be difficult for me to place it in *Wiadomości* because everyone there has his assigned field of competence, and mine is foreign prose (novels in translation). However—let me read the whole ms. first.

I haven't seen you for a long time, dear Professor, as long ago as Kudowa, and each contact with you by correspondence reminds me of times gone by and lost. To my regret, I won't be able to make a stop at Lwów. Should your path, dear Professor, at some point lead you to Warsaw, I would look forward to a visit from you with great pleasure, especially as my fiancée, Józefina Szelińska, knows you well and speaks warmly of you. Please accept my respects and sincere regards,

Bruno Schulz

P.S. I cannot give you a Warsaw address yet; but care of *Rój* or *Wiadomości Literackie* will reach me.
[1936]

TO JULIAN TUWIM

Schulz's contacts with Julian Tuwim[1]*, the most eminent representative of the* Skamander *circle and probably the best-known poet of the prewar years in Poland, were sporadic and never reached any degree of close acquaintance. Tuwim expressed his recognition for Schulz's* Cinnamon Shops *not only in his letter to him, but also by advancing the book for the 1935* Wiadomości Literackie *literary prize. Other Schulz proponents were Antoni Slonimski and* Adolf *Nowaczyński.*

Schulz's letter thanking Tuwim, the only one of this correspondence to survive, represents a literary sketch in letter form, containing motifs, formulations, and metaphorical language that echo in the Sanatorium *collection published three years later. It is difficult to decide whether Schulz in his letter drew on as yet unpublished passages of* Sanatorium *or—as seems more likely—used the letter, as he used correspondence with Debora Vogel to work out* Cinnamon Shops, *to work out ideas and images for his fiction (the story "Księga" ["The Book"]). "The Book," like its neighbor, "The Age of Genius," was to go into Schulz's unfinished novel* The Messiah, *which did not survive the war. When "The Age of Genius" was first printed in* Wiadomości Literackie, *no. 12, 1934, it was identified in a note as a "Fragment from the narrative* The Messiah." *Later the author cut both these pieces out of the scheme of* The Messiah *and inserted them at the head of* Sanatorium. *"The Book," like its companion, was published relatively early (*Skamander, *no. 58, 1935), barely a year after the letter to Tuwim.*

9

My dear Sir:

Thank you! I did not expect it, but in my heart of hearts I counted on, I ardently yearned for a response from you.[2] Buried under the passion and bitterness of that book was this old longing as well. Today you've stilled it in me, sated and filled it to the brim. What fulfillment!

It came a bit late—by no fault of yours.

When you came to Drohobycz years ago,[3] I was in the audience; I stared at you with rebellious hostility, filled with gloomy worship. Ancient history! Certain of your poems drove me to despair with helpless admiration then. I ached—reading them over and over, heaving uphill that heavy boulder of admiration which, just before the top, unable to keep its grip on the steep incline of delight, came hurtling back down each time. They annihilated me, those poems, but at the same time they brought on an exhilaration, a presentiment of triumphant, superhuman powers that would one day be at the command of the happy, unshackled person. At that time I harbored in my mind a sort of utopia about an "age of genius" that supposedly existed in my life once upon a time, not in any calendar year but on a level above chronology, an age when everything blazed with godly colors and one took in the whole sky with a single breath, like a gulp of pure ultramarine.

Julian Tuwim, about 1930.

Such an age never really existed. But in your poems it took on reality, gaudy like a peacock feather's azure-dripping eye, splashing bold color—it was like a nestful of rioting hummingbirds. . . .

You taught me that every state of the soul, followed to sufficient depth, directs us across the narrows and channels of the word —into the realm of myth. Not into the hardened mythology of peoples and histories, but the one that, under a surface layer, murmurs in our blood, is tangled in the depths of phylogeny, branches out into the metaphysical night.

In that mythological deep, I think, you have a pact with Satan. There your poetry becomes transcendental, blatantly irrational in technique, exceeding the limits of feasible things.

Today a great moment of triumph is mine. The spell is broken —everything I absorbed in delight, everything I exalted in, attacks of admiration that felt alien and hostile to me, now confirms me and accepts me.

I thank you!
Bruno Schulz

Drohobycz, January 26, 1934
10 Floriańska

TO TADEUSZ AND ZOFIA BREZA

Tadeusz Breza[1] *made his literary debut with the novel* Adam Grywald *(1936), which Schulz reviewed, and he in his turn was one of the first reviewers of* Cinnamon Shops. *During the years of his association and friendship with Schulz he was the editor of the Culture section of* Kurier Poranny. *In this medium he published his own review (no.3, 1934) as well as other discussions of Schulz's work, such as A. Pleśniewicz's and W. Gombrowicz's.*

The house in Warsaw where Breza lived until the Polish Uprising was among the very few which did not burn down as a result of Hitler's order to "leave nothing standing" after the insurgence. Upon the "liberation" of Warsaw from one occupant by another, Breza found Schulz's letters in his pillaged apartment.

10

Dear Sir:

I need a friend. I need the closeness of a kindred spirit. I long for some outside affirmation of the inner world whose existence I postulate. To cling to it by sheer faith alone, to lug it along with me in spite of everything, is a toil and torment of Atlas. Sometimes it seems to me, even with all the strain of heaving, that I have nothing on my shoulders. I'd like to drop that weight onto someone else's shoulders for a while, straighten the crook in my neck and take a look at what I've been carrying.

I need a partner for voyages of discovery. What is a risk, an impossibility, a whim turned on its head to one person becomes reality when reflected in two pairs of eyes. My world has been waiting for this twosome, as it were: What was once a closed tight place with no further prospects now begins to ripen into colors in the distance, burst open, reveal its depths. The painted scenery

Tadeusz Breza, about 1934.

takes on perspective and slides apart into real vistas; the wall admits us to dimensions formerly denied us; the frescoes painted on the vault of heaven come to life as in a pantomime.

It's good that you aren't perfect, that you're an overconsumer of time. You need to be a vessel full of unofficial events, unregistered activities, which eat your time away under your nose before your official capacity, after much ceremony, decides to sample a bite. After all, there must be somebody to use up time, somebody it agrees with. . . .

People's weakness delivers their souls to us, makes them needy. That loss of an electron ionizes them and renders them suitable for chemical bonding. Without flaws they would stay locked inside themselves, not needing anything. It takes their vices to give them flavor and attraction.

I'm enormously pleased we're going to meet. Please come for a special visit. I will be here until July 1. So far I have no definite plans that might take me away. Maybe we'll dream up something together. First I'd like to show you Drohobycz and its surroundings and see the landscape of my youth[2] afresh through your eyes, guide you into the unwritten chapters of *Cinnamon Shops.* Please come.

With warm regards
Bruno Schulz

Drohobycz, June 21, 1934
10 Floriańska, Drohobycz

11

My dear Sir:

Do you resent my long silence very much? Your last postcard with plans for our meeting found me very ill. I spent the whole vacation flat on my back, dispirited and bitter.[3] I have only been back to work in school about a month. Did you hold my silence against me, or is that "chronophagocytosis" still bothering you, snatching the best bites of time right out of your mouth, along with the best of intentions each morsel is spiked with? Do you realize, my dear sir, we still haven't got together? Where will you be for the Christmas season? What are your plans? I have liquidated my entire fortune in expectation of a leave of absence that I applied to the Ministry for.[4] At this very moment my fate hangs in the Ministerial balance. Should I be granted the leave, I would join you in Warsaw. A sign of life from you, word that you're not angry with me, would cheer me up no end.

My best respects and warm greetings,

Bruno Schulz

Drohobycz, November 13, 1934

12

Dear Sir:

Let me thank you very warmly for your letter and report that I have read your essay in *Rocznik Literacki* (*Literary Yearbook*)[5], which you don't mention in the letter, but which places me at the head of the year's contributors to literature. I consider it an act of great courage that you took such an uncompromising and wholehearted stand in support of your spiritual brothers, shouldering in this way the responsibility for your intellectual sympathies. I am moved and grateful. This support from people close to me cheers me in my state of depression. I am very downcast: I was not awarded the leave of absence I was so much counting on. I'm still in Drohobycz, in the school where the gang will go right on playing fast and loose with my nerves. For you must realize that my nerves have been stretched thin like a net over the entire *handicraft center,* have crept along the floor, smothered the walls like tapestry and covered the shops and the smithy with a dense web. This phenomenon is known to science as *telekinesis,* which makes everything that happens in the shops, the planing shed, and so on seem to happen directly on my skin as well. This perfectly honed signaling system has clearly predestined me for the job of shop instructor.[6]

As long as we're revealing irksome private maladies to each other, I'll let you in on a certain illness that troubles me, one that is also related to time but differs from your symptoms of gastric diarrhea you told me about. Your alimentary canal lets time pass through it too easily, is incapable of retaining it. Mine is marked by a paradoxical fastidiousness: it is dominated by the fixed idea of a *virginity of time.* Just as for some rajah of melancholy and insatiable disposition any woman brushed by a male glance is already tainted and thereby unfit for anything but the silken noose, so for me any piece of time someone has laid claim to, has even casually men-

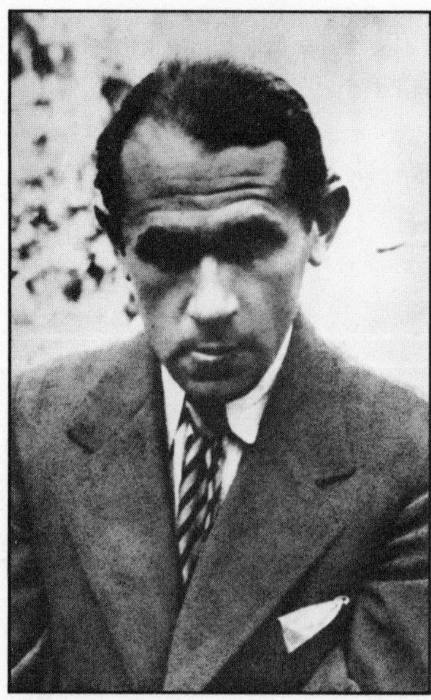
Bruno Schulz, about 1934.

tioned in passing, is already marred, spoiled, unfit for consumption. I can't stand people laying claim to my time. They make the scrap they touched nauseating to me. I am incapable of sharing time, of feeding on somebody's leftovers. (These are the kind of words jealous lovers use.) When I am obliged to prepare a lecture for the next day or buy supplies in the lumberyard, I lose the whole afternoon and evening; I forfeit the rest with a grand gesture. All or nothing, that's my maxim. And since every school day gets profaned in this way, I live in proud abstinence and—do not write. Some sort of feudal mentality lives on in this unbending stance of mine. What do you think, can it be coaxed out, can this tiny sprig of gentryhood be consciously watered and cultivated?

Changing the subject, let me report that I will probably come to Warsaw for Christmas to spend the semester break there. Will I find you there? I look forward very much to a meeting.

With respectful regards and warmest sympathy,

Bruno Schulz

Drohobycz, December 2, 1934

In December of 1934 Schulz did meet with Breza, after which relations between the two writers grew livelier and the tone of the letters less formal.

In the letter below Schulz refers to Stanisław Ignacy Witkiewicz, who was the first influential literary figure to speak in enthusiastic terms of Schulz's gift. Know as Witkacy to his friends, he had severed his connection with Wiadomości Literackie *in 1930 and never published there again. What caused the rift is not clear, but personal conflicts are cited between him and the editors, who were inclined to underrate his writing. The "deep public mourning" Schulz mentions here was over the death of Marshal Józef Piłsudski on May 12, 1935: Schulz's essay, "The Formation of Legends," commemorated Piłsudski's death.*

13

Dear Tadzio:

Don't be upset that I haven't written at all so far. I was immediately swallowed up by the school treadmill. . . . The Inspector has planted himself in Drohobycz and presses down on us like an incubus. Józefina is bored at Janowo and homesick for Warsaw. I still have no official notification of my leave of absence. In these days of deep public mourning I can take no steps in the matter. Have you finished the rewriting job [on *Adam Grywald*] yet? Are you negotiating with a publisher? I am eagerly waiting to see at least a fragment in print.

Concerning Witkacy's article, quite a ruckus developed over my giving it to Grydzewski [publisher of *Wiadomości Literackie*].[8] Witkacy was dreadfully offended and had me withdraw the manuscript at once, and I did so.

I have a request for you. Please don't be angry with me for turning to you, because you are the only one I can confide in about this matter. A certain gentleman of some prominence in society whose favor I value has conceived a most gratuitous desire for a poet's laurels and has begun to write poetry. Not content with this, he has approached me with the request to gather among my friends in the literary world expert testimonials on the value of these verses—since I had let him know that I didn't know how to do this sort of thing. If that expert appraisal turns out bad, the gentleman will withdraw his favor from me. So if scruples of conscience don't stand in your way, be so kind as to write something noncommittally positive about these poems I'm sending you. I am out of my depth, I can't make sense of them.

How is Nyczek doing? Fond greetings to her from Józefina and myself. And a warm hug for you.

Yours
Bruno

Drohobycz, May 13, 1935

Zofia Nycz, known as "Nyczek" to her friends, was Tadeusz Breza's fiancée. The following letter is in two parts, the first addressed to Zofia, the rest to Breza.

14-1

Dear Zosia:

I feel ashamed at not having written to you two for so long, and grateful that you remembered me. I thought of you often, Tadzio and you, but somehow couldn't put pen to paper. The business of my leave of absence is still hanging fire at some commission or ministry; I am thinking of throwing over the whole school job without waiting for a leave.

I should share with you the news that J[ózefina Szelinska]* has been in Warsaw for some little time. She looked for you at the old apartment, then went to the editorial offices and left a note there, which evidently never reached Tadzio.

I am giving you her address—Józefina Szelińska, 45 Koszykowa Street, Apt. 15 (4th floor); telephone 8 27 69, after 4 P.M.—and ask you, if I may, to take her a little under your wing. She is v. depressed. I hope we'll still see each other in Warsaw before the year is out.

Very warm greetings, kissing your hand,

Yours
Bruno

*Schulz's fiancée's name was disclosed in Regina Silberner's *Strzępy Wspomnień (Shreds of Memory)*, London, 1984.

14-2

Dear Tadzio:

From time to time I think of you with longing. Isn't it strange that we never write, that we hear from each other indirectly and in roundabout ways?

I am eager to have your book in my hands at last. Where are you publishing it? That book needs to be produced with elegance and distinction, good paper, beautiful typeface.

My work is going very slowly.[9] The opportunities I've had for it haven't been good. During vacation I couldn't get anything done. Now, when I could write, I have school.

My plan now is to stay a few months at any rate when I get to Warsaw. I'll see if I can make it there, financially and in terms of atmosphere for my work. Let me ask you as well, dear Tadzio, to be friendly to Józefina. It seems you didn't get her note.

Have you written anything else besides the book? Nothing ever gets here—you can't even find *Skamander*.

I'm glad we'll be able to talk and enjoy each other to our hearts' content before long. Stay well, and a hug from

Your
Bruno

November 18, 1935

THE FORMATION OF LEGENDS

Commemorating the death of Józef Piłsudski, Marshal of Poland, on May 12, 1935. Published in Tygodnik Ilustrowany, *no. 22, 1935.*

The legend is the organ by which greatness is apprehended; it is the human spirit's reaction to greatness.

Where people of ordinary caliber and the usual course of history are concerned, psychology, pragmatism, realistic historical methods are adequate. That key opens the workday for us, and many believe it will open anything. This is the credo of minor ages. Positivism is the religion of times that have not known greatness. For greatness is scattered thinly over the map of the world, like glittering bits of pure metal over miles of dull rock. Disbelief in greatness is inborn in the human spirit. There is some elemental pettiness in us that nibbles, gnaws, roots away at the cliff of greatness until finally it is chewed up, ground to bits, dissipated. This is the unending, zealous subterranean work of smallness. In order to understand, man is obliged to reduce. A passion for understanding, digesting, is an elemental force, an automatic reflex of humanity. This is how pettiness gnaws its way through greatness, destroying it. History is full of antheaps and ruins—the withered tumuli of greatness.

Psychology implies the mediocrity of the average, faith in uniformity, the gray commonwealth of the ant. When the nineteenth century pulverized the last great man, the age of psychology dawned like a tedious endlessly sunny day. Humanity heaved a sigh of relief. They vowed to bring forth no more great men. They denied the existence of such persons. The restoration of smallness had begun. With great relief, mediocrity was reinstated, the principle of good sense and rationalism was brought back. The whole fullness of life was divided up, cut into neat parcels, brought under control. The impossibility of greatness was proclaimed, its irrelevance promulgated; an impersonal historical process, numbers, statistics were posited in its place. In these artifacts people sought the key to understanding history.

This is why, when a silent greatness began slowly and imperceptibly growing among us and the first inklings of it flashed out like summer lightning, the first impulse of the populace was to deny it, shut it out, denigrate it. The human mass resists those who lead it toward greatness, especially if that greatness spurns the wiles of seduction, does not wheedle, adulate, or promise. One must surrender one's heart to such greatness if one is to bear it. But who can make up his mind to espouse this sacrificial, unrequited, burning, sublime love? Who can take up the burden of its crushing weight for the rest of time?

When greatness enters the lists of history, the laws of ordinary processes are suspended. Psychology and rationalism, those instruments of belittlement and understanding stand there like spiked artillery, cracked and useless. The intellect retreats, capitulates.

The laws of greatness cannot be reconciled with the modalities of daily thought. The mind wishing to grasp greatness must withdraw to its deepest reserves, and its makeshift construction is that time-honored recourse, legend. Legend is the headline, the first working title of a romance mankind is pregnant with. The borders of a sacred precinct that will hold temples and sanctuaries, an acropolis of the nation is staked out; within it a plaque is fastened bearing the inscription: *Legend.*

The nature of greatness expresses itself in huge antinomies. Here we face a whole series of antinomies, contradictions, paradoxes. But we sense they carry a minus sign only from the perspective of reason. From another, unknown perspective, these contrarities resolve themselves into the highest concord, rightness, and affirmation. In our human language, we must slap them together haphazardly with the sign "not," prop them up only with negations. That one thing whole and indivisible as nothing else on earth we must divide into antitheses and then try clumsily to reassemble it from these parts.

How can it exist, this entity broader and deeper than the nation, at the same time comprising the nation within itself? How can a son of the nation be its father and creator? Will to power, overweening ambition, usurpation—or ascetic humility, renunciation, total sacrifice of self? Pride in, and contempt for, human beings—or the tenderest love and worship? Self-sufficient aloofness, wrapped up in its own greatness, or the loftiest solidarity with the community? Coarseness or sublimity? And we sense

Pilsudski Street, Drohobycz.

that by some profounder law those incompatible qualities do not cancel each other out but add up to some greatly superior sum. A vast agendum is revealed, an enormous task for politicians, historians, strategists, moralists. Specialists will seize on parts of this great discipline, divide it among each other, and measure those superhuman dimensions lengthwise and crosswise by their own yardsticks.

Napoleon merged completely with his acts; he transsubstantiated himself into them, vanished in them. He represented a supreme ability to vest his entire potency in the categories of the real world with nothing left over. He added his own being to the energies at work at a given moment and shaped the course of events. He was a force of nature in the midst of other forces.

But this Other was greater than his acts. None of them was large enough to hold him. He always stood beyond them, towering and inscrutable. He did not use up his reserves to the dregs—as if saving himself for something greater. His strength, the core of his being, remained unconsumed. By virtue of that strength he has laid himself over Poland like a cloud, and endures.

His role in history is only beginning.

Napoleon was all presence and moment, like a splendid set of fireworks with a single mission: to burn itself out utterly. For that Other, acts were not the *ultima ratio.* He launched them from under his cape with distaste, with a heavy and languid hand, when no other way remained: exemplary acts. The moral strength outlasting the act was more important to him. He slowly hoarded it in the nation. He put by an iron capital of power—first of all within himself. Out of this he grew in the eyes of all and took greatness unto himself. He deposited it in himself as in the safest place. He sculpted his own statue. In the end, when he had accomplished his greatness, he left one day without warning, without a word, as if that were not important, since what he left in his place was greatness, bearing the stamp of his features for ever after.

Napoleon stood for nothing but himself. He draped himself in history as in a royal cloak and fashioned a magnificent train out of it for his career. One of the mainstays of his strength was simply that he lacked tradition, was unencumbered by the past. The Other emerged out of the undergrowth of history, out of the mouths of graves, out of the past. He was heavy with the dreams of seers, misty with the teeming visions of poets, burdened with the martyrdom of generations. He was sheer continuity. He drew the past behind him like a vast mantle for all of Poland.

During his lifetime his face may have been the face of an individual. Certainly, those near him knew that smile, that clouding brow, the flashes the moment lit up on his face. To us, from a distance, individual traits increasingly dim and blur, they seem to give out a radiance from within, as of larger, more massive features carrying in themselves hundreds of lost and irrecoverable faces.

In the act of dying, merging with eternity, that face flickers with memories, roams through a series of faces, ever paler, more condensed, until out of the heaping up of these faces there settles on it at last, and hardens into its final mask, the countenance of Poland—forever.

The "Gomber" in the letter below (another two-part letter) is Witold Gombrowicz. The reference is to a fragment of his novel Ferdydurke *(1937), which was published in* Tygodnik Ilustrowany (Illustrated Weekly) *in 1936.*

15-1

Dear Tadzio:

I've thought of you more than once these days and kept making resolutions to write a letter—but I found this hard to bring off somehow. That's why I'm especially grateful you proved better than I and wrote first. I am very, very glad your book is coming out. I can't wait to see some of it. Are you publishing it with *Rój?* I'm so eager to have all of it in front of me.

Those little fragments of mine you read—they were casual freehand sketches done some time ago; I dug them out now as some sort of paralipomena.[10] Your praises are not well founded. They really are on the weak side. The fragment by the Gomber didn't seem *outré.* Only after your remark do I really find it more explicit than, e.g., his "Virginity."[11] But that may be the result of greater daring and awareness of his intentions.

All I have written is a sizable novella ["Spring"] of about sixty printed pages.[12] I plan to have it printed in one of the journals and then publish it along with other novellas in a separate volume. I am not satisfied with it. I have been hankering for some new style. Some of the novellas I can't complete.

Józefina continues on in Warsaw. She is afraid of disturbing you. Perhaps she expected you to ring her up some time. I plan to be there shortly. Has Witkiewicz come up yet?

A big hug, and see you soon!

Yours
Bruno

15-2

Dear Zosia:

Heartfelt thanks for your greetings and for thinking of me. When I'm away, you don't take any interest in Józefina. But I don't resent it—you are probably very busy with your own affairs. It must be lovely for you now where you are living. Józefina wants to go to some place like Leśna Podkowa [a resort near Warsaw] for the summer. Kissing your hand—

Bruno

Droh., May 11, 1936

16

Dear Tadzio:

It makes me sad that we meet so seldom and so briefly, and that we have to hear about each other from third persons. Don't imagine anything within me has put distance between us—though the facts, our rare meetings, regrettably seem to point that way. I think of you always with great tenderness, and at times I feel as one does in one of those dreams when someone long since irretrievably vanished in real life is back in town, yet by a strange procrastination, some incomprehensible distraction, one still hasn't gone to see him, even though he is someone close and dear to us.

I don't know whether Józefina has given you the article about

Grywald[13] I wrote a month ago. I sent a copy to Czarski,[14] but for some reason he hasn't published it yet. I fear you won't like it. The book is exceedingly difficult to make a discursive report on, and still do justice to in conceptual terms.

What are you up to? Loads of work? What's Nyczek doing? When are you getting married? Give her my love.

I am having a pretty sorry and lonesome time. I would like at least to move to Lwów, since Warsaw is evidently a tougher proposition.

Some time ago you had some get-togethers with Józefina as she tells me in a letter, but later those meetings, which Józefina very much enjoyed, petered out—it was probably her fault. She is quite a hypochondriac and full of baseless fears. What are you planning for the holidays?

Warm greetings and hugs from

Bruno Schulz

Drohobycz, November 29, [1936]

17

Dear Tadzio:

I was in Warsaw two weeks ago and wanted to see you, but unfortunately my stay was marked by very unpleasant circumstances: Józefina was seriously ill, and shortly after I fell ill too and spent ten days in bed. Lying in someone else's apartment and down with the flu, I didn't feel like asking you to come. The only person to visit me was Witold [Gombrowicz] who gave me his new novel [*Ferdydurke*] to read. It is almost done, and it is splendid. My piece is still in diapers.[15] I am, however, having a volume of earlier stories [*Sanitorium*] published in *Rój.* They came to 270 pages; with the 33 illustrations it will make about 300 pages. I am very concerned about the plates, fearing that *Rój* might ruin them. I didn't have the feeling that I captured and expressed a full appreciation of the essence of your novel in my review. *Grywald* is very hard to present and characterize in a review. Its form is truly very good. You should have been awarded the Young Writer's Prize.[16] But these matters are decided, I understand, by behind-the-scenes maneuvering. I have taken Józefina to Lwów, where she is still recuperating. She has four weeks of leave. What are you writing now? Will it be something in the vein of *Grywald?* Nałkowska said you should try for a more dramatic subject—then you would write a superb piece! Thank you for thinking of me. To Nyczek, thanks for her greetings, which I warmly return in kind.

Bruno

[February 3, 1937]

18

Dear Friends:

With all my heart I congratulate you two on your beautiful union,[17] long awaited and eagerly anticipated by all your friends. I wish every sort of happiness on that beautiful partnership of yours, which is one of the dearest and most luminous centers of finest humanity, warmheartedness, and nobility of mind in literary Warsaw.

I am sorry to have to sadden you with the news that my relationship with Józefina has completely broken down. She finally grew tired of my hopeless situation, the difficulties in the way of a move to Warsaw, which she attributed—rightly, I admit—to my lack of practical sense. I don't even know where she is now, since she has broken off even written communication with me. I am going through a difficult time. I long for the end of the school year and a change in my place of residence.

My most sincere wishes of all good things to you,

Your devoted Bruno Schulz

June 8, 1937

19

My dears:

It will be a pleasure to send my autograph to Maria Leśnobrodzka—her enthusiasm is contagious. It is very nice for an author to learn he is getting through.

My thanks to you, dear Tadzio, for your words—positive and negative. I think you are right in both cases. I don't have to tell you how happy I would be if you were to write something about the book. So little has been written on it so far. The press is virtually silent about it. My sincere thanks in advance.[18]

To you, dearest Nyczek, go my thanks for remembering me with your greetings and news. Embracing you both fondly, I close in haste, for your package, postmarked the 21st, reached me only today.

Bruno Schulz

February 24, 1938

TO ZENON WAŚNIEWSKI

Zenon Waśniewski[1] differs from most of Schulz's correspondents in this volume by having gained a somewhat adventitious access to Schulz's life and mind more than twenty years after their first slight acquaintance, made between 1910 and 1913 when they were both attending Lwów Polytechnic. Waśniewski's architectural studies there were interrupted by World War I; Schulz had to leave school mainly because of his father's long (and ultimately fatal) illness. When Waśniewski accidentally came across Schulz again, they had in common their three years at school and the fact that they were both graphic artists (though poles apart in their themes and techniques) who were teaching at provincial high schools. Their correspondence (shortened by fifteen letters in this edition), and Schulz's use of the formal second person plural—not used in most of his letters—makes it plain that Schulz quite lacked the resolution to break off an exchange that was unfruitful and not entirely congenial. As a result he spent endless hours composing empty letters of apology for not writing sooner and for failing to contribute work to Waśniewski's magazine, Kamena (Camoena).

But the letters here do include some discussion of Schulz's work in the graphic arts and shop talk about teaching. In Letter 24 the mention of the art dealer Leszcyayc and an excursion to Truskawiec, a resort town where Leszcyzyc frequently mounted exhibitions, is one of the relatively rare occasions that Schulz refers to his career as a graphic artist per se. *Schulz's art had been exhibited at Truskawiec some years earlier, and the account of Juliusz Flaszen,[2] who met Schulz there, is a revealing glimpse of Schulz early in his career and of the provincial world in which he moved:*

I made Schulz's acquaintance at Truskawiec in the years 1928–29; I don't recall the exact date. He was then a teacher at the classical high school of Drohobycz. He came to Truskawiec fairly often in the course of his vacations, and there we met and became friends. He was morbidly shy; I was right, I think, in setting him down as suffering from an inferiority complex.

One day he brought along his paintings and drawings and asked for my opinion. The greater part of this work consisted of pen and pencil sketches which in their thematics and technique recalled Rops. The chief motif was male sexual enslavement to the beautiful contours of the female body; the women finely drawn, their nudity treated in the Ropsian manner, wearing either nothing but black stockings and small slippers, or wide hats and some scrap of fabric across their hips, and invariably holding a little whip in their tiny hands; the men in poses of servility, the fear in their eyes set off by glints of desire. There were few oils; they showed a strange but attractive color toning, chiefly light violet and sky blue. The foreground was occupied by scenes similar to the above; the background or landscape was hardly elaborated.

The entire compositional impulse and conception of this artist was dominated by the tyranny of the female body over the slavish sexuality of man.

There was an undeniable nobility in the draftsmanship, fine control over brush and stroke, beauty in the nudity of the figures, and a mastery of light and shadow. There was no slavish dependence on any school, no mannerism, but an outstanding originality in the treatment of a given theme. Looking at Schulz's work, you felt certain that you were encountering this form of art for the first time.

Upon acquainting myself with his portfolio, I advised him to arrange an exhibition of his work at Truskawiec, where a good many educated people from all over Poland congregated in the main seasons. Schulz adopted this idea. The owner of the Truskawiec resort at the time, Rajmund Jarosz, mayor of Drohobycz, a well-disposed and influential man, was happy, upon my intercession, to put the banquet hall at Schulz's disposal free of charge. Schulz exhibited some fifty or sixty works, which immediately fascinated the viewers. One day, though, an indignant Schulz dropped in, exclaiming: "Can you imagine this? I have been summoned to the Resort Administration and informed that some senator taking the waters here has categorically demanded that my exhibition be closed, since in his view it was repulsive pornography! He has lodged a complaint with the state authority, demanding immediate action!"

The senator in question was the well-known leader of the Christian Democrats and professor at the Lwów Polytechnic, Thulie, then aged about eighty.

I calmed Schulz down and called the whole business a stroke of luck—provided it took the desirable course, and the state official really were to close the exhibition down on these and not any other grounds. I counted on the professional solidarity of [Schulz's] sculptor colleagues who would not tolerate such interference by unqualified agencies in matters of artistic creation, which was not subject to any prescriptions of societal hygiene. I explained to Schulz that if the intervention by old Thulie—whom the famous essayist and critic Boy-Żelenski had sarcastically nicknamed St. Thulia—were successful and the incumbent state administrator, Porebalski, were cowed into arbitrarily closing the exhibit, an outcry would be raised by the literary journals, the dailies, the party press, etc., and Schulz's name would become famous overnight. Unfortunately this was not what happened. The administrator, advised of the matter by Rajmund Jarosz and a handful of friends of Schulz's like myself, declined to intervene in a matter totally out of the realm of his authority and suggested to the senator that he bring the matter up in the Sejm—which was not in session during this parliamentary vacation period. The tempest in a teacup died down and was soon forgotten.

Schulz sold almost all his exhibits—at wretched prices, needless to say. His self-esteem was so low that he always feared to overcharge and felt sufficiently rewarded by people's buying his work at all.

Zenon Waśniewski, about 1938.

Schulz walking with a group at Truskawiec, a health resort, about 1930.

20

Dear Fellow Student:

I am truly embarrassed to say that I don't remember. I can't locate a face in my memory to attach to that name. Would you be good enough to help me with some detail, some event or picture going back to those days? If you sent me a photograph or at least a description of your physical appearance! With your letter I caught a breath of times gone by and forever lost, or so it once seemed. This makes me feel pleasant and a little sad. Did I possibly once draw you a little portrait in your notebook?

In any case, sincere thanks for your letter and the splendid magazine [*Kamena*]. I never would have thought the town of Chełm could boast such a monthly—on such a high level. It was a pleasure to look at your beautiful lino prints, and I enjoyed tasting the poems here and there. Excellent translations of Russian poetry. I'll be glad to send along a piece of prose. I won't be in bad company there.

I beg you not to infer from my poor recollection any disregard or inattention on my part. Nothing of the kind was intended. I simply haven't what you might call a biographical memory. Whole districts of my vita have flown away without a trace along with the people in them. How much farther could fate have driven the analogy between us? We were at the Polytechnic together; both of us pulled out before graduation and ended up in the teaching profession. Add to these a shared weakness for literature and painting! Do you teach crafts too? I am so sick of them I could throw up!

I look forward with pleasure to further news from you. Meanwhile, I send best regards and a warm handshake.

Bruno Schulz

P.S. Have you ever come across any of my etchings?[3] Give my respects and appreciation to Mr. Jaworski.[4]

Drohobycz, March 15, 1934
10 Floriańska

21

Dear Classmate:

Of course I remember you, and now your face springs vividly before my eyes! I have thought of you more than once and asked myself what might have happened to you. Only in the meantime your name got detached from your features. When the name turned up by itself years later, I didn't recognize it and couldn't place it anywhere. Now I remember perfectly that we kept company from time to time; I recall outings and conversations. You were a dour sort of person, on the taciturn and introverted side. Have you stayed that way? But it may have been just the set of your eyebrows and eyes that created that kind of gentle Slavic gloom.

Thank you with all my heart for helping out my memory, for that fragment of my biography you gave back to me. Many thanks, too, for the gift of those sketches. They will be a dear memento

Bruno Schulz with students, 1926.

for me. I recognized the little portrait sketch of myself at once; the person drawn in profile with an aquiline nose and a five o'clock shadow is our fellow student Cygie from Łódź. I also recognized Sadłowski the assistant.

I am very happy to have [Aleksander Blok's] "Garden of Nightingales"[5] with your fine woodcuts. I am still unable to respond in kind with my own book, since I haven't a single copy left. I have written to *Rój* asking for a few copies, but they haven't sent any yet. I am also going to send you some of my etchings whenever I find the time to prepare the prints. I didn't answer you immediately because I was busy preparing for a demonstration class in handicrafts (carpentry) in the presence of an inspector and a professional instructor;[6] luckily I didn't do too badly. All this bores me to distraction; I wish I could free myself of it somehow. Metalworking is added the second year.

I see from the photograph that you come from a landed family; your interests and sense of class suggest perhaps that you are still rooted to some degree in the gentry. Your vacations are always spent in the country, on your own or someone else's land—I like that very much.[7]

I am not sure yet where I'll spend my vacation. Right after the Easter holidays I'll have a few days in Warsaw. I can be found in the boardinghouse for public school teachers at 4 Marszałkowska Street—in case you happen to be in Warsaw also. I am very eager to get together with you. I see you have developed in a direction I didn't foresee. I never suspected you of literary inclinations.[8] It would be good to meet somewhere during the summer. We'll stay in touch, I hope, and come to some agreement in due course. I took great pleasure in this whole episode of finding you again after so many years, and I thank you once again for all those gifts and mementos. I am returning the photos of yourself and your family; the sketches, taking advantage of your kindness, I keep.

Could what I am to send for *Kamena* be a prose fragment or does it have to be something complete? I take it a fragment would be all right. I'll send one soon.

Yours
Bruno Schulz

Drohobycz, March 24, 1934
10 Floriańska

Sketch for title page of *A Book of Idolatry*, drawings, about 1920.

22

My dear Classmate:

In the press of time before my trip to Warsaw, here are just a few words of gratitude for your long letter. Unfortunately, my schedule in Warsaw is so jammed it leaves me no time to drop in at Chełm, however badly I want to.

Nor have I had a chance so far to make a fair copy of a fragment of my manuscripts. I'll do it after my return.

I am sending along a small print[9] as a down payment for more to come. With warm regards, I remain

Yours sincerely
Bruno Schulz

April 2, 1934

23

Dear Classmate:

Don't hold it against me if my replies are late and sparse. I too am moved and elated by our strange reunion. I read your confession with emotion and suspense. If I do not respond with as generous an outpouring, it is because of a strange constraint I have been subject to for some time, some sort of joylessness, depression of spirit, for which I can't find sufficient grounds. I must have some nervous disorder. Right now I have good cause for satisfaction; I could afford a little gaiety, but instead I feel an indistinct fear and worry, a sense of desolation. I neglect important correspondence that I care about, I don't write anything; even trying to make a copy of something already written I run up against an insuperable aversion. Yet the

"Dedication," a self-portrait from *A Book of Idolatry*.

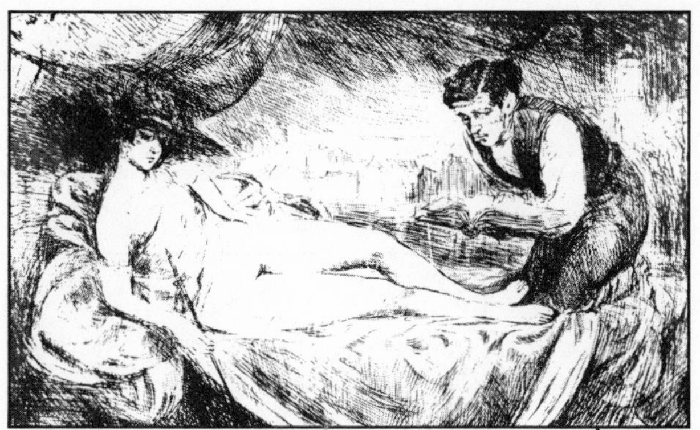
"A Book of Idolatry," a cliché-verre etching from the cycle of the same title.

world has just now been possessed by such an improbable glory of spring, with all its mild airs, radiant light, and promise—but all it does is bring home to me that I've left springtime behind for good.

Don't hold it against me that I keep procrastinating about sending a piece of prose for *Kamena.* I haven't a large supply; it needs selecting, completing, revising, and copying out. This will get done—and soon. I haven't anything to contribute to the Mickiewicz issue. My acquaintance with Mickiewicz dates back to school days. Nor can I offer graphic work for that or any other issue. My technique is a laborious one. It isn't aquafortis etching but the so-called *cliché-verre* technique, using a glass plate. You draw with a stylus on a black gelatin layer covering the glass, and the translucent negative drawing obtained in this way is treated like a photographic negative, i.e., it is printed in a photographic copying frame onto light-sensitive paper, developed, fixed, and rinsed. The procedure is like photo printing. The cost is considerable—so is the labor. I have an offer from *Rój* for ten to twenty folios; I am not taking the offer up although I could make several hundred zlotys out of it. It is not a technique for mass production.

I well understand your impatient yearning for wider horizons. I have felt the same and still do. Finding you was a strange and beautiful event for me. We will probably keep in contact always from now on, but you mustn't expect me to write letters as rich in content as yours are—for the reasons mentioned above. Please don't let this offend you and keep you from writing more; I find genuine pleasure in reading your letters.

For the time being, I send you my warm regards.

Sincerely yours,

April 24, 1934 Bruno Schulz

Pencil draft for *Idolatry*.

"Tribe of Pariahs," from *Idolatry*.

"Primordial Fable," cliché-verre etching from *Idolatry*.

24

Dear Classmate:

Your long silence has been weighing on my conscience whenever I've thought of you. I had the dim feeling that I hadn't been as friendly in my last letter as I ought to have been after those warm letters of yours. Your fair, straight Slavic soul does not understand the twisted and winding paths followed by mine, which is murky and meandering, full of knots and tangles! I urge you most sincerely, dear classmate, not to entertain the suspicion that I might want to keep my distance from *Kamena* or yourself—even though I haven't sent the promised fragment. I have a very real respect and sympathy for *Kamena* as a journal that holds high the standard of pure, uncompromising poetry. Take it rather, because it's true, that I am sunk in a deep prostration of spirit and feel that I will never write another thing! I try to comfort and persuade myself that I am neurotic, but this aversion to the pen has lasted over six months now, and that after all is food for thought. From older fragments I have picked one, not a fragment really but a more or less completed piece, called "*A Night in July*,"[10] and have earmarked it for *Kamena.* And now I can't find the energy to correct and transcribe it from a slightly rough draft! I have the feeling I might profane this work, which grew out of some sort of inspiration I can no longer match. Have I published anywhere else in the meantime—even though all journals are open to me? Really, how can you talk about my having reservations toward *Kamena*?

I am grateful to you for writing, though, in spite of the opinion

"The Enchanted City," from *Idolatry*.

"Undula at the Artist's," from *Idolatry*.

you hold of me. It's a good thing you did, because God knows if I could have made myself take up the work again otherwise; and it would have been a pity to lose my hold on a piece so steeped in the essence of our past and bulging with the capital of our youth. You ask, "What the hell is depressing you?" I don't know how to answer that. The sadness of life, fear of the future, some dark conviction that everything is headed for a tragic end, a decadent *Weltschmerz* or devil knows what. No, I am not withdrawing from our correspondence, I want to keep it up, though I may not be capable of the effusions you expected from me. Don't take offense at this or read into it any reservations against you personally. I would not want to do without your letters, and beg you to maintain your lovely warmth of feeling and your captivating spontaneity. I feel these qualities more vividly precisely because I lack them myself. I am terribly eager to get together with you. Where are you off to June 20? Perhaps it's a place I could somehow reach during the vacation. I am truly happy to hear a little jaunt to Italy is in the cards for you. You have long deserved that, enthusiast of beauty that you are! There's no chance of my joining you. My salary comes to 240 zloty. *Cinnamon Shops* didn't earn me a grosz. On the contrary, the book cost me several trips to Warsaw.

Rój[11] did promise me some sort of bonus in case the printing was sold out, but I doubt they will honor the promise. It was very nice in Warsaw. I had six days there. I spent them mainly with Nałkowska, my patroness and, I can say, friend. I visited Tuwim (who was recovering from an illness) and Aleksander Wat, and I saw Ważyk, Brucz, Gojawiczyńska.[12] What I am going to do over the holidays I don't know yet. What I should do is hole up in some

"Infanta and her Cards," from *Idolatry*.

village and write. I may go to Zakopane for my health. It depends on whether I can get a grant. Isn't *Kamena* going to be coming out anymore? I would like to stay in touch with you over the vacation. Write me where you're going to be. I know Leszczyc [an art dealer],[13] but only casually. The excursion to Truskawiec [now Truskavets, U.S.S.R.] will give me a chance to ask him about prices.

I send you warm greetings and hugs. Don't forget me!

Bruno Schulz

Drohobycz, June 5, 1934

25

Dear Classmate:

Unfortunately nothing can come of my trip to Lwów. My sister (the elder, who is widowed) suffers from a severe nervous disorder, and I can't leave her. I'll probably have to place her in some boardinghouse in Truskawiec, but for the present she won't hear of any move.

I must thank you with all my heart for so many tokens of genuine solicitude and sympathy. I hope we get to see each other in the course of the vacation. Maybe I'll visit you at Zwiniącz.[14] Can you imagine, the day I received your suggestion to go shares on a lottery ticket, the little shopkeeper where I stepped in to pick up some paper offered me a quarter ticket for 10 zloty? I didn't have the money so I didn't buy it. Maybe a chance was there—a hint of fate? No one ever offered me a ticket before. I am really sorry that we won't be able to meet now in Lwów. But maybe you could scoot over to see me in Drohobycz?

I have registered for a three-week summer course in handicraft shopwork, to be held in Żywiec starting July 2. I don't know if I'll go, although I badly need to because of the course in metalworking I am to teach next year, which I can't bring off without training. Back in our time, how on earth did we manage to avoid taking this subject, which has now ousted drawing?

My depression is not letting up, unfortunately. Perhaps it has to do with the unhappy conditions at home (my sister's illness). Thanks so very much for your words of comfort and moral support.

Don't forget me, and drop me a line from Zwiniącz. Is it a pretty place? Is it in Podolia [now a region in the U.S.S.R. called Podolsk]? Forgive me for sending only a few lines today—more soon.

Warm greetings and hugs,
Bruno Schulz

Drohobycz, June 23, 1934

Poor health dogged most of the Schulz household. Hania Hoffmanowa, Bruno's widowed older sister, "was an invalid who suffered from a neurotic condition," according to Schulz's cousin and family physician Dr. Hoffman. "After taking up my medical practice I was frequently called by Bruno to attend to her. She used to have attacks at night (cardiac symptoms, convulsions, etc.). Bruno would come to me in a state of panic, and we would spend several hours at her bedside together. After medication the attacks passed, only to recur after a week or a month. Bruno himself was in delicate health. I examined him frequently and diagnosed a heart defect in a recessive phase." Schulz also suffered from kidney stones.

26

Dear Classmate:

It has lain heavy on my conscience that once again our correspondence has lapsed through my fault. I didn't attend any courses because I got turned down the day before departure; and it was just as well, for a few days later I became seriously ill and am only now slowly recovering. I am beset by some urological trouble, very unpleasant and dispiriting, a condition that killed all energy and initiative in me. So I wasted my vacation in morbid brooding, sourly tracing the sinister and degrading symptoms of my malady. Only a week ago did I go to a specialist in Lwów, who pushed the whole business onto the road to recovery. I have an awful reluctance to go back to the school. The thought of teaching metalwork, which I haven't the faintest knowledge of, seizes me with despair. What's more, everything about this rotten job bores and repels me beyond limit. Imagine, on the same day I got your letter suggesting our going shares to buy a lottery ticket, I dropped in at a stationer's for notepaper and the attendant offered me a quarter ticket. I had no money and didn't buy it. As it so happens, a ticket bought at this very shop just won 300,000 zloty. The ticket was divided into quarters or eighths. I know a man, a judge, who won 60,000 zloty. If I had bought a ticket then, maybe neither of us would be teaching school today, we'd be traveling somewhere in Italy or Spain.

Exhausted as I am by my illness, I am going to apply for a sick leave of several weeks.[15]

I have known Wojtów[16] for a long time but expect no favors from him. Even if he wanted to, what could he really do for me? I'm sorry now I didn't accept a proposal put to me in Warsaw to join the staff of a daily and work as a journalist.

I haven't written a line the whole vacation; so much time lost. And here I had planned to enter *Ilustrowany Kurier Codzienny*'s[17] novel contest.

That's all my news this time. A hearty hug, and thanks for keeping in touch.

Your
Bruno Schulz

Drohobycz, August 28, 1934

27

Dear Classmate:

Pardon the pencil, but the fact is that a temporary shortage of ink has befallen my "studio" and caused the entire scholastic administration to go on a pencil diet.

Please, I beg you, don't ever think when my answer to something is delayed that it is because of my feeling out of sympathy or disgusted. If I am any judge, we will probably always remain in this relationship of warm and intimate exchange. Imagine, I saw one of your gouaches at Leszczyc's in Drohobycz—a garden or summerhouse, you know, with a bright distant landscape shining through nearby trees, and a group of people and a dog.

I was impressed by the technique these gouaches show, its difficulty and precision, and the luminosity and purity of the colors. You must surely get a feeling of satisfaction from these productions, from the calm mastery of them. I like them better than the woodcuts. Leszczyc told me he sold several little pictures and would be able to sell them all if they were a little cheaper; people go for them. He wants to exploit you, it looks to me, even though he is a likable person. I feel guilty when I contrast your hard work with my laziness. So much work at the school and still such a surplus of energy and initiative! You ask how I got involved in crafts. It happened very simply: all by itself. This process of slow metamorphosis of graphic artists into common laborers may be observed in all state high schools, where Drawing, as an optional subject, functions solely to boost the staff budget. Here in our high school we now give—for all the artificial and overstretched expansion of the subject—12 hours of Drawing. The budgeted curriculum calls for 27 hours!

Right now I'm on sick leave. I'm afraid to count up the days left till it runs out.[18]

Many many thanks for *Kamena.* I feel guilty about accepting it like that, as if it were my due, when I should be paying for a subscription. It is unethical.

I am going to send you a small prose piece.[19] Oh, how splendid it would be to have a year's leave of absence![20] If I got one, I'd be sure to visit you at Chełm. I haven't seen "people" in such a long time. What one meets here can only be matched up to that term with a certain loose approximation, a sense of figurative irony. Life could be pleasant . . . I choose to end on this optimistic note, the moreso as I have to go to the school to find out how the matter of my leave is progressing.

Warm greetings and hugs,

Bruno Schulz

Drohobycz, September 14, 1934

"In the Garden," cliché-verre etching from *Idolatry*.

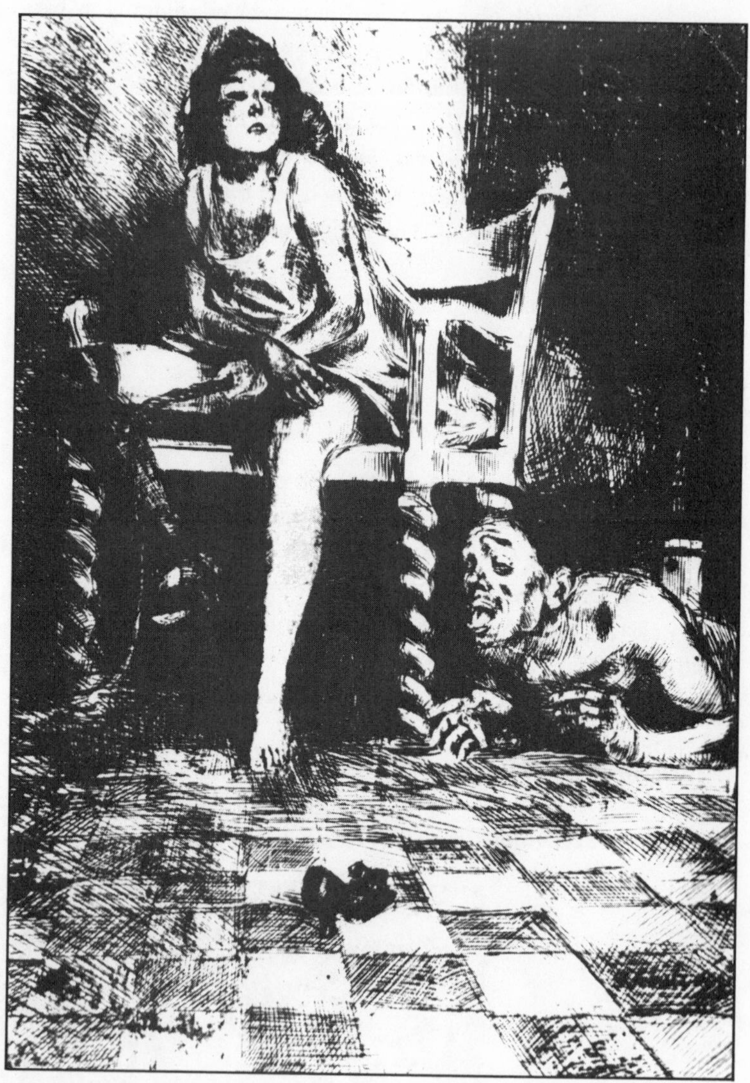

"Wild Beasts," from *Idolatry*.

"Undula, Eternal Ideal," from *Idolatry*.

Cliché-verre etching from *Idolatry*.

TO THE EDITORS OF *SYGNAŁY*, TADEUSZ HOLLENDER AND KAROL KURYLUK

Sygnały (Signals), *which was initially under the editorship of Tadeusz Hollender*[1] *(1933–1934), late in 1934 passed into the hands of Karol Kuryluk,*[2] *the founder of the journal. Kuryluk was not a participant in any private or personal correspondence with Schulz; his presence here is due only to the intermittent contacts Schulz had with* Sygnały. *These contacts were initiated by Kuryluk, who paid Schulz a visit in his cottage in Drohobycz and invited him to submit contributions to his journal. Linked from early adolescence with the revolutionary workers' movement, Kuryluk was more of a social, political, and cultural activist than a literary editor; the latter he treated as a sideline. He saw Schulz's creative potential not only in literature but also in graphic and sculptural arts. He expressed this judgment, among other occasions, in his report covering the exhibition held by the Association of Sculptural Artists in Lwów in December 1935, where he mentioned Bruno Schulz's drawings in first place among outstanding work (*Tygodnik Ilustrowany*, no. 5, 1936). The letter below was probably directed to Hollender; the others to Kuryluk.*

28

Dear Sir:

Right after my conversation with Karol Kuryluk I had to leave Drohobycz unexpectedly and did not get back until day before yesterday. In haste I made a fair copy of one novella,[3] hoping it might reach you in time for printing.

Your letter was delivered to my temporary address, missed me there, and reached me only today.

With kinds regards and greetings I am

Bruno Schulz

Drohobycz, September 28, 1934
10 Floriańska

Left: Karol Kuryluk, about 1930.

Right: Tadeusz Hollender, about 1930.

29

My dear Sir:

I am certainly aware of the founding of *Sygnały,* I even read it with interest when a copy comes my way.

I am glad to let you have Wilhelm Korabiowski's[4] manuscript. I will send something more eventually.

I well remember the summer day you came by with Madame Baranowska. Or was it autumn?[5] Please give my best regards to Korabiowski, whose performance in "The Merry Wave" I genuinely admire.[6] I don't know his prose yet.

When you have a chance, please give my regards to Maria Kuncewicz,[7] who I am told will be in Lwów this week.

I remain, with fond regards, yours

Bruno Schulz

Drohobycz, March 19, 1936

30

My dear Sir:

You are most welcome to a fragment from Kafka's[8] *The Trial;* I am sending along two to choose from. The one called "The Henchmen" is shorter but less representative of the whole. The other, which I have given the title "The Parable of Entry into the Law," contains the essential idea of the work.* I have added a short introduction about the nature of Kafka's literary work.

The latest issue of *Sygnały* looks very interesting. You won't believe this, but I haven't been able to read it straight through yet. I will thus reserve my critical remarks for my next letter.

A clasp of the hand and fond greetings,

Bruno Schulz

Drohobycz, May 12, 1936

*But is a trifle heavy, perhaps.

AFTERWORD TO KAFKA'S *THE TRIAL*

Schulz, who read Kafka's works in German and early recognized his genius, is credited with introducing Kafka's work to Polish letters. The afterword to the Polish edition of Kafka's The Trial, *which Schulz called an "Introduction" when he sent it to the editor of* Sygnały *with part of the translation, appeared in print only once—in 1936, when* The Trial *came out in book form. It was not reprinted in the postwar reissues, or included in a collection of works by Kafka titled* Prose *published in Poland in 1964. The translation was not actually Schulz's but Józefina Szelińska's, with Schulz's corrections and with his name attached to ease its acceptance for publication.*

Only a few of his minor stories saw the light of day during Kafka's lifetime. The unimaginable sense of responsibility, the quasireligious rigor of judgment he applied to his work allowed him to rest content with no single achievement and compelled him to cast away fruit after fruit of his inspired and happy talent. At that time only a small coterie of friends was even aware that here was creative genius on a grand scale, reaching its maturity before their eyes, grasping for ultimate goals, struggling to solve life's deepest problems. For him, writing was not an end in itself but a means of attaining a higher truth, of finding the proper way to live. It is its tragic destiny that the life rushing with desperate urgency to the light of faith does not find it, and goes off into darkness after all. This explains the last will of a writer who, dying before his time, consigned his entire literary oeuvre to destruction. Max Brod, appointed executor by Kafka, resolved to defy his wish and publish the surviving remnants of Kafka's literary estate in a series of volumes that established Kafka's position among the spirits which represent his generation.

All that rich, dense body of work, ripe and realized from its inception, was even at its earliest an inspired account and testimony from the universe of deep religious experience. Once and always under the spell of an otherworldly, religious sense of reality, Kafka's unwavering gaze penetrates the structure, organization, and underlying order of this hidden reality and sets its boundaries, where human life impinges on the nature of God. He is a bard and worshipper of the divine order; a bard of a strange stripe, to be sure. The most poisonous and scornful slanderer could not depict this world with more twisted caricature, through figures so overtly compromising and absurd. The sublime nature of the divine order, according to Kafka, can be rendered only by the power of human negation. This order is so far beyond the human range, so greatly transcends all human categories, that its sublimity is measured by the force of disapproval, resistance, and elemental rebuke that man marshals against those high authorities. How else, after all, could the human condition react to the usurpation of those powers except by protest, sheer lack of comprehension, shattering bursts of outrage?

The hero of *The Trial* subjects the entire hierarchy of the "judiciary" to just such bursts of outrage during the first court hearing. He attacks it passionately, threatens it with his apparent success, turns from accused into accuser. The seeming consternation of the Court, its withdrawal and perplexity, which symbolizes the fundamental incommensurateness of its majesty with human categories, excites the hero's audacity and reforming zeal. This is the way the blinded nature of humans reacts to the incursion of those powers, to a confrontation with them: by exaggerated self-assertion, that hybris of the ancients which is not the cause but a by-product of divine wrath. Jozef K feels a hundred times superior to the Court, its alleged trickeries and deceits fill him with disgust and contempt. To these traits he opposes human *raison d'etat,* civilization, work. Comical disillusion follows. All his superiority and reason do not shield him from the inexorable progress of the prosecution, which barges straight into his life as if all this were utterly beside the point. Feeling its ring drawing tighter and tighter around him, Jozef K dreams endlessly of the possibility of eluding it after all, of living outside its realm; he deludes himself that it might be possible to cadge something out of the Court by backstairs maneuvers involving women, who are, according to Kafka, intermediaries between the human and the divine; or by means of a beggarly painter who is rumored to have "connections" with the Court. In this way Kafka brands, holds up to unremitting ridicule, the dubious and hopeless nature of human endeavor in relation to the divine order.

Jozef K's mistake lies in clinging to his human reason instead of surrendering unconditionally. He persists in his stubbornness, submits endless petitions in which he attempts to present, day after day, his airtight human alibi. All these efforts and "legal recourses" drop into a mysterious void, never reaching the exalted authorities they orbit around. Human traffic, with this violently centripetal universe it is forever bumping up against, must always take the form of misunderstanding, failure to coincide, random shots that never find their target.

In the next to last chapter, which may be regarded as the key to the whole work, yet another aspect of the matter is developed in the prison chaplain's parable: it is not the law that pursues the guilty person, but rather he or she engages in a lifelong search for "entry into the law." It looks as if the law were hiding from man, wrapping itself up tight in its inaccessibility and holiness, but counting at the same time, surreptitiously as it were, on the sacrilegious invasion, the intrusion of man. The defense of the law that the chaplain undertakes in the astounding exegesis of this parable picks its way along the very edge of sophistry, borders on falsehood and cynicism—the hardest test to which devotion to the law may be put, the peak of self-denial to which it may rise.

In this work Kafka depicted the intrusion of the law into man's life, presenting it in a somewhat abstract manner. He did not demonstrate it concretely in a "real" individual fate. Right down to the end we never find out what Jozef K's guilt consisted in, we never come to know the form of law his life was to have fulfilled. Kafka only renders the atmosphere—the climate and aura—of a human life's involvement with the suprahuman, with supreme truth. The feat of artistic genius performed in this narrative lies in the fact that for these matters, which possess neither shape nor expression in human language, Kafka has found an adequate corporality as it were, a substitute material in which to build their structure and fashion it down to the smallest detail.

The perceptions and insights Kafka means to give expression to here are not his exclusive property. They are the common heritage of the mysticism of all times and nations, which has, however, always been couched in a language that was subjective and extraneous, the adopted language of certain esoteric communities and schools. Here for the first time the magic of poetry has created a species of parallel reality, a fictional body upon which mystical experience can be demonstrated; not substantively, to be sure, but in such a way that even the uninitiated may feel the chill breath of its distant majesty and realize that they are being offered a poetic equivalent of the actual experience.

In this sense Kafka's procedure, the creation of a *Döppelgänger* or substitute reality, stands virtually without precedent. The dual nature of his reality is achieved with the help of a kind of pseudorealism that merits special attention. Kafka sees the realistic surface of existence with unusual precision, he knows by heart, as it were, its code of gestures, all the external mechanics of events and situations, how they dovetail and interlace, but these to him are but a loose epidermis without roots, which he lifts off like a delicate membrane and fits onto his transcendental world, grafts onto his reality. His attitude to reality is radically ironic, treacherous, profoundly ill-intentioned—the relationship of the prestidigitator to his raw material. He only simulates the attention to detail, the seriousness, and the elaborate precision of this reality in order to compromise it all the more thoroughly.

Kafka's books present neither allegory, nor analysis, nor exegesis of a doctrine; his fiction shapes a poetic reality in its own right, rounded, hermetically sealed on all sides, self-justified and self-supporting. Aside from its mystical allusions and religious intuitions, the work lives its own poetic life—polysemantic, unfathomable, not exhausted by any interpretation.

The present narrative, which Max Brod received in manuscript from the author in 1920, is incomplete. A number of chapter fragments that were to find their places somewhere before the last chapter were omitted from the book by Brod, who acted upon Kafka's statement that the trial, ideally speaking, had no end, and that further elaboration would add nothing of substance to the meaning of this fiction.

THE ANNEXATION OF THE SUBCONSCIOUS: OBSERVATIONS ON MARIA KUNCEWICZ'S *THE FOREIGNER*

The novelist Maria Kuncewicz, whom Schulz mentions in Letter 29 and in later letters to Romana Halpern, was considered one of the most "Western" writers among her contemporaries. She made her debut in Pro Arte et Studio *in 1918, circulated in the same milieu as the Skamandrites, and championed Schulz's work in Warsaw's literary circles. In this review of her second novel* Cudzoziemka (The Foreigner), *published in* Pion, *no. 17, 1936, Schulz echoes and elaborates some of the themes developed in his afterword to* The Trial.

Kuncewicz's *The Foreigner* is one of those books that do not end at their back covers but, stepping over them, try to transplant their rootstock of problems in the reader, then sprout and take on new life in him. The resonance of this work is rich and lingering, as though it meant to abide within us and generate a secondary growth of issues and reflections in our minds.

As for literary gender, this novel is a portrait: We have to postulate a special genre for *The Foreigner* even if it should turn out to be the sole specimen in the category. It is a portrait assembled by the apparently incommensurable means of narration and novelistic plot. Unlike a biography, which presents its subject in a process of sequential dynamic development, the portrait has the contours of its physiognomy fixed from the start; development tunnels into depth and becomes dramatized analysis. The actual biographical passage of time is arrested, and the various episodes of a life are arranged not chronologically and pragmatically, but according to their deeper characterological meaning for the line of fate etched in the human palm.

It has been said of Rembrandtian portraits that in some manner they encompass the whole biography of the sitter, the balance sheet of his or her life. They are the definitive precipitate, so to speak; petrified biography. In Kuncewicz's book we confront the opposite process: The petrifact, the inanimate physiognomy, revives, sprouts with life, explicates its entire contents. I have long had the idea that you could distill an entire story or novel from the face of a person you meet, somehow remobilizing back into biography what had congealed into an end product in that face. I had no inkling, though, that this could be carried out on such a monumental scale.

The essence of the novel is movement and action; a portrait is static. Kuncewicz solved this dilemma by means of a novelistic trick: She used the device of confession. Trapped within a fate she does not understand, equally misunderstood by her environment, the heroine finally gains insight into her enigma shortly before her death and confesses before her daughter, rendering the account of her whole life.

This confession provides the novel's main flow. Into it the author has built a whole system of dams and dikes in which she catches the secondary currents, the backwash, and this undertow puts her back into various regions of the past and crisscrosses her heroine's life story with a branching network of canals. But against all these currents the narrative somehow makes steady headway, throwing up a fine spray of psychic insight, pressing on to the great estuary, the broad delta of the confession that swallows up all those tributaries and side streams.

The portrait is one of an evil woman, a Jezebel and witch never before depicted in Polish literature on such a broad scale and with this kind of reckless abandon. We are miles away here from the vamps and female demons, those cheap, counterfeit, coquettish sublimations of evil; this is malice in its common animal vulgarity. In the first stratum of the portrait, the underpainting, so to speak, the heroine confronts us with just that sort of unkempt, comic, pitiable spite. Kuncewicz's rendering is so splendid and convincing that it leaves us wondering where we have met this character before. Kuncewicz does not spare her heroine, does not tone down or retouch. Courageously, inexorably, she provokes the reader's antipathy, disapproval, even mockery. But this plucky ruthlessness pays off generously on a higher level of psychological persuasiveness.

Human wickedness, that primal snarling spite the individual directs against the entire world, can be a splendid, fascinating phenomenon in its elemental outbursts; even in minor manifestations it is not without a certain charm. Fundamentally, wickedness is an atavistic reaction that goes back to brutal primeval times, when direct terror was still an efficient and successful regulator of human relations. Relapses into this uncontrolled reactive mode thus tend to be regarded as disgraceful and ludicrous. On the other hand, blasts of spite hold a certain romantic appeal, a pathos of naiveté that provokes and entertains in its role as a spontaneous eruption of the life force from effete civilized forms. Wickedness has something of the aborigine's club to it, comic and touching in a European's hand. There is a disinterested candor in it, a rising above utilitarian motives, an implacable profligacy of emotion spent on self-assertion; something spontaneous and self-propelled, moreover, like a fit of madness that disarms and to some degree propitiates us. That sort of instinctive and innocent malice occasionally merges its symptoms with those of another variety, which is basically inverted love—a complicated, twisted affair whose origins lie in the straits of hysteria.

Accumulated charges of psychic energy sometimes find themselves suddenly blocked without release in the human soul, at which point they may discharge themselves, far from their dynamic sources, in fits of rage and spite. The malice of our heroine appears to have that involute and equivocal binary source, and therefore is by turns amusing and engaging, amazing and pathetic.

Had the author confined herself to this aspect of Róża, she would have presented a lively and memorable portrait, monumental in its unity. This is how those around her must have seen her, if such a person actually existed, and as such she deserved to be immortalized for the purity with which she embodied the demonic female. But the author does not leave her character there; she carries the case of Róża through many courts of appeal, develops her set of problems on a number of levels. Each time Róża emerges an utterly different person. What has already seemed the bottom layer of her personality draws back, exposing farther and lower planes. By this gradation of the issue of Róża's nature, this descent to ever deeper levels of predicament, the author keeps us in constant tension and dazzles us into profounder amazement at each stage.

As long as we see her in the context of everyday life, Róża is merely a shrew. The flat background provokes bursts of ordinary spite, as it were, highlights the mask of the common scold. In this mode, Róża is constantly subject to discharges of the wicked element, which presses for relief with the inexorable force of a machine. But placed in exceptional situations, festive surroundings, Róża changes completely, becomes a different being. This woman is actually predestined for the grand, heroic life, for the great fullness to which music, or the highest exaltation of love, offers the key.

On those rare convivial occasions when it is granted her to rise from the flatness of the everyday into a world of beauty, the convulsive cramp of her nature loosens, and she lights up with an inner glow, becomes magnificent, a perfect instrument of the beauty of life. At those times she fascinates those around her and works a peculiar magic on them. Then she radiates with a fire that energizes life around her, kindles it to a strange intensity, makes it luscious, beautiful, and ardent. Under her spell life rises to a larger dimension, people overstep their boundaries, outdo their potential. She vibrates with a passion for greatness that inspires and transforms. The seemingly disruptive ferment of malice and irritation, excitement and fever proves creative and takes on a new life—as war waged against all that is mean and petty in people and things.

At those times no one, however badly hurt, can resist her, everything is forgiven her, all pulses beat fast and hard.

To the author's great credit, she has been able to make that polarity of Róża's nature plausible and prevent the violent leaps between bathos and exaltation she has her perform from shattering the unity of the character. Róża lives on a shuttle between the uplifting power of a muse and the crass vulgarity of a termagant; but this swinging of the pendulum not only fails to detract from the authenticity of either mode of being—they seem rather to justify and uphold each other. Only the sundering of the character Róża into two such contradictory figures vouches for the genuineness of each. The whole irritating fauna of spite, cattiness, arrogance, and hauteur gains in that juxtaposition a foil against which it seems to assume a new and deeper meaning. Her mood swings, her raptures, her musings, on the other hand, gain in the contrasting spectacle of the mundane and the comic a certain realistic counterpoise that saves them from artificiality.

How is it credible that this egoist devoid of love, kindness, empathy, or forbearance toward anyone, who makes a habit of flinging handfuls of gritty truth into everyone's eyes and has never bid for anyone's favor—how is it such a creature rouses enthusiasm anywhere she cares to step down from her glorious isolation? That one friendly smile from her is all it takes to open all arms to her? The secret lies precisely in her self-sufficiency and independence from the environment, the fact that she reposes entirely in herself. Those around her are all under some control, all are dependent on someone or something they need.

She alone among these crippled and fragmentary beings is whole, fierce, and proud; she needs no one, she is beginning and end and absolute center, a perfect monad. The malice she permits herself is her triumph on the summit of that independence, the surplus of her self-sufficiency. That is the secret of her ascendancy, her metaphysical domination of her milieu. Nothing fascinates people as much as substantiality, fullness of being. The author does not spell out this truth, or even formulate it at all; she knows how to convey it without words—the greater art.

It would seem that the author might close her analysis with this facet of the character. But the analysis proper has not even begun. She now rolls back the walls of the psychological interior like scenery on a stage and discloses the deeper background of the business. In retrospect, those manifestations of demonic spite become comparatively innocuous, for they take the form of rows, hysterical scenes, and social scandals. A dilated malignity is now revealed that is greater and more menacing. It ruins the life of her husband, Adam, it hovers like a fatal power over her children's lives. There are moments when evil power confronts her with criminal temptation. Róża toys with the idea of murdering her son, engineering her daughter's death. The author no longer conceals the fact that something is very skewed here, that Róża's rage is misplaced and vents itself against a surrogate in the wrong territory. All those irresponsible acts of desperation are actually gestures directed elsewhere, expressive behavior improperly addressed. We now pass with the author into another psychological dimension, a province marked by another mechanism of processes, another technique of motivation: the subconscious.

Kuncewicz conceived the excellent idea of employing something like the technique of free association associated with psychoanalysis. By the first pages of the work she has smuggled in, incognito so to speak, the underlying mise-en-scène of this life. She does it in anecdotal fashion, evoking a faded scene from early childhood: We see Róża, an immature young girl from Taganrog full of curiosity about life, by the stove with Michał, and his enchanting words—*diese, diese, o ja, wunderschöne Nase** —words that trace out the boundaries of Róża's destiny. What appears so unobtrusively in the language of the conscious mind holds the whole meaning of a life in the subconscious. This was the text of Róża's fate, the couplet she would recite endlessly, each time with a different intonation, each time closer to understanding—until, at a late hour in her existence, she understands it completely.

Everything later life was to write over this text, which encompasses the full tragedy and bliss of Róża's lot, is only in the nature of a palimpsest made to obscure its true meaning. Those words woke her up to her own being, made her into a woman. And when Michał, the only lover of her life, later abandoned her, her womanhood shut down and entrenched itself forever in those fateful words.

* "This, this, oh yes, absolutely lovely nose."

Psychoanalysis is familiar with those accumulations of disjointed psychic energy with no outlet that become fixated on certain words, certain compulsive thoughts or actions. The question arises whether experiences of psychoanalysis are legitimately subject to literary treatment.

I tend to think that, to the uninitiated, psychoanalytic reasoning is not entirely persuasive. The mechanisms of subconscious events and their logic are unlike those we are accustomed to encounter in belles lettres. In the novel the ultimate and decisive argument is not truth, but verisimilitude. The revelations of the psychoanalysts, though genuine, will remain unconvincing to the uninured mind for a long time to come. At some future point, when our introspective faculties have been sufficiently sharpened by the insights and methods of psychoanalysis to allow us to catch the subconscious mechanisms red-handed, and when our minds are used to the mechanisms of these processes, the time for psychoanalysis in the novel will have come. Kuncewicz's novel, however, contradicts this prognosis. It does seem to demonstrate that the procedures of psychoanalysis are already ripe for literary deployment. But I suspect that this is because of a certain distortion of the actual workings of the subconscious, brought about by an unsanctioned attempt to fit them into the hierarchy of conscious psychic processes and make them similar in structure—a strategy, by the way, that I consider admissible, even necessary, in the interest of intelligibility.

Let us return once more to Róża's decisive childhood experience. It was by this encounter, this text, that she learned how to read her life. And when this text was taken from her, she refused to accept any other, to entertain any counterproposal from life. At this point her life collapsed and became blocked. From then on, all that came her way—marriage, children, their careers and happiness, the things that fill the life of a normal woman—was to her like an alien, extraneous, unreal shadow life. Thus her terror before death, which is devoid of meaning when it does not seal a destiny fulfilled.

A life caught in the jaws of this kind of complex, however, still has another road to freedom open to it: sublimation in art, ambition, a career. Róża tries to escape her complex through all these hatches. The most tragic of these ventures are her attempts to take flight into the realm of music, for Róża is a gifted if not fully trained violinist. The reader is profoundly shaken by the spectacle of Róża's struggle for a higher level of being and fullness of feeling, predestined as she is by nature for a grand, spacious, elevated life. The setting for this is Brahms' violin concerto in

D major. The passage where Róża, having plumbed the full abysmal depth of her fate, rises through the bars of her cage into the lavish profusion of a moonlit night, hallucinating liberation with the aid of this half-illusory music, is one of the summits of Polish prose. No one in our literature has written like this about music before. Here Kuncewicz finds a veritable new language for rendering what music is—that glistening body of sounds—and touches the juncture where music passes into metaphysics.

Róża's life is not extrinsic, does not evolve by way of external events and encounters in the real world. Despite its seeming expansiveness, this life is intrinsic, focused inward. Its single true adventure, Michał's love, shrunken in the gray mists of childhood, has moved beyond time and reality to become eternal. By this adventure, both a source and an unattainable goal, her life measures itself. But can one resurrect what is gone forever, live by what has been canceled, withdrawn, annulled? *Si flexere nequeo Superos, Acheronta movebo.*† To the parched soul nothing is impossible. Róża struggles in the coils of her unhappiness until her strength gives out and the fierce passion subsides. Her fate, set on finishing her off, makes her softer, more compliant, more amenable to compromises.

Róża has an encounter in Królewiec where she consults a doctor who takes a somewhat unusual attitude toward her. Undeterred by her fundamental hostility and intransigent stance, he gives her good and warm advice. Róża reacts with contempt and arrogance, then scornfully dismisses the whole episode. Some time later, though, after her return to Poland, Róża's mind reverts to the incident and reviews it. This happens at the stage when her organism's deep instinct senses its approaching end. Róża then reedits the experience in her mind, interpreting it now out of the depth of her longing, fantasizing that the wheel has come full circle, that what was impossible has come to pass in this very episode. For the physician happened to use the same words as Michał; from his lips came the same fateful refrain, the text of her complex, and this was sufficient for the original mise-en-scène of her life to become actuality. The doctor assumed Michał's place, he *was* Michał. Michał never betrayed her, God heard her prayers back then and kept him faithful. Her children are Michał's children. All the martyrdom of life with Adam was one long bad dream. Róża now wakes up from it and once again becomes the unripe young girl full of longing, her whole unlived life, *her* life, still lying before her, untouched. Those words of Michał's and the attendant mise-

† Translator's note: Misquoted: should be: *Flectere si nequeo superos, Acheranta movebo,* "If I cannot bend the gods, I will unleash Acheron [Hades]." Vergil, *Aeneid,* vii, 312.

en-scène are somehow eternal and emblematic. Discrepancies of time, place, and person are irrelevant to the psyche, hence they vanish before the essential semantic identity. Róża cannot be redeemed except by the words uttered that single time, the couplet that was her curse; and if fate will not come to her rescue, she will create the redemptive scene, her beatification, herself—hallucinating it in the hour of her death.

Róża attains grace; the armor of malice, compulsive ambition, passionate will to greatness crumbles. She revokes her life, her heroic attitude to it, her blasphemous posturing; she demobilizes and disarms the entire apparatus of her life. "Not ambition or art, nor travel nor wealth —a smile is what is vital for living," she tells Marta; "the kind of smile that rises from an utterly satisfied heart."

It is not fanciful to say that this hallucination is a reward, Heaven's compensation to Róża, who, beaten down so long by life, finally understood what fate asked of her, opened up and undid the hard knot of her obduracy.

This then is how far the author had to reach to solve the issue of Róża, an issue that in its first stages appeared a relatively uncomplicated psychological problem.

So it comes to pass that, when we pursue an inquiry into a character beyond a certain depth, we step out of the field of psychological categories and enter the sphere of the ultimate mysteries of life. The floorboards of the soul, to which we try to penetrate, fan open and reveal the starry firmament. The case of Róża ceases to be a matter of psychology and becomes simply a matter of man, a matter that has been tried before one supreme tribunal or other since time began. Into the clinical case, the psychoanalytical interview, eternity steps unnoticed, and it transforms the psychoanalytical laboratory into eschatological theater.

Such extension of psychoanalysis, beyond its proper scope in the province of human life and its problems, where its dialectic becomes ambiguous and flickering, is the cupola over the entire analytical model, the dome that caps a complicated, rich, muscular edifice.

Let me devote a few final words to the novel's structure. By the example of this involved, opulent, multiply interconnected structure one can observe how the construction of a work arises from the articulation of content, from the mental penetration of the subject matter in various directions. In certain aspects, the construction of this book recalls the multiplex structure of a dream; like a dream, it may be read many times according to a variety of keys, each version unlocking a deeper sense of the matter.

Kuncewicz has unconsciously based the composition of this book on the procedure devised by psychoanalysis for the relief of neurotic symptoms. This makes certain leitmotifs recur frequently, submerge and resurface, guided, as in free association, by the subterranean dynamic of the subconscious. This technique imparts a quasimusical character to the composition. The undulation of motifs continually returning in different keys, the oscillation of the narrative among constant allusions, mental assonances, correspondences, rapports—fuse into a final impression of an immensely finely spun, highly interconnected artifact of multiple determinants—like a fugue.

31

Dear Editor:

I take the liberty of sending you a piece of prose that seems remarkable to me. Written by a young woman,[9] it is more than a promise of fine things to come; I find unusual virtues in it.

I put it before you for your kind appraisal and would be delighted if you could find space for it. This would serve as a great incentive to the young author to make a commitment to serious work.

In any case I would be glad to have your opinion; and please preserve the manuscript.

With my respects and warm regards,

Bruno Schulz

Drohobycz, September 4, 1938
8 Floriańska[10]

32

My dear Editor:

I will be happy to contribute to the December issue. I am not sure yet what I am going to pull together for it, but most likely it'll be *belles lettres.* I will send it in by the indicated deadline.

With my respects and warm regards, I am

Bruno Schulz

Drohobycz, September 24, 1938

33

My dear Editor:

Enclosed please find the promised piece of narrative prose ["*Ojczyzna*" ("Fatherland")] for the December issue of *Sygnały*.[11]

I would be grateful if galleys for proofreading could be sent to me since, given my handwriting, misprints are apt to be particularly painful.

With my respects and cordial regards, I am

Bruno Schulz

November 4, 1938

TO WACŁAW CZARSKI

CHIEF EDITOR OF *Tygodnik Ilustrowany*

34

Dear and respected friend:

Heartfelt thanks for your kind and lovely letter, your words of comfort and encouragement. I do need them, for I am at the end of my strength. I don't know if I can stand this drudgery much longer. School today is not the school of an earlier day, that veritable idyll among professions—almost a sideline, maintaining a modest position on the backdrop of life. Since it cut its teeth, it has run rampant with shameless presumption, it has turned demanding, raising ever more baldly a claim to be the entire content of a person's life. School tolerates no competition. It lost long ago that beautiful modesty which predestined it to be the income-yielding profession of people possessed of some mission, some lofty but unprofitable task.

What am I to do? Am I to renounce what I regard as my vocation, my peculiar mission?

Am I to take manual labor as the sum total of my aspirations?

By my very nature I am not made to offer resistance, stand up for myself, defy the will of another person. I do not possess the necessary strength of conviction, the narrow faith in the rightness of my cause, for that. Why am I, lover of nature and her elemental portents, condemned to resist her, smother her natural, beautiful whims and impulses that erupt in children, repress her primal vandalism? No—that struggle against a united front, a likable gang of twenty-six boys (that is the enrollment in each course) equipped with hammers, saws, and planes, is no honorable struggle, and the violent and desperate measures of intimidation I must resort to in order to keep them in check fill me with disgust. Every day I leave that scene brutalized and soiled inside, filled with distaste for myself and so violently drained of energy that several hours are not enough to restore it.

In the afternoon, too, for that matter, I have various things to see to in the workshop.

Why won't you rescue me, dear and kindly sir? Why is Mr. Zawistowski taking so much time to pave the way for the renewal of my petition for leave?

Could you let me have two more weeks in which to complete the illustrations to "Eddie"[2]? I really haven't had the time. My autobiographical piece—an interview with Witkacy in the form of an exchange of letters, an epistolary interview—has been sitting at Witkiewicz's in Zakopane for a week, and I fear it may never see the light of day.[3] If I weren't afraid to hurt Witkiewicz, I would send it to you for the *Tygodnik* as an interview conducted with myself. Except for this, I'm not writing anything, just dreaming about it; I hardly find the time to get anything read.

Gombrowicz hasn't sent me the piece by him I was to illustrate. He must have changed his mind.

I commend myself very kindly to your memory and add my respects and best wishes.

Bruno Schulz

[Winter 1934/1935]

TO WŁADYSŁAW ZAWISTOWSKI

DIRECTOR, DEPARTMENT OF ARTS, MINISTRY OF RELIGIOUS BELIEFS AND PUBLIC EDUCATION[1]

35

Dear Chief of Section:

Though already verbally apprised of your communication by Mr. Wierzyński[2] and Mr. Czarski, I am profoundly moved and more grateful than I can say, not least for the decisive and definite form it took in bringing me the fulfillment of my ardent desires. If one may speak of bliss, then today I feel in my heart that deep calm, that solemn and slightly rueful sense of fulfillment which is bliss.

How can I thank you?

From my worthy spokesmen you have learned with what distress I submitted to the demands of a school routine alien to my temper and how much I suffered under this yoke. With what sighs of relief, with what sense of limitless liberation I will now return to the concerns I believe I am destined for!

I am a little frightened by—the responsibility I am now taking on. I am reassured, however, by past experience, which has never failed to show that my short periods of freedom were periods of productivity. Released from outside pressure, my nature in some way returned to its native dominion, its normal functions. Left to itself, my mechanism—began creating.

Concerning the details of the arrangement made on my behalf,

Untitled pencil sketch, probably 1920s. Imaginary scene near Drohobycz marketplace. Compare to illustration for "The Book."

Untitled pencil sketch, 1930s.

I am full of appreciation and gratitude. The combination of an increase in my salary (after deducting the cost of my replacement) with a ministerial subsidy strikes me as a model of innovative ingenuity. I would never have hit upon such an idea. I am grateful beyond measure, my dear Chief, for what you have done for me.

My application to the school board for leave will be handed in to the principal today; the petition to the Ministry for a stipend I take the liberty of attaching here. Should anything in its content or form be inappropriate, I would be glad to have you send it back for emendation.

Commending myself henceforward to your kind favor, I am, with sincere respects,

Bruno Schulz

Drohobycz, March 19, 1935
10 Floriańska

36

My dear Chief of Section:

With the memory of your great favor fresh in my mind, and aware of your uncommonly kind disposition toward me, I have decided—finding myself in a quandary, though perhaps one of minor import—to appeal to you as to the Palladium of Polish art and literature, and ask for your assistance.

"Encounter." Pencil or charcoal, about 1920. Original of this and of "Undula Strolling" are lost; these reproductions are from the Yiddish journal *Custztajer* (*Contribution*), Lwów, 1930.

For many years I have dreamed of going to Paris, to experience the art of France at long last and breathe its atmosphere of aesthetic purity. But now that I am in a position to use some modest book royalties for a few weeks' stay in France, I am running into a great deal of trouble with government regulations. The Foreign Exchange Administration has declined to issue me the necessary letter of credit, and the county authorities in turn will not issue the required tourist (i.e., reduced rate) visa without this L/C.

I imagine these restrictions are aimed at purely recreational travel by ordinary tourists, but the bureaucratic machine is unable in its ponderous course to allow for exceptions without the intervention of loftier powers. But if the Ministry of Religious Beliefs and Public Education lent its support to my request in the form of a recommendation of the applicant to the Ministry of the Interior, emphasizing the artistic-creative nature of my trip, I have little doubt this would remove all obstacles.

May I submit, dear sir, a most earnest plea to you to lend me such support?

Committing this matter—one so vital to my future artistic development—to your kindly care, I look forward to a favorable outcome and remain, with deep respect,

Bruno Schulz

Drohobycz, June 21, 1938
10 Floriańska

TO KAZIMIERZ TRUCHANOWSKI

Kazimierz Truchanowski[1] *before the war published the novels* Ulica Wszystkich Swiętych (All Saints' Street, *1936*) *and* Apteka Pod Słańcem (Pharmacy Under the Sign of the Sun, *1938*). *Though the following letters indicate that Schulz was flattered to have attracted a follower, by December of 1936 he had come to regard Truchanowski's work as an "involuntary parody" and poor imitation of his own (see Letter 43). Truchanowski defended himself in his article* "Czy naśladnictwo?" ("Mimicry?") *in the magazine* Studio, *nos. 5–6, 1936.*

During the war he worked as a gamekeeper in the forests of the Kielce region, taking part in organizing aid to partisans, Jews, and fugitives from German POW camps. He was one of the group that planned to spirit Schulz out of Drohobycz and hide him in an isolated forester's lodge in the Spały (Kielce) country.

37

Drohobycz, October 10, 1935

My dear Sir:

Your feeling of connection to my work touches me. I thank you from my heart for your words of sympathy and solidarity.

Messiah grows, little by little; it will be the continuation of *Cinn. Shops.* Parts of the novellas have already appeared in journals. The novella *"Edzio"* ["Eddie"] was published in issue no. 4 of *Tygodnik Ilustrowany.*[2] The translation from German [of *The Trial*] is finished, it just needs going over and copying out. I am putting that off until the winter, since I'll be in Warsaw then and can get it done personally at *Rój.* I have very little time, since I teach shop in school twenty-seven hours a week—though leave has been promised me.

As for illustrations, I haven't illustrated *Cinn. Shops,* I only have plans to, and for that I intend to learn how to make woodcuts. So I cannot help you with these illustrations. If you are interested,

"Undula Strolling," pencil, about 1920.

though, I may send you two older sheets;[3] with no money involved, however, because I only accept money from rich Philistines. I'll send them on as soon as you give me your Warsaw address.

You ask if I would undertake to illustrate your work. Please forgive me, but I can't do it. I don't even have the time to illustrate my own things or to write; I mustn't devote what time I do have to illustrating other people's work. Still, I'd be glad to see some of it. You might send me a moderate-size sample.

I'll be very glad to get together with you in Warsaw. For the moment, warm greetings and my respects, and please let me hear from you.

Bruno Schulz

38

Dear Sir:

Now that I think of it, during our meeting I didn't really get to the bottom of you, to those layers that would have been the most intriguing. You must be full of interesting things inside; I'd like to spend a week or two in the country with you some time. You must be an ideal companion, a fellow spinner of fantasies, wanderer, and hiker.

Do you like children's tales of adventure, for example? Would you like to live with me and some other person on a desert island, a self-sufficient fastness slightly menaced by wild animals, pirates, and so on? Have you read Stevenson's *Treasure Island*? Have you never thought of writing such a book for children and childlike fantasizers?

Untitled pencil and India-ink wash, 1920s. Schulz on the left. Collection of the Museum of Painting, Lvóv, U.S.S.R.

Untitled oil, about 1925.

You touch a sensitive spot, asking about my *Messiah.* I'm getting nowhere with it. The Kafka translation has already gone to the printer. I take it you have read the extract in the *Tygodnik Ilustrowany.*[4] Did you like it?

I apologize for having forgotten to sign the two sheets. I'll write you presently about the drawings. Please excuse my not writing oftener.

Consider me your devoted friend and well-wisher. I look forward to another meeting and send you warm greetings.

Bruno Schulz

March 4, 1936

I am sending you "*Father and Adela.*"[5]

Should I return the manuscripts to you? I like the father's roaming the streets on his way to the station very much.[6] The top hats in "Guests"[7] are splendid, too, and the mannequins the guests turn into.

39

Dear Sir:

Please forgive me for having left two letters unanswered. The blame lies with the enduring depression that weighs down my life: I feel I can't give anything of myself, whereas you expect and anticipate so much. I simply have nothing with which to respond to your enthusiasm. Besides my barren condition as a writer, I am beset by a multitude of material and personal worries. Next month, for example, my stipend (150 zloty) runs out and I won't have any income since I am not on salary. So far spring has been fairly hard, tart, and inhospitable and has brought me—nothing. Every day I go to see a friend [Emanuel Pilpel][8] who is dying of cancer. It makes me feel bad to puncture your legend about my good fortune. I face a difficult marital problem, the undermining of my union with a loving, brave, unusual woman because of my material circumstances.

I read your radio play with interest. Apart from my subjective interest, I can tell you nothing about it, I simply feel incompetent in the matter. You should show it to Irzykowski in Warsaw; he deals a lot with scenarios for radio and can give you valuable hints about radio conditions. He may also be of help to you; he likes young, undiscovered talent. Shall I send your manuscript back?

My translation of Kafka is going to come out shortly; I'll send it to you when it's published. Besides that, by the end of the vacation I plan to publish a volume of short stories [*Sanitorium*] which have already appeared in journals, plus one longer one.[9] I would like to have these come out with illustrations. I am not touching *Messiah.*

Please pardon my not writing much. I hope we'll see each other, and then we must have some long talks. In the meantime I wish you a happy holiday and all good things.

Bruno Schulz

Drohobycz, April 11, 1936

TO STANISŁAW IGNACY WITKIEWICZ

The following interview with Schulz was conducted by S. I. Witkiewicz through a questionnaire and published in Tygodnik Ilustrowany, *no. 17, 1935. Stanisław Ignacy Witkiewicz (1885–1939) was perhaps the most versatile Polish artist of the century: prose writer, dramatist, philosopher, painter, aesthetic theorist, he pioneered in all these areas. The allonym "Witkacy" was derived from his signature on paintings, which cannibalized IgnACY WITKiewicz in an effort to avoid confusion with his father, the distinguished but less innovative painter of the same name.*

Witkiewicz was the first significantly influential literary figure to champion Schulz's work, publicly assigning the author of Cinnamon Shops *a place second to none in contemporary Polish literature. He did this at a time when the forty-year-old provincial had been no more than noticed in some literary or paraliterary coteries; Schulz's extraordinary imagination had not been fully assessed even by the editors who had accepted some of his work. All the actual letters written by Schulz to Witkiewicz went up in smoke when Warsaw underwent its first (partial) incineration by the Germans in September 1939. After the German invasion of September 1, Witkiewicz, with thousands of other refugees, fled Warsaw toward the eastern provinces, where the Polish army was hastily attempting to form a second front. Witkiewicz had foreseen the possibility of a Fascist invasion from the west and a Communist invasion from the east, and on September 17 his worst fears were realized. On September 18, the day after the Russian invasion, he died by his own hand.*

What follows is the introduction furnished by Witkiewicz to the 1935 interview. Taken together with his extensive study of Schulz published in Pion (Probe), *nos. 34 and 35, 1935, under the title* "Tworczosc Literacka B. Schulza" *("B. Schulz's Literary Work"), it is testimony to Witkiewicz's pioneering role in discerning Schulz's highly original literary genius and its symbiosis with Schulz's visual art. This assessment became generally accepted in Polish criticism only years later. In the rest of the West the very awareness of Schulz's existence was delayed more than twenty years by the Fourth Partition at Yalta.*

INTERVIEW WITH BRUNO SCHULZ

My acquaintance with Schulz dates back ten years.

At that time he showed me his graphics. It was they that stayed in my mind while the image of their creator vanished from it like dust in a hurricane.

I later received two of his sheets from Stefan Szuman, professor at the Royal Jagiellonian University of Wilna [Kraków], another admirer of Schulz's graphic and literary art, which gave me the opportunity for a closer look at and into them. At that point we renewed our acquaintance, or more properly, friendship; and my reading of *Cinnamon Shops,* which left me thunderstruck, provided the occasion for closer intimacy.

I did not know until recently that where drawing is concerned, Schulz was practically self-taught—a fact which can only serve to enhance one's admiration for his astonishing and peculiar talent. As a draftsman and graphic artist, he belongs to the realm of the demonic. To my mind, the beginnings of this trend in art appear in certain works of earlier masters who do not specialize in it yet, as it were—e.g., in Cranach, Dürer, Grünewald—when they paint with a strange certainty and licentious relish scenes that are hellish rather than heavenly, resting their brushes there with a clear conscience from (one may assume) tedious and externally imposed sanctities. I claim Hogarth, too, for the company of the demonists.

The true creator of this trend, however (where overt content, realistic substructure, pretext for Pure Form are concerned), was Goya. From him come the demonists of the nineteenth century such as Rops, Munch, even Beardsley. The point here is not the paraphernalia of demonism (witches, devils, etc.) but that evil which is the matrix of the human soul—egoism which makes allowance only for kin; rapacity; avarice; sexual lusts; sadism; cruelty; craving for power; oppression of all around—upon which only by dint of proper training grow other, nobler qualities, which, incidentally, may be observed in seminal form even among animals.

This is the general territory of Schulz's imagination; his special area within it is female sadism, linked to male masochism. In my view, woman by her nature (one must marvel that she still is such, having such organs and means of operation—marvel, admire her, and praise the powers responsible for the division of the sexes) must in principle be psychically a sadist and physically a masochist, while man must be as a rule psychically a masochist, but physically

Stanisław Ignacy Witkiewicz ("Witkacy"), about 1930.

Untitled pencil sketch, 1930s.

sadistic. Schulz drove the expression of both these psychic couplings to the extremity of tension and almost monstrous pathos. To him, the instrument of oppression of men by woman is the leg, that most formidable part—besides the face and various other features—of the female body. It is with their legs that Schulz's women tease, trample, drive to sullen, helpless madness his dwarfish men-freaks, cowed as they are by erotic torture, degraded and finding supreme painful relish in their degradation. His graphics are poems of pedal atrocity. Notwithstanding their dreadful mugs, one has the impression that Schulz's dames carefully scrub their feet with brushes twice a day and have no corns. Otherwise the impact would be downright appalling—and morally it is appalling even so.

Apart from this theme, which is treated with unusual expressive power, some of Schulz's compositions seem almost to approach the ideal of Pure Form in the matter of design and distribution of dark and light planes, as well as in slight deformations which impart an uncommon directive tension to the masses involved. . . . [omission]

I have the impression that in Schulz's case we find ourselves, if not in the realm of genius (which inheres precisely in proportions, not just in the mere tension of unrelated elements), then certainly at its border. The same is true of his writing (*Cinnamon Shops* and the stories published in *Tygodnik Ilustrowany, Wiadomości Literackie,* and *Sygnały* of Lwów), which is provisionally revealed to us in the form of pieces strung on a common thread of place, time, and recurrent characters—the author and his surroundings—but not clearly connected by any shared idea or plot. This makes of them neither short stories nor an integral narrative but items interrelated by the unconscious metaphysics of the author's mind and the uncanny strangeness that radiates even from his style—whose elements, along with the purely literary and philosophical values of his works, I intend to analyze in a separate study. . . .

BRUNO SCHULZ: AN ESSAY FOR S. I. WITKIEWICZ[1]

The beginnings of my graphic work are lost in mythological twilight. Before I could even talk, I was already covering every scrap of paper and the margins of newspapers with scribbles that attracted the attention of those around me. At first they were all horses and wagons. The action of riding in a wagon seemed to me full of weight and arcane symbolism. From age six or seven there appeared and reappeared in my drawings the image of a cab, with a hood on top and lanterns blazing, emerging from a nocturnal forest. That image belongs to the basic material of my imagination; it is a kind of node to many receding series. To this day I have not exhausted its metaphysical content. To this day the sight of a carriage horse has lost none of its fascination and troubling power. Its schizoid anatomy, sprouting antlers, whorls, knotholes, outcroppings at every extremity, was arrested in its development, as it were, at a time when it still wanted to reproduce and branch into other forms. And the wagon is a schizoid structure, too, derived from the same anatomical principle—multiarticulated, fantastic, made up of sheet metal warped into flipper shapes, of horse hides and huge clattering wheels.

I don't know how we manage to acquire certain images in childhood that carry decisive meanings for us. They function like those threads in the solution around which the significance of the world crystallizes for us. Another of those images for me is that of a child carried by its father through the spaces of an overwhelming night, conducting a conversation with the darkness. The father caresses the child, folds him in his arms, shields him from the natural element that chatters on and on, but to the child these arms are transparent; the night cuts straight through them, and over the father's soothing words he hears its sinister blandishments without interruption. And oppressed, full of fatalism, he answers the night's importunities with tragic readiness, wholly surrendered to the mighty element from which there is no escape.

There are texts that are marked out, made ready for us somehow, lying in wait for us at the very entrance to life. This is how I absorbed Goethe's ballad,[2] with all its metaphysics, at age eight. Through the half-understood German I caught, or divined, the meaning, and cried, shaken to the bottom of my soul, when my mother read it to me.

Such images amount to an agenda, establish an iron capital of the spirit, proffered to us very early in the form of forebodings and half-conscious experiences. It seems to me that all the rest of one's life is spent interpreting these insights, breaking them down to the last fragment of meaning we can master, testing them against the broadest intellectual spectrum we can manage. These early images mark out to artists the boundaries of their creative powers. The works they create represent drafts on existing balances. They do not discover anything new after that, they only learn how to understand better and better the secret entrusted to them at the outset; their creative effort goes into an unending exegesis, a commentary on that one couplet of poetry assigned to them. Art, for that matter, does not resolve that secret completely. The secret stays in a tangle. The knot the soul got itself tied up in is not a false one that comes undone when you pull the ends. On the contrary, it draws tighter. We handle it, trace the path of the separate threads, look for the end of the string, and out of these manipulations comes art.

"The Isle of Cythera."

Untitled pencil sketch, 1930s.

If I am asked whether the same thread recurs in my drawings as in my prose, I would answer in the affirmative. The reality is the same; only the frames are different. Here material and technique operate as the criterion of selection. A drawing sets narrower limits by its material than prose does. That is why I feel I have expressed myself more fully in my writing.

The question of whether I'd be able to interpret the reality of *Cinnamon Shops* in philosophical terms is one I would much rather avoid.* It is my opinion that rationalizing one's awareness of what inheres in a work of art is like unmasking actors, means the end of enjoyment and impoverishes the problems inherent in the work. The reason is not that art is a crossword puzzle with the key hidden, and philosophy the same crossword puzzle solved. The difference lies deeper than that. In a work of art the umbilical cord linking it with the totality of our concerns has not yet been severed, the blood of the mystery still circulates; the ends of the blood vessels vanish into the surrounding night and return from it full of dark fluid. A philosophical interpretation only gives us an anatomical sample dissected from the total body of the problems involved in the work. Just the same, I am curious how the philosophical credo of *Cinnamon Shops* would sound in the form of discourse. It would have to be an attempt to describe the reality given there rather than a justification of it.

*In the manuscript Schulz himself inserted the word *pose*. Isn't this addition, itself, the pose? (Interviewer's comment)

Cinnamon Shops offers a certain recipe for reality, posits a certain special kind of substance. The substance of that reality exists in a state of constant fermentation, germination, hidden life. It contains no dead, hard, limited objects. Everything diffuses beyond its borders, remains in a given shape only momentarily, leaving this shape behind at the first opportunity. A principle of sorts appears in the habits, the modes of existence of this reality: universal masquerade. Reality takes on certain shapes merely for the sake of appearance, as a joke or form of play. One person is a human, another is a cockroach, but shape does not penetrate essence, is only a role adopted for the moment, an outer skin soon to be shed. A certain extreme monism of the life substance is assumed here, for which specific objects are nothing more than masks. The life of the substance consists in the assuming and consuming of numberless masks. This migration of forms is the essence of life. Thus an all-pervading aura of irony emanates from this substance. There is an ever-present atmosphere of the stage, of sets viewed from behind, where the actors make fun of the pathos of their parts after stripping off their costumes. The bare fact of separate individual existence holds an irony, a hoax, a clown's stuck-out tongue. (Here, it seems to me, we have a point of contact between *Cinnamon Shops* and the world of your paintings and plays.)

What the meaning of this universal disillusioning reality is I am not able to say. I maintain only that it would be unbearable unless it was compensated for in some other dimension. In some sense we derive a profound satisfaction from the loosening of the web of reality; we feel an interest in witnessing the bankruptcy of reality.

There has been talk about the book's destructive tendency. From the viewpoint of certain established values, this may be true. But the work operates at a premoral depth, at a point where value is still *in statu nascendi.*

As a spontaneous utterance of life, a work of art poses tasks for ethics, not the reverse. If art were merely to confirm what had already been established elsewhere, it would be superfluous. The role of art is to be a probe sunk into the nameless. The artist is an apparatus for registering processes in that deep stratum where value is formed. Destructive? But the fact that these contents express themselves as a work of art means that we affirm them, that our deep perception has spontaneously declared in their favor.

To what genre does *Cinnamon Shops* belong? How should it be classified? I think of it as an autobiographical narrative. Not only because it is written in the first person and because certain events and experiences from the author's childhood can be discerned in it. The work is an autobiography, or rather a spiritual genealogy, a genealogy *par excellence* in that it follows the spiritual family tree down to those depths where it merges into mythology, to be lost in the mutterings of mythological delirium. I have always felt that the roots of the individual spirit, traced far enough down, would be lost in some matrix of myth. This is the ultimate depth; it is impossible to reach farther down.

I later found an imposing artistic realization of this idea in Thomas Mann's *Joseph and His Brothers,* where it is carried out on a monumental scale.[3] Mann shows that beneath all human events, when the chaff of time and individual variation is blown away, certain primeval patterns, "stories," are found, by which these events form and re-form in great repeating pulses. For Mann, these are the Biblical tales, the timeless myths of Babylon and Egypt. On my more modest scale I have attempted to uncover my own private mythology, my own "stories," my own mythic family tree. Just as the ancients traced their ancestry from mythical unions with gods, so I undertook to establish for myself some mythical generation of forebears, a fictitious family from which I trace my true descent.

In a way these "stories" are real, represent my way of living, my personal fate. The overriding motif of this fate is profound loneliness, isolation from the stuff of daily life.

Loneliness is the catalyst that makes reality ferment, precipitates its surface layer of figures and colors.

1935

THE MYTHOLOGIZING OF REALITY

In 1936 Studio *published two notable pieces: "The Mythologizing of Reality" (*Studio, *nos. 3–4, 1936), an important essay on aesthetics that echoes and develops themes found both in his essay for Witkiewicz published in* Tygodnik Ilustrowany *and in his afterword to the translation of* The Trial; *and later in the year the witty exchange (though it was no less serious, at least on Schulz's part) between Witold Gombrowicz and Schulz, which was widely regarded as the literary equivalent of a scuffle or "dust-up" between rivals. Schulz's admiration for Gombrowicz's work is evident from his writings, however, and as vigorously as he championed Gombrowicz's* Ferdydurke, *he just as vigoriously argued that he and Gombrowicz were not part of the same school.*

The essence of reality is Meaning or Sense. What lacks Sense is, for us, not reality. Every fragment of reality lives by virtue of partaking in a universal Sense. The old cosmogonists expressed this by the statement, "In the Beginning was the Word." The nameless does not exist for us. To name something means to include it in some universal Sense. The isolated word as a mosaic piece is a late product, an early result of technology. The primeval word was a shimmering aura circling around the sense of the world, was a great universal whole. The word in its common usage today is only a fragment, remnant of some former all-embracing, integral mythology. That is why it possesses a tendency to grow back, to regenerate and complete itself in full meaning. The life of the word consists in tensing and stretching itself toward a thousand connections, like the cut-up snake in the legend whose pieces search for each other in the dark. This thousand-formed but integral organism of the word was torn apart into syllables, sounds, everyday speech; and in these new forms, adapted to practical needs, it was handed down to us as a handy code of communication. In this way the life of the word, its development, was shunted onto a new track, the track of mundane life, and subjected to new rules of order. But if for some cause the restrictions of pragmatic reality loosen their grip, if the word, released from their restraint, is left to itself and restored to its own laws, then a regression, a reversal of current, occurs; the word strives for its former connections, wants to complete itself with Sense. And this striving of the word toward its matrix, its yearning for the primeval home of words, we call poetry.

Poetry happens when short-circuits of sense occur between words, a sudden regeneration of the primeval myths.

As we manipulate everyday words, we forget that they are fragments of lost but eternal stories, that we are building our houses with broken pieces of sculptures and ruined statues of gods as the barbarians did. Even the soberest of our notions and categories are remote derivatives of myths and ancient oral epics. Not one scrap of an idea of ours does not originate in myth, isn't transformed, mutilated, denatured mythology. The most fundamental function of the spirit is inventing fables, creating tales. The driving force of human knowledge is the conviction that at the end of its researches the sense of the world, the meaning of life, will be found. It seeks out sense at the very top of its scaffoldings and artificial stackings of level upon level. Yet the building materials it uses were used once before; they come from forgotten, fragmented tales or "histories." Poetry recognizes these lost meanings, restores words to their places, connects them by the old semantics. In the poet's mind, the word remembers, so to speak, its essential meaning, blossoms, unfolds spontaneously according to its own inner laws, regains its wholeness. Thus all poetry is mythologizing and strives to restore myths to the world. The mythologizing of the world is not over yet; the process was only halted by the development of knowledge, *scientia,* diverted into a side channel where it courses on without understanding its identity. But science, too, only fabricates its own world myth because myth is embodied in the very elements themselves, and there is no way of going beyond myth. Poetry reaches the meaning of the world intuitively, deductively, with large, daring shortcuts and approximations. Knowledge seeks the same meaning inductively, methodically, taking into account all the materials of experience. Fundamentally, one and the other are bound for the same goal.

The human spirit is indefatigable in supplying glosses to life by means of myths, in "making sense" of reality. The word itself, left to its own devices, gravitates toward sense.

Sense is the element that involves mankind in the process of realization. It is an absolute given that cannot be derived from other givens. Therefore what makes sense to us cannot be defined. The process of imparting meaning to the world is closely bound up with the word. Language is man's metaphysical organ. Nonetheless, in the course of time the word becomes static and rigid, stops being the conductor of new meanings. The poet restores conductivity to words by new quasi-electric tensions that are produced by an accumulation of charges. Mathematical symbols are extensions of the word into new realms. The image, too, derives from the primal word, the word that was not yet a sign but myth, story, sense.

We usually regard the word as the shadow of reality, its symbol. The reverse of this statement would be more correct: reality is the shadow of the word. Philosophy is actually philology, the deep, creative exploration of the word.

1936

TO WITOLD GOMBROWICZ

Witold Gombrowicz (1904–1969) wrote stories, plays, diaries, and the novels Ferdydurke, Pornografia, Trans-Atlantic, Possessed, *and* Cosmos, *which won the International Literary Prize in 1967. During the thirties Gombrowicz maintained close contact with Schulz, who had a very high opinion of Gombrowicz's works, lectured on them, and wrote an extensive essay on* Ferdydurke, *Gombrowicz's best-known book.*

As an emigré writer (Gombrowicz left for Argentina in 1939 and did not return to Europe until 1963), Gombrowicz produced an essayistic "Diary" in three volumes (I:1957, II:1962, III:1970 [posthumous]), which includes a discussion of Schulz on the occasion of the publication of a collection of Schulz's work in French translation (B. Schulz, Traité de Mannequins, *Juillard, 1961).*

The open "letters" that follow were part of an exchange by Schulz and Gombrowicz suggested by the editor of Studio, *Bogusław Kuczyński, and published in* Studio, *no. 7, 1936.*

OPEN LETTER TO BRUNO SCHULZ

40-1

My good Bruno,

Bogusław would like us to write for him in *Studio;* wouldn't it be better to write in *Studio* for oneself—or still better, to write each other?—yes, writing letters back and forth is really the most pleasant, but how much more enticing still to take aim at a concrete person than to shoot off into empty space a bulletin that is addressed to everyone and therefore to no one. For a long time I've racked my brains over what kind of thought I could fire off to you, dear Bruno, but absolutely nothing occurred to me until yesterday I bumped into the opinion of a certain doctor's wife whom I once met by accident on Line 18. Bruno Schulz, she said, he's either a sick pervert or a poseur, but most probably a poseur. He's only pretending.—She said this and got off, for the streetcar had just stopped at Wilcza Street.

Thus I shoot you with this woman's opinion; I hereby inform your personage publicly and formally that this doctor's wife regards you as a madman or a poseur. And I challenge you to take your stand against this woman. So: a specialist's better half, whose opinion you already know, lives in Wilcza Street. There, in Wilcza Street, she lives and has a negative opinion; there, she circulates it to chance acquaintances who take her at her word. There, Bruno, at 102 Wilcza Street, this unpleasant opinion grows and prospers, the unfavorable view of a member of a vast social and cultural milieu who is very decided in her notions. What are you going to do with her opinion? Will you, following the example of the overwhelming majority of your literary colleagues, assume a pretentious attitude, that is, an attitude full of demands and complaints against the general public because of its lack of understanding and too-low level? No, Bruno, not for a minute did I suspect of you the shamelessness and banality of a commonplace reaction by a hack whose sacred reputation has been injured. And neither do I believe that you will blush naively and cry, as happened in France to one of our most popular female writers when she was told that Polish literature was rather lowbrow. . . . Or perhaps, indulging in your masochistic tendencies, you will humiliate yourself and fall at the dainty toes of the satisfied doctor's wife. That way you would at least be able to enjoy the female and, against her will, get some sensual pleasure out of her. Hey, Bruno, I join you officially and formally in holy matrimony with the verdict of this woman, I deliver her verdict on you, I load it on your shoulders and buckle you up with it, I ram into the consciousness of Bruno Schulz the verdict of a woman, marry this man with a spouse through the legal bond of her verdict. What will this Bruno Schulz of yours do, then, in such a situation—this very Schulz whom you write books to and who must represent you, how will you wind up your Schulz and put him in position facing this person? My God, I have no desire to give form to my thoughts, it's hot, the devil composed this letter; if Bogusław hadn't

Witold Gombrowicz, about 1933.

gotten sick, then we wouldn't have to do it. But consider: the cruelty of a thing lies in the fact that all objective arguments serve scarcely any purpose. How, in effect, is one supposed to argue to a woman met by accident that one is neither crazy nor a poseur! Here it is a question not of content but rather form. Before the tribunal, which is composed of some accidental readers of *Studio,* I challenge you to a formal fight with a woman who is, like the others, also accidental. The tribunal will not concern itself with your argument; for that we have neither time nor common, generally recognized criteria. There are too many of our own matters to be carefully dealt with for us to deal with other matters as well. We will simply have a look and determine if that Schulz who was taken by surprise on a flat road by a silly run-in with a woman is capable of preserving good, sovereign form or if he, to our malicious pleasure, is compromised. And remember that your attitude must not only be subjectively right but, worse, must have the appearance of correctness for people who observe from the outside. If, for example, you explain that the opinion of the doctor's wife didn't faze you at all, we will not believe you, for on what basis are you supposed to be less touchy than we are? The tribunal that must pass judgment on you will judge you according to its own standards.

With complete premeditation I present you and no one else with just this question. Your philosophical, artistic, and poetic style does not predestine you to a squabble with mothers of doctors' children. Your form is manifested *in excelsis!* Get back down here on earth! Dance with an ordinary woman! Show how you defend youself against a chance encounter! Show what style you use to destroy her or lift yourself above her or keep your distance; show us this expression on your face, give us one look at it, how gentle Bruno shakes off the opinion of the doctor's wife from Line 18. What good would your form be if it were only being put into use at two thousand meters above the level of life? One must play the game with people on every level and in every possible situation. Our attitude toward matters of stupidity is perhaps even more important than our attitude toward the great, wise, principal problems.

That damned Bogusław! Good-bye, Bruno.

With deepest respect,
Witold Gombrowicz

40-2

TO WITOLD GOMBROWICZ

You'd like to lure me into an arena, dear Witold, beset on all sides by the curiosity of the mob, you would like to see me as the enraged bull in pursuit of the doctor's wife's fluttering banner; her flimsy amaranthine peignoir is supposed to serve as your cape, behind which the thrusts of your sword await me.

It would have taken a more provocative color, dear fellow, an arrow with more poison on it, and a poison that works more fatally than the spit of the doctor's wife from Wilcza Street. You would have had to launch a much cleverer doctor's wife at me, a more seductive woman, one it would be worth taking on one's horns. You somewhat overestimate my sensitivity, trying to foist this rag-stuffed puppet on me. Scarred old bull that I am, with the best of will I can't do more than lower my head and glare with threatening, bloodshot eyes around the picador's lances you have stuck me full of. Alas, I lack the noble fire and that blind tempestuous fury that might have plunged me forward, as you planned, into a magnificent assault. And you had staked out the territory for me ahead of time, closed and barred the side exits in order to get me smack in the middle of the arena. You spoiled the contest for me from the start, you handpicked the audience, fine-tuned the acoustics of the place, laid out in detail what was expected of me. But what would have happened if I had turned out to be an unconventional bull, a bull without honor or ambition in his breast, if I had spurned the audience's impatience, turned my back on the doctor's wife from Wilcza Street you are pushing me on and, tail up for battle, made a rush at you instead? Not to bump you off your feet, O noble toreador, but to take you on my back if this is not megalomania—and carry you out of the arena, beyond the confines of its rules and statutes.

Because, to put it plainly, I don't believe in the sacred code of arenas and forums, I despise and deprecate it whereas you, who are dazzled by it, have filled its margins with brilliant glosses full of mockery—truly a strange form of worship, that manages to leap on top of its idol with somersaults of irony!

You'll agree, then, dear Witold, to call off this curious tauromachy, leave the ripped-up puppet lying on the sand and, with the mutters of the disappointed crowd rising behind us, walk side by side at an easy gait, bull and toreador, to the exit, freedom, absorbed in intimate conversation even before we leave behind the outer circle of the arena.

Really, what kind of paradox is this? You a defender of the public arena and its massive acoustics! What, after all, are the acoustics of forums and arenas, what truths and arguments find expression there, and what gives them such an irresistible appeal to our hearts and convictions? What part of our essential selves hurries to meet them, full of affirmation and nodding approval, against our better judgment? Do you admire and cherish that popular joke, the joke with crowd appeal, the joke that hits the enemy from behind his reasons and arguments, sentencing him to mockery, knocking the weapon out of his hand without any crossing of swords on its merits? Are you reduced by directness of effect, the immediate irrational solidarity of all doctors' wives from Wilcza Street, the applause of all those people who are ordinary, flesh-bound, and mediocre? What's more, aren't you able to sense, aren't you astonished at this involuntary sympathy and solidarity with what at bottom is alien and hostile to you growing out of the depths of your being? Let me tell you, then, that what appears to you as some sort of malign force transcending the individual is only a weakness of your own nature. It is the mob within us that applauds, dear Witold; the mob deeply rooted inside, casting spells, gives off its collective grunt, smothers our better knowledge and causes our hands to lift convulsively with blind acclamation. These are reflex motions of the herd that dim our clear judgment, introduce archaic and barbaric modes of reasoning, open the arsenal of an atavistic and discarded logic. This kind of joke appeals to the mob in you, at this signal a dark, inarticulate mob rises up in you, like a bear trained to the sound of a gypsy's flute.

The doctor's wife from Wilcza Street! Did you mean to upset my plans, confuse my feelings, confront me with a representative of a consolidated tight, powerful guild and lay out the grid for our contest right next to the well-marked battlefront of sex? Did you plot, in your craftiness, to lure me into that marshy border region you know so well, where the compass needle of our feelings begins to whirl, where the magnetic poles of moral values switch charges in a strange ambivalence, and hate and love alike lose their clarity in a great general confusion? Oh no, dear Witold, I have liberated myself from this sort of thing; I've learned by this time how to counteract this great confusion, to separate and seal off what is alien to me. Certainly, I appreciate and admit with all my heart that the doctor's wife has beautiful thighs, but I put this matter in its own place. I can ensure that my worship of the doctor's wife's legs does not filter down into a totally inappropriate area. And the steadfastness of this worship does not prevent me from nourishing a sincere contempt, on the intellectual level, for her philistine dullness, her prefabricated thinking, her entirely alien and hostile mentality. Of course—I confess it frankly—I hate the doctor's wife from Wilcza Street, a creature leached void of any substance, the pure distillate of a doctor's wife, the textbook case of a doctor's wife or simply of a wife . . . though on an altogether different plane I find it difficult to resist the charm of her legs.

Granted, this iridescent ambivalence, this Januslike duality of my nature, which changes depending on whether I happen to consider the doctor's wife as the owner of her legs or of her intellect, is a puzzling phenomenon that gives cause for reflection, provokes philosophical generalizations and metaphysical perspectives. It seems to me that here we may have caught red-handed one of the basic antinomies of the human soul, as if we had struck a quivering metaphysical nerve.

I am not in favor of easy simplifications, but until psychology can shed more light on these matters I propose we accept, as a provisional hypothesis, that our sexuality together with its whole ideological aura belongs to another era of development than our intellectuality. I generally think that the organization of our psyche is not uniform at all in the matter of the developmental levels of different spheres, and that its antinomies and contradictions may be explained by the coexistence and overlap of many simultaneous systems. Here is the source of the confusing, multitrack nature of our thinking.

I have deliberately descended into the realm of sexuality because under the pressure of everyday life we have long been accustomed to keeping its transactions under separate accounts. But at this spot the multilayered structure of our psyche is quite evident. It becomes less evident in the realm of general moral, biological, and social value formation, and here I encroach on your highly personal domain. I recognize your peculiar irritability regarding this topic, your frankly pathological (and therefore creative) anxiety. This is a sore point where your hypersensitivity reaches its peak, it is your Achilles heel that itches and rankles you as if some new organ wanted to sprout from it, a kind of new hand more prehensile than the other two. Let us try to confine and isolate this especially painful and sensitive place, locate it with surgical precision, even if it is metastasizing and starts spreading in all directions. I have the impression you are troubled and disoriented by the existence of some unwritten code of values, some anonymous Mafia, something evading the control of *consensus omnium*. Behind the official values that we sanction and profess lies hidden some unofficial but powerful conspiracy, an elusive underworld system—cynical and amoral, irrational and mocking. That system (for it does absolutely possess the features of a consistent system) lends its sanction to the untruths of a perverse woman, sets up paradoxical hierarchies, gives shattering force to a shallow joke, gathers us up against our will or wisdom under the power of a collective guffaw. This intangible system that cannot be localized anywhere, that slips between the cells, as it were, of our value judgments, evades responsibility and eludes every attempt to capture it or pin it down. Anything but solemn or serious this unsolemn and unserious system kills with the powerful weapon of ridicule; it is indeed a peculiar and troubling phenomenon. I don't know if anyone is free from its fascination.

I consider it a great service that you were the first to direct our thoughts and feelings to these matters. If I am not mistaken, you were the first to succeed in smoking out the dragon from its myriad hiding places and bringing him within arm's length. I'd like to crown you ahead of time with the laurels of the dragon's future slayer, for I consider that anonymous system as something evil that must be overcome. That is why I worry about your all too protracted collusion with it, your long-winded whispers and shady dealings, your whole two-faced muddled policy. For heaven's sake, come to your senses! Shake off this blindness! Understand finally where the enemy is and where the friend! You, predestined dragonslayer, armed by nature with formidable instruments of murder, you with your fine sense of smell that tracks the enemy to its deepest hiding place—lay hold of him by his lying tongue, twist it in his maw with two snaps of the teeth, seize, choke, tear out his throat!

No, really, Witold, I believe you. You are only charming him with a magician's sleight-of-hand, fumigating him with the incense of praises, hypnotizing and immobilizing him in the pose of timeless idol you impute to him. Oh, well, I will second you in this. Let us enthrone the doctor's wife from Wilcza Street, hosanna, hosanna, let us prostrate ourselves before her. Let her sprawl, push out her white belly, swell up with pride—the doctor's wife from Wilcza Street, the timeless idol, object of all our yearnings, hosanna, hosanna, hosanna. . . .

While she sits there all carried away, overflowing her banks, with sky-blue eyes that flicker over us unseeing, let us analyze her face, test her expression, sink a probe to the bottom of that unfathomable visage.

You say this is the face of life? You say not only that we, the brighter and better, have the right to make fun of the doctor's wife, but also that you acknowledge her equal right to scorn, disdain, and ridicule? In that case you stand on the side of inferiority against superiority. You try to compromise our actions by casting before our eyes the massive torso of the doctor's wife, and you identify with her thick-headed chuckles. You claim that in her person you defend vitality and biology, against abstraction, against our detachment from life. If this is biology, Witold, then you must mean the force of her immobility; if this is vitality, you must mean her heavy passive mass.

But the avant-garde of biology is thought, experiment, creative discovery. We, in fact, are this belligerent biology, this conquering biology; we are the truly vital.

Don't laugh. I know what you're thinking, what a low opinion you hold of our life. And that pains me. You compare it with the life of the doctor's wife, and that life seems real to you, more firmly rooted in the soil, whereas we, creating up in Cloud-cuckoo-land and devoted to some chimera under hundreds of atmospheric pressures of boredom, distill our products that are useful to almost no one. Boredom, Witold, blessed boredom! It is our lofty asceticism, our high breeding, that doesn't allow us to dine at the lavish banquets of life; it's the incorruptibility of our taste, pledged to new and unknown sensations.

In conclusion, permit me to tell you in a few words where I would like to see you, where I see your rightful place and proper station. You have the stuff of a great humanist. What else can your morbid sensitivity to antinomies be if not a longing for universality, for the humanization of the not yet human realm, for the expropriation of separate ideologies and their annexation to a single great unity? I don't know how you will bring it to completion, but I think that this is the positive meaning and sanction of your efforts which, until now, were no more than a routing out and forcing into the field of fire the game of that half-human preserve.

With greetings to you, I am
Yours
Bruno Schulz

July 1936

TO ANDRZEJ PLEŚNIEWICZ

Andrzej Pleśniewicz[1] had studied history with Professor Marceli Handelsman at Warsaw University. In the thirties he was on the staff of the quarterly Verbum, *the vehicle of a group of influential Catholic intellectuals, and also published essays and reviews in the leading literary journals. During the Occupation he remained in Warsaw, taking part in underground literary work with such leading writers as Nałkowska and Breza. As a surviving participant in the Warsaw Uprising, he was driven out by the SS, reached an intact Mazovian village, and worked there as a laborer until the Liberation in late 1944, when he attempted to return to Warsaw to salvage his manuscripts but died before reaching his destination.*

A critic of rare gifts, outstanding especially for his fine aesthetic sense and the polish of his essays, he reviewed Cinnamon Shops *under the headline "Little Town of Fantasy" in* Pion *no. 4, 1934, and dealt with the Schulz-Gombrowicz exchange in a guest editorial in* Kurier Poranny *(*Morning Courier*) that year.*

41

Dear and esteemed Andrzej:

Your letter pleased me. For some reason I hadn't felt sure that you really meant what you promised. There was a time when I put everything I had into letter writing, then my only creative outlet. It's a shame we can't carry on our correspondence retroactively. Nowadays I can't write like that any more, and in retrospect that time—not very remote—seems rich and full and blossoming compared to the grayness and fragmentation of the present. You have the type of handwriting I like. I've had good experiences with people who write like that.

You overrate the advantages of my situation in Drohobycz. What I miss even here is quiet, my own quiet of the Muse, of a pendulum slowed to its own calm gravitational rhythm, marking a clean path undeformed by any alien pull. That silence—substantive, positive, full—is almost creative in itself. The things that I sense want to be uttered through me occur above a certain threshold of quiet; they take shape in a medium brought to perfect equilibrium. Even the peace I experience here, though more nearly perfect than in that happier period, is no longer enough for the demands of an ever more delicate, more exquisite "vision." I find it harder and harder to believe in this vision. Yet those very matters demand a blind faith, demand to be taken on credit. Only when they are won over by this kind of faith do they barely consent to materialize, to assume a certain degree of existence.

What you say about our artificially prolonged childhood—our immaturity—takes me a little aback. After all, the kind of art I care about is precisely a regression, childhood revisited. If it were possible to reverse development, to attain the state of childhood again, to have its abundance and limitlessness once more, that "age of genius," those "messianic times" promised and sworn to us by all mythologies, would come to pass. My ideal goal is to "mature" into childhood. That would be genuine maturity for you.

I live quite alone here. I have taken on the sad duty of visiting a friend who is dying of cancer.[2] Spring is giving me the itch to go hiking with someone, a sort of high school camping trip. A friend, a painter, may come on a visit.

About my work I had better keep silent; it's all so trifling and futile. If you see Witold [Gombrowicz], give him my warm greetings and tell him he shouldn't be angry that I haven't written to him yet.

I must close. Accept my cordial thanks for letting me hear from you, with my respects and a warm clasp of the hand,

Bruno Schulz

Drohobycz, March 4, 1936
10 Floriańska

I hope to have news from you soon, and to resume our correspondence.

42

Dear Andrzej:

Thank you most sincerely for the fine and thoughtful defense you put in for me in the columns of the *Kurier Poranny.* Was this cause really worth breaking a lance for? I have the impression that my dust-up with Witold takes on retrospective meaning only in the light of the epiphenomena in its wake.[3] In itself it was actually trivial and laughable. I was surprised to have it taken so seriously. Be that as it may, I am sincerely grateful to you.

Facts and deeds speak louder than intentions, and intentions unsupported by facts don't warrant belief. That's why you may not believe I often thought of you in Warsaw, and if no meetings resulted, it wasn't my doing. I regret our contact took such an unproductive turn. I don't know myself whose fault it is that I saw so little of you, Breza, and Witold, although we have so much in common linking us.

I have come to see that my chronic depression derives from a quietist and eudaemonic disposition, from spending every other minute testing the balance of satisfaction in exploring the art of happiness. Every other minute I ask myself the question: Do I have the right to be satisfied, is the undertaking "Schulz" worth carrying on, does it justify further investment? And from the answer to this happiness questionnaire, I deduce a defeatist or optimistic attitude —mostly a defeatist one. Yet the question ought to be: Have I achieved the maximum of what was feasible in the given period? To build a life on work, on activity, declaring independence from the barometer of happiness—this is the right way to organize a life.

I can't make up my mind to turn over a volume of short stories [*Sanitorium*] to the publisher—distaste for decisions. Is this some sort of disease?

What are you up to? What are you writing? Who are you keeping company with? What's interesting in literature? I'd be very happy to hear from you. I probably won't go to Warsaw for the holidays.

Warm greetings and hugs,

Bruno Schulz

Drohobycz, November 29, 1936
10 Floriańska

43

Dear Andrzej:

Your friendly and unexpected letter gave me great pleasure. Just yesterday I wrote you a letter, and before I had a chance to send it off (no envelope) there was your answer, so to speak. What is the letter you write about that you got no answer to? Since the last letter I had from you we saw each other in Warsaw, after all. Did you write to me after that? Could a letter have been lost? I feel a little at fault over seeing you so seldom during my stay in Warsaw. I believe it was really up to me to take the initiative there. But this won't be our last chance.

Your article sounded a very pleasant note to me, and my judgment of it may not be objective for that reason. I fancied Witold might have attacked you more effectively. His position is very strong and hard to overthrow. What you say about the artist's objectivization of experiences, about the distance between life and art, I too have thought, in almost identical terms. Also about the fallacy of demanding that the artist should be what the Gomber calls a writer "in the full sense." To my mind, this criterion of his for the writer does not pertain to the artist's essence at all; it pertains to his social veneer in terms of life and society and things of that sort. [As you say,] material personal advantage gained from mastery of the word "cannot be" the criterion of artistic value. All this you formulated most incisively. In general, I must say, we coincide on many points (as I had occasion to remark in earlier correspondence), and in the way we conceptualize problems we move on parallel tracks, as it were.

It is good to hear that you take an interest in me personally. Unfortunately I have nothing happy to report about myself. I fall out of one depression into another, and this paralyzes my rate of activity. I am beginning to think that the responsibility for my meager output must be assigned to a lack of discipline or techinque for living, an incapacity to organize my day. I suffer from the misconception that literary creation can begin only when all difficulties have been cleared away over the entire range of one's life, when no threat lurks, and the breath of serenity wafts over the "soul" at peace. But you have to wait a long time for that to happen. All it takes is some little thing due but undone, some perceived lack of worth, to spoil my urge to write.

Have you read my "Spring"[4]? I am not satisfied with it myself, that's why I seek outside affirmation.

No, I haven't applied to the Ministry. Thank you so much for your kind offer. I presume that it is not in your power to induce the Minister to give me a position in Warsaw? I have sent in a request to the district school board for reassignment to Lwów.

Truchanowski's book [his first, *All Saints' Street,* 1936] is the sort of thing that totally depresses me. I look on it as an involuntary parody of my book, a caricature generated by the author's ineptitude and naïveté. This person's faculty of self-criticism seems to be paralyzed. He doesn't notice, or else doesn't care, that he repeats my turns of speech, statements, and formulations in a bungled and trivialized form. Have you seen some of the misbegotten copies of paintings that dabblers produce? In those, the features of the original are coarsened, twisted, and deformed in a similar manner. My distaste stems from the nausea that seizes me when a clumsy, untutored, primitive type of mind touches my inventions with a coarse hand. In these hands they metamorphose into cartoons. That book may do me a lot of harm, for our reader is not the conscientious type who would care to return to *Cinnamon Shops* to check for the differences between Truchanowski and myself. In this way his counterfeit prose may set itself up in the reader's mind in the place mine belongs. If you feel as I do, my very strong wish is that you would warn the reader of this danger and dig a trench between us. That my fear isn't groundless is demonstrated by Laszowski's [the critic linked in those years with the extreme Right] review, in which the trashiness of Truchanowski's book provides the opening for an attack on myself and my whole genre.

What are you working on besides review articles? Anything of your own? I understand very well your need for isolation and quiet. As for Napierski's review,[5] I didn't quite make it out either, but I ascribe this to its profundity and the difficult paths of argumentation he leads you through. Don't you agree?

Sincere thanks for remembering me, along with my respects and fond greetings.

Bruno Schulz

December 1, 1936

TO MENDEL NEUGRÖSCHL

44

Dr. M. Neugröschl[1]
Vienna
Sterng[asse] 11

Dear Dr. Neugröschl:

Miss Debora Vogel,[2] a dear friend of mine, has informed me that you expressed some interest in my book, *Cinnamon Shops,* in a letter to her.

I take the liberty of sending you a copy of this book under separate cover. I would be very glad if you were to consider parts or even all of it worth the labor of translating. In case you do, please consider the present letter my grant of translation rights.

I apologize for the damaged condition of the book; I have no other copy handy, and I doubt you greatly care about having a new one.

Yours very sincerely
Bruno Schulz

Drohobycz, November 4, 1936
10 Floriańska

TO MIECZYSŁAW GRYDZEWSKI

45

To the Editor,[1] *Wiadomości Literackie*

In issue no. 762 of your journal there appeared a laudatory review by Emil Breiter[2] of my book [*Sanatorium*] *Under the Sign of the Hourglass.* It contained the following passage. "[Schulz] has already succeeded in launching a literary movement which, apart from a few inept latecomers, has produced important talents, as for example Gombrowicz, who have begun to seek new and independent modes of expression."

I find this judgment difficult to endorse.

Gombrowicz is an exceptionally autonomous and indigenous phenomenon that carries its sources and resources within itself. He operates in an absolutely different dimension of reality from mine and belongs—certain appearances notwithstanding—to a quite different species of writer and a different intellectual formation.

In view of the total incommensurability of our inner worlds, the question of precedence in time is quite irrelevant, yet even here the primacy is unquestionably Gombrowicz's. His first work, *Memoirs of the Time of Immaturity,* which already showed him as a completely crystallized and matured creative personality, appeared in 1933, whereas my *Cinnamon Shops* only saw the light of day in 1934.[3]

It seems to me that we may dispense with arguments to combat this mistaken notion, since its psychological sources become obvious upon closer inspection. What led to the association of our names and respective works were certain fortuitous similarities, such as our nearly simultaneous emergence, our brusqueness in dealing with conventional reality (which has different origins, though, in our two cases) and, above all, the defiance of classification the two phenomena share.

In the final analysis, this coupling of our names and our literary work by an illusory equal-sign is damaging to us both, since it undervalues each writer's essential autonomy and integrity.

Bruno Schulz, Drohobycz

[published: June 19, 1938]

TO GEORGES ROSENBERG

Georges Rosenberg, or Gregory R. Marshak, was the brother of Schulz's friend Maria Rey-Chazen. Schulz met him during his three-month stay in Paris.

46

My dear Sir:

I am moved by your beautiful gift, which is precious to me as a token of your consideration and subtle attention. My heartfelt thanks for it, as well as for giving so much of yourself to me all that time—and I remained under your spell throughout our acquaintance. I confess that this mixture of subtlety and a generous nature, self-discipline and freedom, independence and restraint, suits me admirably. Your charm was the greater for being upheld by a very discreet and restrained goodness. Please forgive my clumsy effort to analyze something integral, irreducible, and undefinable—*individuum est ineffabile*—but such is the vice of the writer, who has to divide everything into its natural elements, discuss it, chew on it; just as, by the way, we used to chew on various topics during our nights in Paris, not stopping before any barrier, shattering with the license of free spirits all resistance offered by things equivocal, touchy, and shameful. It is a postulate of humanism for that matter, the humanization of the whole range of life, so that there will be fewer and fewer things avoiding the light of thought, shying away from the word. What is put in words is already half under control. Let me once more note the ease of communication that set in between us from the first moment. This brought about a kind of collegial bond in humanism, a common platform of humanism that was our springboard, our stockpile, and the court of appeal to which our thoughts had recourse.

Thanks to your tact, which also derives from humanism, our conversations never overstepped a certain objectivity that was binding on us both. Strictly private as they were, they did not become intimate. We broke them off long before they could reach the boundaries of our minds, and thus they left behind incentive and appetite for resumption. I predict we could have kept ourselves in this keyed-up state of animation for quite some time. I hope the possibility of further developing a relationship that promises such good and interesting things may be granted me. I have not yet reported to Maria[1] about our meeting; I still owe her an answer to her last letter.

Warm regards to you, and please let me hear from you again.

Bruno Schulz

Drohobycz, October 28, 1938
8[2] Floriańska

P.S. I see to my chagrin that I noted down only your telephone number.

TO ROMANA HALPERN

Romana Halpern (1900–1944) was a divorcée in her thirties, a former student of theater greatly interested in literature and writing, and well connected in the art world of Warsaw. Daughter of the well-known journalist Aleksander Kenig, she attended but did not graduate from theater school in Lwów, took up secretarial work, and occupied a fairly responsible post in a film import company in Warsaw, where her former husband also worked. She became active in the literary and artistic life of the capital as a participant and organizer, and for a time was very close to S. I. Witkiewicz, through whom she met Schulz. Her correspondence with Schulz, judging by what is left, ultimately developed into a less interesting exchange than Debora Vogel's, perhaps because her gifts were more social and linguistic (she was at home in five languages) than literary, and because Schulz came to look upon her mainly as a troubleshooter. Their relationship lasted over three years, and his letters to her make up the largest, if not the most important, group of letters so far collected.

Romana and her son escaped from the Ghetto in 1942. She was able to hide him in a remote boarding school, take on a false identity, and work as a Pole in a German firm in Kraków until 1944, when she was recognized and killed by the Germans shortly before the Liberation of the city by the Russo-Polish armies.

47

I have a very bad conscience about you, even though I might be able to justify my failing in my own mind, citing the disruption and disorganization of my time in Warsaw. I won't try to exonerate myself; there are excuses that seem all the more spurious and made up the more accurately they try to set forth the true state of affairs. It's good you brought Rilke to my mind. When creative reverses (which nobody else knows about) depress one, the mention of his name does one good. The presence of his books is a guarantee that the mute, convolute mass of what remains unformulated in us may yet reach the surface, miraculously sublimated. The precision and purity of Rilke's distillates are a cheering thing to us. My attempts to write are really agonizing. A writer (my type of writer, anyway) is the most wretched creature on earth. He has to lie incessantly, has to represent as valid and real what is actually in a miserable state of disintegration and chaos within him. The idea that I might mean to somebody what Rilke means to me strikes me as equally touching and humbling as it is undeserved. I am not taking it wholly seriously, either.

It will be very nice to stay in touch with you. I wonder what the substance of this contact will be.

I am sending you a copy of *Cinnamon Shops* under separate cover, and assure you of my esteem and sympathy.

Bruno Schulz

Drohobycz, August 16, 1936

Portrait of Romana Halpern, by S. I. Witkiewicz. Pastels, 1928.

48

Please forgive me for answering so late, and under altogether changed circumstances, in which the problems broached in our correspondence have become strangely dated. The now-interrupted concerns in which I was formerly deeply engaged have receded into the distance. I am going through very tangible and severe personal problems. My fiancée (did you know of her existence?) wants to throw me over; she sees my return to Drohobycz as the opportunity to break off contact with me. I can't deny she has a case, unfortunately. She has been waiting for me too long and is wasting her days in loneliness at a bleak job in the Bureau of Statistics. In my distaste for practical affairs I neglected the matter of our marriage when the time was right and she asked me for it. Now the technical difficulties are even greater, but I still have the impression that if I managed to get the formalities out of the way, all would not be lost yet.

The question is only whether you are interested in my personal affairs. You wanted contact with a poet, and what you find is a man absorbed in the most mundane of concrete matters. Unfortunately I am nothing but a private individual now, suffering in the human way, who has had the ground pulled out from under him and doesn't find any meaning to his life. She, my fiancée, represents my participation in life; only by her mediation am I a human being and not just a lemur or gnome. She loves me more than I love her, but she is more of a life necessity for me. By her love she has redeemed me, who was nearly lost and marooned in a remote no-man's-land, a barren underworld of fantasy. She brought me back to life and the earthly realm. She is the closest person I have on earth.

Do you know that, before I met you, Szturm[1] wanted to direct me to you in connection with this very matter, in the hope that you might have some advice for me? The problem is precisely that of my marriage to Józefina Szelińska. I don't know what I built my hopes on. Do you have some expertise in the matter of civil marriages? Could you, and would you, do something for me? Forgive me for applying to you with this matter. Let me put the case before you—maybe you'll find some way out for me. I would be endlessly grateful to you. Let me lay out the facts:

My fiancée is Catholic [. . .]. I don't care to accept baptism, though. The only concession I made for her was to give up membership in the Jewish community. Under these circumstances it's possible to get married only under German law, which is in force in the former Prussian-annexed territory, at Katowice, for instance. I understand that a marriage license can be obtained only after three months of residence in the district of Silesia. It's possible to get around this rule by a pro forma registration at some Silesian locality. Are you familiar with these matters? Are you acquainted with someone, some lawyer, who might undertake this action? Perhaps you know someone who had a civil marriage ceremony under German law in the recent past? Are you in a position to do something for me?

These are the problems my thinking revolves around these days. I must have Józefina's (this is my fiancée's name) closeness and connection with me assured in order even to function. That is the zero level from which I rise on the scale of fantasy. Right now I can neither write nor draw. I await impatiently your kind reply. A few days ago I had a card from Witkacy.

With warm greetings and regards,
Bruno Schulz

Drohobycz, September 19, 1936

49

Dear Madam:

I can report that the misunderstanding between myself and Józefina has been set right again—for how long, I don't know. Let me thank you so much for the information you furnished and your kind warm words. With joyful astonishment I ask myself what I did to win your friendship, how I could have deserved it. Is it not undeserved good fortune that a book might gain one friends, among other good things? However—I accept it with gratitude. I am having a better day today, one of the placid and restful kind. I am in bed with a touch of fever and haven't gone to school. It's a cold, raw, inhospitable day, all prose and bleakness. Benign spirits have taken position about my bed, however; next to me lie two volumes of Rilke I was able to borrow. From time to time I take a few moments to enter his tense and difficult world, walk under the multiple vaultings of his skies, and then return home. I don't know whether you're acquainted with Rilke. I regard his *Neue Gedichte* as the summit of his creation. What he wrote later—*Duino Elegies,*

Sonnets to Orpheus—is already too esoteric and abstract. I also have my drawings next to me, and at times it seems to me that they are really good and that I am capable of doing even better ones. My great enemy is lack of self-confidence, of *amour propre*. Long months pass when nothing I do wins my approval, no idea that comes up satisfies me, there is nothing I like. This state of self-discontent sentences me to inactivity. Yet at times I feel that my severity is justified and that I am right to consign underdone and imperfect items to perdition. There is only this flaw in the argument: In the beginning it's better to stay with such imperfect pieces, fall into the rhythm, get stimulated and intoxicated, and somewhere at the boundary of personal potential find perfect things. Your concern that life in a partnership could yank me out of the proper climate for literary creation made me think. True, the solitary life may have been the source of my inspiration, but does life as a couple really break down this solitude? Doesn't one stay alone just the same? And why do all poets ultimately trade in their solitude for a life *en deux*? I have a human fear of aloneness, of the sterile life of the unnecessary person beyond the pale I tried to portray in "The Old Age Pensioner."[2] Hence my excursion into matrimony. For that matter, it is the person who is closest and dearest to me to whom I mean a great deal; isn't that a fine thing —to mean everything to someone?

Have you read my "Spring" in the September issue of *Skamander*? The October issue will have the second part of "Spring," the better part, I think. I would like to know a little more about you, about your life and your past. Would you mind writing a little about yourself? Once more, warm thanks from your devoted and thankful

Bruno Schulz

Drohobycz, September 30, 1936
10 Floriańska

50

Dear Madam:

Was there something in my last letter to offend or hurt you? Why have you fallen silent? Did my letter perhaps fail to reach you? You seemed genuinely eager, after all, to begin a serious correspondence with me! Did something disappoint you? I often think of you, but not remembering how you look frustrates me. I only know that you wore morning slippers on very small feet and that later, when you put on a hat, you suddenly looked different, younger. What are you doing? I recently read André Gide's *The Dungeons of the Vatican.*[3] A splendid story! You absolutely must read it. Did you read my "Spring" in the recent issues of *Skamander*? I fear your silence signifies either low spirits or disappointment. I would be glad to hear that its causes are less serious.

My relationship with Józefina has improved, although the basic situation is the same—i.e., the obstacles in the way of getting married persist—and so does our enforced separation. I get brief notes from Stas Witkiewicz now and then. Do you see anything of Szturm? I would like you to start a genuine correspondence—initiate a discussion, bring up some problem. I don't know if I am making this up, but didn't you tell me about your little daughter? Where is she? Is she a big girl? Please let me have a word or two in reply! With warm regards,

Bruno Schulz

I plan to go to Katowice on November 1 for two days to sniff out the terrain in the matter of my marriage. Have you got any advice for me?
[no date]

51

Dear Romana:

What you say of the worry you have about your little son[4] troubles me. But aren't you perhaps going a little too far in your distress, which is unfounded, it seems to me? As far as I know, swollen tonsils and low-grade fever or even higher temperatures are a very common childhood illness. There have been a number of cases even in my own family. These children grew up into healthy young adults. I also suspect that you are overly distressed by the child's being in bed. Bed rest is necessary, and the child does not take it as badly as you think. I myself once had to stay in bed for six months—I was twenty-two then—and in retrospect that time doesn't seem like the worst of my life. Don't despair, dear Romana, you will see that tonsillitis pass and the little boy come out of it without a blemish. (I have no idea why I thought you had a little girl.)

I am also dismayed by what you write about Józefina Szelińska. While I am convinced that you judge the matter by surface appearances and don't really know Józefina, something of the threat you hold over my head has communicated itself to me. Let me tell you truthfully that fear of loneliness is not the deepest motive linking me to Józefina. Would you believe me when I say no woman has ever bestowed such feeling and such passionate love on me? I will certainly never in my life find another being so completely filled by me. This great feeling of hers enslaves and obligates me. I couldn't throw away a feeling like this, which comes to one once in a lifetime. It is beyond my strength. Besides, I am very much attached to her, I love her and feel good being with her. I can't imagine that our married life will be philistine and middle class, as it appears, ahead of time, to your imagination. Józefina likes my writings very much, every new piece of mine gives her the greatest pleasure. Do you really see such a menace to my writing in this union? I wonder what Szturm thinks about this. Have you ever talked about it with him?

Thank you so much for your efforts on my behalf. I am touched and really grateful. I am so happy about your friendship, which fell so undeservedly to my lot. I never got to Katowice. I am informed that filing for fictitious residence is out of the question in Katowice, because the authorities are aware of the abuses people commit, but it can still be managed in provincial Silesia. I really wish I could have this business behind me. I can't stand being involved with government offices, and I don't know how to handle these kinds of

Jews at the Sabbath meal. Pencil sketch, 1930s.

Untitled pencil sketch, 1930s.

matters. I am highly inept when it comes to things like this.

I am not complaining, but I live in very straitened and confining circumstances. I live in two rooms with my widowed sister, a very dear person but sickly and sad, an old cousin who looks after the household, and a nephew, a young man of twenty-six who is something of a depressive.[5] This is why I believe marriage will be a change for the better for me. Only I don't know whether I can manage to maintain two households, for my family lacks any income. Szturm and others have made efforts to find me a post in Warsaw, but so far without result. I am very much worn out by, and bored with, school—I now teach in grade school—I wish I could get on without a position and live for my writing alone. Perhaps I ought to isolate myself totally, like Rilke, live alone and not have anybody.

When you wrote me once about your loneliness, I felt for you so much, I regretted I wasn't free. Please don't laugh. You also have a friend in Szturm, a wonderful, unusual person. What do you talk with him about?

Please let me know if your little son is better, if his temperature is down, and what the doctors say. You mustn't worry about this; it's harmless and always passes. How old is he?

Many many thanks again and warm regards.

Bruno Schulz

Please give my best to Szturm.

[no date]

52

Dear Madam:

My thanks for being in touch and for sharing opinions that are always interesting to me because they concern my business, and people are insatiable listeners when someone wants to talk about them—hence the success of fortunetellers, palmists, and the like. Since I last wrote you, things have taken a very bad turn, not externally, but my morale has gotten much worse. I am in the lowest possible spirits. I have been telling myself I am neither a painter nor a writer, I am not even a decent teacher. It seems to me I have been swindling the world by some sort of flash or glitter when there is nothing inside me. I tried to renounce creativity and live like an average person, but this feels very sad. Besides, my daily existence depends on my art, since I use values borrowed from art to prop up my spavined instructorhood. In my imagination I have already been fired from my job and plunged into abject poverty. When I see the town idiots and the ragged beggars, the thought springs to mind that I may look like that soon. You know—I am unsuited for any honest job. I can't help it, I am able to find no charm in teaching, and I can't live without some charm, a little spice, some sort of piquant sauce to go with life. In this I differ tremendously from my fellow teachers. I feel like idling, doing nothing, rambling, enjoying the landscape, the sky ushering in another world with little afternoon clouds. Maybe then the music would come back to me, a wave of prose would well up. My official duties fill me with fear and loathing and cast gloom over any *joie de vivre.* In this time of unemployment all you hear are threats and reprimands. The concept of duty rises to apocalyptic heights. The menace of staff cutbacks hangs over everyone. A few months ago you could still have the sense of being in a safe port, of having an anchorage for life in our profession. There was a little peace and joy. Now they have driven joy out of our lives, and without joy, without a small bonus of cheer, I can do nothing creative. But please don't tell Szturm about my distaste for my work; he doesn't like that in people, although he is so indulgent generally.

On one point you are in error, and that is when you think that suffering is necessary for creative work. This is a worn old cliché that may sometimes be borne out, but not for me. I need blessed quiet, a little wholesome joy on the side, a contemplative sweet tooth for silence and serenity. I don't know how to suffer. But for all I know, I may be wrong.

I don't correspond with any other woman besides Józefina. It's a pity we didn't know each other a few years ago; I was still able to write beautiful letters then. It was out of my letters that *Cinnamon Shops* gradually grew. Most of these letters were to Debora Vogel, the author of *The Acacias Are Blooming*. Those letters are mostly lost.[6]

Reading the current literary journals is a galling experience for me. I see that other people are writing and I am not. My sincere thanks—but don't bother sending me *Wiadomości Literackie*, I don't know if I'll read it. Szturm—I don't know what to write to him. I am depressed, groundlessly, and in that condition I am an egoist wrapped up in his own affairs. How is Szturm going to understand that—he who is wholly devoted to others, lacking a private life, the antithesis of egoism?

Please don't worry about Stef [Romana's son]. This business has to take its little time, but it will pass. You'll see.

With warm regards to you, fondly

Bruno Schulz

November 15, 1936

Do you really still like *Cinnamon Shops*? Do you believe in my gift? Please give Witkacy my very best.

Can you do something in the matter of my fictitious residence in Silesia? Proof of a few weeks' residence is sufficient in the outlying parts of Silesia, I was told by a Katowice attorney. How does one go about that? But please don't concern yourself with this. You have worries enough of your own, and then there is Stef's illness. I'll wait till he is well.

53

Dear Romana:

You inform me so casually about losing your job, as if it were some trivial fact! Surely you must have foreseen this quite some time ago? Do you have prospects of another? Can't Szturm see a way out, won't he use his influence? Strange that your little son's tonsillitis should drag on like this! Perhaps there is something else behind it? Let me know how he is now and what the doctor says.

Do you ever run into people we both know at literary evenings? Who are you acquainted with there? I haven't written about the letter exchange with the Gomber because, when you come right down to it, the affair was trivial—who knows why it stirred up so much talk? Gombrowicz is a very interesting writer, one of the most intriguing we have. Do you know his *Memoirs of the Time of Immaturity*? Please, you really must read it, it's an eye opener. I haven't been writing about my coming to Warsaw because I didn't know how things were working out. It now looks as if I'm not going at all, or only for a very short time. Józefina is going to Janow near Lwów. We'll see each other at Lwów. I may come by myself to see to the publication of my short stories. Before that, I want to settle the matter of our marriage and make the trip to Katowice. Right now I am looking for somebody in the Silesian countryside who might be willing to register me as living with him. I don't know anybody. I don't even know the names of these places. Maybe you have some advice on this?

The reason I haven't written to Szturm is that I had the feeling I would be needlessly bothering him—busy as he is—with the obligation of replying; I consider it sinful to take from him the little scrap of time that others haven't managed to tear from him yet. How could you imagine I had conceived a dislike for him? How can he assume this? How can anyone be offended with Szturm for anything? I have nothing but esteem and warmth for that man; I'll write him shortly.

I am coming to the conclusion that the prime cause of my depression is inactivity, unproductiveness. And the cause of my inactivity, in turn, is the mistaken idea that I am able to work only when everything is in good shape and I am content and have some peace of mind. The truth is that one has to make oneself work whatever one's mood is, make oneself independent of serenity and changeable moods; not ask for contentment, for happiness, but build one's life on work, effort, results. If I could bring this off, I would be happy.

Last week I was in Lwów, where I visited my old friend Debora Vogel—a dear, noble, wise person—and my relations there. I volunteered to give a lecture on Thomas Mann[7] in the casino of arts and literature. I haven't begun work on that yet.

Please don't be angry with me for today's skimpy letter, and write again soon. I read your letters with great pleasure and . . . ease.

With fond regards, I am
Bruno Schulz

November 29, 1936
I'll send the drawing separately.

54

Dear Romana:

Your letter saddened me. To my amazement I recognize, sign after sign, the image of my own depressive states. How alike people are, after all! Just as all have the same limbs and organs, so they experience the same internal states. Would books and works of art and their kind of communication be possible if it were otherwise? But the great novelty for me is your prose sample! Your writing is excellent! The question is only whether you have a greater supply of material and wouldn't run out of steam on a larger project. Do try it out! I am struck by the strong element of narcissism in this short piece. I wouldn't have attributed this to you. It is a quality that never fails to fascinate me in a woman, as an expression of a fundamental otherness, a harmony and self-affirmation that are unattainable for me. That is what will forever remain alien to me, therefore alluring and yearned after. For my part I am far from narcissism, and it strikes me as some kind of metaphysical privilege to surrender to it so without care or scruple. Do go on writing! Your final effect is very good.

What advice do I have for your condition? Some sort of work! It is the best anesthetic. I talk like a moralist, though I am far from heeding those worn-out saws. I speak from the viewpoint of internal hygiene and effectiveness of living. That is our sole salvation. Ask Witkacy if he could keep on living and not go mad or kill himself if he hadn't any work.

I am reading *Nightmares* by Zegadłowicz.[8] The book interests and greatly stimulates me. Behind it I see the contours of another book I'd like to write myself. Thus I actually can't tell if I am reading the first book or that possible but unrealized one. That's the best way to read—reading oneself, one's own book, between the lines. This is how we used to read in childhood, and that is why the same books, once so rich and full of pith, are like trees stripped bare of leaves when read in adulthood—stripped, that is, of the commentary we used to putty over the gaps. The books we read in childhood don't exist anymore; they sailed off with the wind, leaving bare skeletons behind. Whoever still has in him the memory and marrow of childhood should rewrite these books as he experienced them. Then we would have the real *Robinson* and the real *Gulliver* back again.

I am glad your little son is so much better. Didn't I tell you it would pass? And still you are unhappy and have other worries. What's going to happen about your job? Could you possibly get a job with GUS [the Central Office of Statistics]?[9] How is Stas [S. I. Witkiewicz] doing? Could you ask him to give me advice about establishing residence in the Silesian countryside? He has connections there. Or could Szturm possibly do something? It would have to come off soon because I want to go to Katowice about the twentieth. Please get after them. I am now trying to get transferred to Lwów. At Christmas time I plan to go to Warsaw for a few days. We'll see each other then, needless to say. Fond greetings from

Bruno Schulz

Drohobycz, December 5, 1936

55

Thank you so much for your letter. I was just having pangs of conscience, reproaching myself for having hurt you. Several times I inquired of Lieberwerth[10] by letter how you and your little son were doing. Somehow I couldn't make myself write. It's a good thing you gave yourself a push and broke this silence. Why on earth should I bear you any grudge?

Since you know about the other matter, you are probably aware that relations between me and Józefina are broken off or at least, I like to imagine, merely suspended for an indefinite time.[11] I feel very sorry for her, I don't know how she is getting on after all she has been through; she doesn't answer my letters. I feel sorry for both of us and for all our common past that is now condemned to extinction. I won't find anyone like her again.

My life is quite miserable just now, I am not writing at all. What buoys me up is the hope that maybe during the holidays I'll be able to spend a few weeks entirely alone—with no one but myself—though I'm not sure I'll be able to stand it alone with myself. I'd like to bury myself somewhere in total seclusion.

My book is due to come out in May; it gives me no joy but fills me instead with stagefright and misgivings. How is life treating you? How is your little boy doing? I wish you would write about yourself at some length. Thank you so much again for thinking of me. That will have to be it for today.

Bruno Schulz

April 30, 1937

Publication of his second book, which Schulz was anticipating in May, was much delayed; Sanatorium *didn't appear until November (see Letter 63).*

56

Dear Romana:

I don't know if this letter will still reach you. It is a great pity you didn't write earlier because until recently I was in your proximity, at Boberka near Lomna, and we might have seen each other. I am just back from the place, where I was bored stiff, regardless of what I always think about the beneficent effect of solitude on me. I am sorry to hear you have gone through unhappy times. If I am going through them now, it is on a general and philosophical level rather than a personal one. Of course I would gladly get together with you, but my mobility is very much hampered by lack of funds. You would have to be awfully close, e.g., at Truskawiec—which is actually very beautiful. What does that fellow Hatlingberg write about love? Where I am concerned, I look for a medicine against incapacity for love rather than love itself. I envy people who know how to love.

Heartfelt thanks for your readiness to offer me help. Do you think you might try to find me a position in an editorial office in Warsaw, for example? I'd better not prolong this letter or it won't reach you in time. My surname has always been the way you just wrote it. Very warm regards to you and all the best,

Bruno Schulz

Drohobycz, July 24, 1937

57

Dear Romana:

One might suppose your question regarding my proposed visit could be answered without difficulty, clearly and definitely. That isn't the case, however. My reaction to your invitation is a mixed one: It is made up of alternating impulses and inhibitions. I am afraid to put our acquaintance to the test of several days in conditions that are somewhat depressing to me. I search my mind for the origin of my reluctance, for what it is that disheartens me about this plan—which is, after all, something to look forward to. Well, it's funny what species of dejections a nervous temperament like mine is subject to: first the idea of so unusual an undertaking as a trip exclusively for pleasure, that is, the absence of the sanction provided by some serious goal; then, the risk of failure, of the disappointment I might cause you or experience myself; next, my limited means, the need to be careful with money and to avoid putting you to expense. Maybe I should have kept quiet about all this, since I did decide to come. But since you demanded candor, here you have it—and for me this candor is a sort of reassurance in case the enterprise miscarries, a deflection of responsibility. This isn't a very gentlemanly trait, but that's the way I am. So I leave it to you to decide whether, in the face of these inhibitions of mine, you want to receive me and share the risk of the venture. As for the impulses that incline me to visit you, I will limit myself to stating that they are there, without proceeding into a closer analysis. So if you want me to come, please let me know right away how much longer you are staying there, and if it would suit you if I came Thursday or Friday. I have had the proofs of my new book *[Sanatorium]* in the house for over three weeks and haven't gone over them out of distaste for the job. I have to do it before I leave, or it will be a load weighing on my mind.* I'd also like to write a review commissioned by *Wiadomości*[12] of a book by Karen Michaelis.

With warm greetings,

Yours
Bruno Schulz

Drohobycz, August 3, 1937

* In addition to reading proofs, Schulz may have written dust-jacket copy for *Sanatorium.* The unattributed blurb printed on the flap of the first edition may be Schulz's own work, with some modifications by *Rój's* publicity staff. This adds a curious small paragraph of literary analysis to the self-appraisal found elsewhere in his letters and essays:

> The keynote of this new prose fiction of Schulz's is the dream of a renewal of life through the power of delight, the unleashing of inspiration, the primeval human belief that the dammed-up loveliness of things, hampered and hidden though it is, only awaits an inspired being to break its bonds and release a flood of happiness over all the world. This ancient myth of the mystics becomes flesh in this work, takes the shape of a peculiar eschatology, a wreath of legends plaited from strands from all cultures and mythologies and transformed into a fascinating tangle of fabulation. It is worth emphasizing that this fabulation, for all the wealth of its cultural elements, is strictly private and *sui generis,* that a wholly novel terminology is used, that a new organ, as it were, has been created for age-old human dreams. Those reveries about shuffling off the coils of the body, about a revaluation of life through poetry, have found in Schulz a new homeland, a climate all their own, in which, watchful, they burgeon forth in tropical vegetation: a legendary childhood of wonder, elation, and metamorphosis. There is the uncanny and the commonplace, wonderworking and street magic, dream worlds and realism; and all is shot through with the most colorful and dazzling invention.
>
> An author who illustrates his own books—this urge to accomplish the whole of a piece of work with one's own hands surely is akin to the dedication of medieval priests and craftsmen.

58

Dear Roma:

I want to thank you so much for those few days we spent together. I fear you were a bit disappointed in me; as for me, I returned home strangely full of life, strengthened, and mentally active. This lasted the whole week. During that time I did a great deal of thinking, reading, note taking. I was in good form, so to speak. All I needed to feel completely well was that "legitimation" of myself—some kind of result. I thought about you, too, and the sources of a lack of productivity—on the part of a person so richly and variously endowed by nature. You really should muster all your energies and force yourself to produce. For people of a certain makeup, a life without creative activity lacks all zest.

I also reflected on my own barren condition, which has gone on for such a long period. I justify it and exonerate myself—though this is hard to explain. I found a passage in a letter of Richard Wagner's that I could personally endorse with my signature (*si parva cum magnis . . .*).[13] The passage runs: "Actually I harness myself to the yoke of work—each time—with despair; when I conclude it and again have to face that life full of toil and unspeakable strain, when I immerse myself in the world of fantasy to make up for the abnegations suffered in this world—then I demand support. I cannot then live like a dog, sleep on straw, and drink stale swill: then I must feel uplifted in spirit, must feel myself affirmed and stilled on all sides—if indeed I am to succeed in the superhumanly difficult task of creating a world that does not exist. . . ."

As for myself, I would want to have, over many months, unbroken free time for thinking, reading, inner labor. There's so much to think through, so much to sort out. The business of my intellectual nourishment is so badly organized, too. I hunger for ideas, books, new systems of thought. And I want those periods of depression, which paralyze me, to stop coming back. Maybe I should seek treatment by a psychiatrist. These depressions disorganize me, making continuous work impossible. Out of seven days per week they may poison six.

It is possible that I'll go to Warsaw one of these days. [Marian] Kister (of *Rój*) is calling me about various decisions regarding my book. In that case I will come to you first, of course.

Did you go to Kazimierz? Did you perhaps see Lieberwerth?

Have you been in touch with Szturm? Please give him my best

regards. I have been about to write to him for a long time, but somehow I don't get to it easily. Too many sad memories are linked with his person.[14]

Now for one other matter I want to bring up with you. I have been approached by the parents of a boy who was once my student and who was later jailed for alleged subversive activities while studying at Ljubljana in Yugoslavia. What is needed is an inquiry at our Foreign Office, where they have a petition by the parents of the ex-prisoner. This young man is gravely ill with a lung disease. He was on the point of death in jail at Belgrade, but by a miracle he made a comeback and was released after three and a half years. Without waiting for a passport he had applied for to be issued, the police packed him off to the Hungarian border (harassment, clearly). In Hungary he was arrested for being without papers and was detained in the so-called *Schubhaus* in Budapest pending receipt of documents. The Polish consulate at Belgrade informed the family that the passport had been sent to the Hungarian police. Since that time several weeks have passed with no further news either from the young man in detention or from the Polish consulate at Budapest or from the Budapest police, despite numerous inquiries. The family has asked the Foreign Office to instruct the Polish consulate at Budapest to intervene. Again no answer. Now it is a matter of speeding up the intervention, since the released prisoner is ill and living in the worst possible conditions. Do you know anyone who might bring this matter up in the Ministry and reinforce the family's petition? The name is Izaak Feuerberg.[15] Please send me word about what might be done, if anything.

Fond regards to you and greetings to Stefanek.

Bruno Schulz

August 16, 1937

59

Dear Roma:

Thanks for your prompt answer and kind words. When one has no self-assurance and faith oneself, someone else's is very welcome even if it doesn't quite replace one's own. What I lack is not so much faith in my own gifts but something more pervasive: trust in life, confident acquiescence in a personal destiny, faith in the ultimate benevolence of existence. I used to have these without even being aware of it. That faith, that confidence opens up stores of creative energy in us, it is the rich, satiated, warm climate in which those late and barely accessible fruits ripen. Cases in which the deficits and tragic turns of life serve as a stimulus are incomprehensible to me. That kind of creative process must be completely different from mine.

If I want to capture the essence of my present condition, what comes forcibly to mind is the image of a person shaken out of a deep sleep. He wakes up to the light of day, still sees the world of dreams as it sinks into oblivion, still feels the softness of dreaming under his lids—and all at once the new, sober, brisk waking world presses down on him; still full of inner languidness he lets himself be drawn, feet dragging, into its affairs and processes. Thus inside me my specific being, my exceptionality, immerses itself in oblivion, so to speak, without dissolving. What shut me off from the world's onslaughts recedes gently into the background, and I, like an insect released from its cocoon, exposed to the tempest of an alien light and the winds of heaven, commit myself to the elements, in a way for the first time. Where this may lead me—I don't know. Whether this new sobriety is only the emptiness following an engulfment by creative nebulae or a fresh hunger for the world, a new confrontation with the outer element—I don't know. The peculiarity and unusual nature of my inner processes sealed me off hermetically, made me insensitive, unreceptive to the world's incursions. Now I am opening myself up to the world, in a way for the second time, and all would be well if it weren't for that terror and inner shrinking, as if before a perilous venture that might lead God knows where.

What about you? What's your state of mind like? Who have you been in touch with? Has Witkacy written to you at all? I don't know if I am coming to Warsaw now, I'm waiting for word from *Rój* on that score. I have a nephew in Warsaw, Wilhelm Schulz,[16] an engineer, a very capable and bright young man (very good looking, too), who would gladly go out of his way to help me get out of Drohobycz. May I direct him to seek inspiration and guidance for action from you?

Thank you so much for taking up the case of that poor F. [Feuerberg] with such zeal. He is no relation of mine, only a former student and an unfortunate boy. He has very poor parents who can't do anything for him. I will tell them what to do and await the result. Please don't be angry with me for bothering you with this affair, but you haven't taken up an unworthy cause.

With warm greetings, and hoping to hear from you often, yours

Bruno Schulz

Drohobycz [between August 20 and 26, 1937]

60

Dear Romana:

Please don't hold it against me that I rewarded your efforts and your caring with—a refusal. If you care to take a closer look at my circumstances you will realize that I was unable to accept this proposition. I mentioned to you once that I have three dependents (a sister, a cousin, and a nephew) whom I can't simply throw to the mercy of fate. I now earn about 300 zloty a month. If I were to get a post in Warsaw on similar terms, I would make the move; I could subsist there on 200 zloty a month and send 100 zloty to my family. But at Ramberg's[17] I'd be working two to six hours and would make at most 100 zloty. For such a handful of hours I can't throw over a civil service post (at rank VII) that guarantees me a pension. I haven't enough courage, enough drive or incentive, to take such a risky step. I flatter myself that one could find something better, after all, if one went at it full steam. This is no hint to spur you to greater efforts! I know well the kind of difficult circumstances you work in and you don't have an easy life. With all this I didn't expect you to find the time and the goodwill to think of me. Nor do I see how you could do any more for me—though I'm not quite giving up hope. Please don't be upset that I permitted myself a jocular addition to my recommendation of my nephew as a form of inducement, i.e., that he is handsome (this is, as a matter of fact, one of his salient traits). I harbored no hidden thoughts when I wrote this. For that matter, on further reflection I have backed off the idea of getting you two together; I'm afraid my nephew is too independent by temperament to work as one of a team. In his time he generated a great deal of activity for my benefit; with great zeal he went to see Wierzyński, Szturm, and Czarski on my behalf. By now, though, he is much too absorbed by his own career to involve himself so intensively. As for Gombrowicz, I will try to take the initiative in getting you acquainted; he is well worth your knowing. May I simply let him know that you would like to meet him? That would be the simplest.

I can't recall what I wrote you about in my last letter. My own diagnosis of my psychic state and inner situation changes constantly and takes on new shapes. It seems that the world, life, is always important to me solely as raw material for writing. The moment I cannot make creative use of life, it becomes either fearsome and perilous to me, or fatally tedious. To sustain curiosity, creative incentive, to fight the process of sterilization, boredom—these are my most important and urgent tasks. Without the zest this adds to life I would fall—alive—into a lethal lethargy. Literary art has accustomed me to its stimuli and sharp sensations. My nervous system has a delicacy and fastidiousness that are not up to the demands of a life not sanctioned by art. I am afraid this school year may kill me. When I had more youth and vitality I managed to tolerate it somehow. Now it makes my gorge rise. As an antidote to that oppressive school waltz, what about—debauchery? The thought has gone through my mind. But it threatens too much nervous shock and exhaustion (in the difficult and dangerous conditions I face here: small town . . . teacher). In order to write I need to have an especially benign and favorable climate around me—a good portion of belief in myself, quiet, security. . . . I am now richer and more mature than when I wrote *Cinnamon Shops.* I lack only that naiveté, that insouciance. Back then I felt no responsibility on my shoulders, no burden, I wrote for myself. That makes it much easier. I understand perfectly why someone like Berent[18] reads no reviews of himself and avoids the press. He creates an artificial solitude around himself, an emptiness within which he works. That's what it takes. It is true that in Warsaw I wouldn't have this creative isolation. On the other hand, I wouldn't face death by tedium, creeping boredom, horrible vomiting fits from the drabness of life. After a certain time I would remove myself to a place of quiet to write. One can accuse me of many contradictions in what I say, but you will understand me if you put yourself in my situation mentally.

Perhaps you could borrow Husserl[19] (the German philosopher) for me somewhere. Maybe I will turn to Witkiewicz for this. In any case I would like to subscribe to some large lending library in Warsaw that sends out books to the provinces. Or would it be better to do this in Łódź?

Are you disillusioned with me? Won't you do anything for me

anymore? I sense, I know, and you don't need to convince me, that you want to help me very much. You are now the only one who really cares about doing this. Remember me and write soon. With fond greetings,

Bruno Schulz

August 30, 1937

61

Dear Roma:

Ever since my return from Warsaw I have enjoyed what felt like a period of healing and surcease. Instead of irritating and troubling me, the meeting with Józefina had a soothing effect. I found her completely calm, reconciled to our parting, and this sobered me. Her value to me grows or declines in proportion to the vacillations my imagination undergoes regarding her attachment to me. Since this matter is not an easy one to decide and keeps presenting different facets of itself to me—depending on the memories that rise in my mind—my depression and regret lie always in ambush, ready to pounce. Now, for instance, it occurs to me that her calm, whether prompted by pride or the dictates of self-control, may have been feigned. But let that be as it may.

What partly accounts for my good spirits is—please don't make fun of me—your insight, or is it intuition, that predicted a productive period in my writing. Do you remember? Added to this was a certain sense of abundance and potency, a command of adequate resources and reserves. Given the fact that I keep thinking about being translated into a Western European language, it occurred to me to write something [a novella, *Die Heimkehr*] directly in German.[20] I have put this into practice and have begun to write a German draft (over twenty notebook pages long by now). Until today I was fairly well satisfied with it, but today I suffered the first attack of doubt, which threatened to make me scuttle the undertaking. Still, I may rescue it yet. The language poses no serious difficulty for me, I move in it with almost perfect freedom; yet the work suffers from a certain incapacity to rise to the supreme effort, the flight of originality—the fundamental disease that has stricken my writing. Only after copying it out will I be able to judge whether the work is worth anything.

I have had no reply from Italy to my suggestion about [a translation of] *Cinnamon Shops.* It surprises and worries me. The proposition came from the Italian side and was very warm in tone. Why is there no answer now to either of two letters? (I take it I have told you about their proposal?)

What's new with you? Are you still plagued by overwork? Is the termination of your department that you wrote me about irrevocable? Do you have any plans or prospects yet? What are your personal feelings? Do you see anybody? Have you seen Szturm? Parallel to this I am writing to Gombrowicz about you. I have an idea I'll succeed in bringing you two closer to each other. Right now, of course, he is ailing and not in his best form.

I would like to get a few words from you soon and find out all about your external and internal state. Will you write?

With all best wishes,

Bruno Schulz

Drohobycz, September 29, 1937

A DESCRIPTION OF THE BOOK *CINNAMON SHOPS*

Schulz's hopes to have his work published more widely in Europe were raised, in part, by the invitation, mentioned in Letters 61 and 62, from an Italian publisher to submit Cinnamon Shops *for translation. Toward this end Schulz wrote a succinct analysis of the book in German—apparently the one language he and his would-be publisher shared.*

This book represents an attempt to recreate the history of a certain family, a certain home in the provinces, not from their actual elements, events, characters, or experiences, but by seeking their mythic content, the primal meaning of that history.

It is the author's conviction that there is no way to plumb the deepest level of biography or make out the true shape of personal destiny either by describing the external curriculum vitae or by psychological analysis, however deeply the latter might probe. The ultimate given data of human life, he submits, lie in a spiritual dimension, not in the category of facts but in their transcendent meaning; likewise, a curriculum vitae that aims to elucidate its own semantic structure, that is honed to be sensitive to its own spiritual significance, amounts to—myth. That murky, portentous atmosphere, that aura which condenses around every family history and illuminates it, as it were, with mythic flashes—as if it embodied the ultimate secret of blood and kinship—is the poet's way of glimpsing that history's other face, its profounder gestalt.

Stryjska Street, the model for "The Street of Crocodiles." From a 1910 postcard.

Here the author feels close to the sensibility of classical antiquity; he regards his creative imagination and its phantasmagoric inclination as being derived from a "pagan" concept of life—having to do with the fact that for the ancients, too, the genealogy of the clan became steeped in myth at two or three generations' remove, and the backward look exposed a family history which found its solution and dissolution in mythology.

This book, however, is not a repository of a mythology culturally grounded in *res gestae,* bearing the stamp of history. The elements of the mythological idiom operating here rise out of that misty region of early childhood fantasies, forebodings, anticipations, terrors which is the true spawning ground of mythical thinking. It seemed worthwhile to condense that mythical suspension into a coherent, densely meaningful world of legends, to let it ripen into a kind of personal and private mythology without sacrificing its substratum of authenticity.

At center stage we see the enigmatic figure of "Father," a merchant by profession, who presides over a cotton goods shop, holding sway over a swarm of darkhaired and redheaded clerks. We see him harried, in a perpetual dither, constantly setting himself against the nature of things, launching attacks against it by means of the most hazardous experiments. This severely tested man, a quintessential victim, was condemned to pursue his meditations on the redemption of the world in solitude, almost breaking under the strain of his metaphysical mission, surrounded by a lumpishly unconcerned environment insensitive to his metaphysical woes. His problematic and heretical experiments touch the roots of the world's mystery. He is forever tempted to lay impious hands on the secret sensual nodes of the world's cohesion, to run caressing and provoking fingers over the most sensitive sources of its mystery.

Father to an avian brood beyond counting, reared in the hidden recesses of his domicile, he looses vivid squadrons of peacocks, pheasants, and pelicans out the windows into the evening landscape, he the headquarters of their soarings, turns, and wheelings—until his archenemy Adela, the housemaid, scatters the dense flocks to the four winds. After this defeat he begins, in his deserted quarters, to shrink and dry up, a little more each day, indulging now in silly games, now in pointless chatter, gradually loses himself in the chambers of his relatives' vast apartment, preserving some possible semblance of life in the shape of an old stuffed condor; and finally one night pays a brief visit to Mother as a traveling salesman.

In a running feud with the cockroach tribe that inundated the apartment one day with its teeming black hordes, he becomes inadvertently trapped by his corrosive hatred in those labyrinths of feeling where revulsion transforms itself into sinister seduction—and bit by bit he assumes the manners and way of life of the detested species. Now and then the author allows him time off from this conversion to revert back to himself, and presently we see him again as he lectures on puppets, tailors' dummies, and a "heretical Demiurgy" before an audience of little dressmaking flunkies, a learned dissertation in which he challenges the Demiurge's exclusive right to create and, by perverse and sacriligious methods, scrutinizes the genesis of life.

Thus the author has him pick his idiosyncratic way from adventure to adventure, failure to failure, in the company of the narrative's other characters and happenings, within the boundary of the brightly colored landscape that, in constantly mutating forms, keeps company with his exploits.

62

Dear Roma:

I am out of luck with Gombrowicz. He is having fits of the blues and avoids people. He promised me he would telephone you when he felt better. Witkacy has written to me. He has broken with Gombrowicz but made it up with Marusia Kasprowicz[21] and is often at her house. He advised me to change my subject matter completely "to make the oviducts *[sic]* taut for a last squirt of sperm." But please don't quote this sentence back to him, or he will complain of my indiscretion; though the potency in question is mine, not his.

I finished my German novella quite some time ago, but the copying goes very slowly because of various other occupations and lack of confidence in what I have written. It is going to be a pretty long business, in its subject matter related to *Sanatorium Under the Sign of the Hourglass.*

I am afraid that the Italian project is still hanging fire somehow —no answer to my memorandum about *Cinnamon Shops* as a bilingual. This scheme came about through the intermediacy of M. Chasin [also Chazen] a pianist I met in Zakopane who has fantastic connections abroad.

Why are you so downcast? What could give you a little bit of calm and prop up your morale? How does bobbed hair suit you? I am glad you're done with substituting. Ah, if you could only earn a little money and go abroad for a few weeks! I have the same dream. . . . I haven't thought of Józefina lately. Last week I went through such a powerful attack of domestic hostility that I thought this time I would carry out the separation [from his family] and live apart. Somehow the rift has been papered over again, but quite possibly I may move out. What do you advise me to do? The family income will suffer, since I'll have to pay for room and separate maintenance.

Please don't resent my writing so rarely, I have a lot of school and other chores. I'll write again soon. So far nothing worth translating for you has come to hand. With fond greetings,

Bruno Schulz

October 10, 1937

63

Dear Romana:

Please don't think I've forgotten about you, but what with constant spells of grief and depression I never get to the point where I can cast my thoughts in the form of a letter. But such a long silence as has fallen between us is beginning to trouble me. How are you doing? How is your little son? Are you still so loaded down with work? How's your mood?

Untitled pencil sketch, possibly a study for a scene in "Tailor's Dummies."

My last few days passed under the thunderous, dazzling impact of Gombrowicz's book [*Ferdydurke,* just published]. All attempts at classifying this work fail. It is a book on an altogether grand scale, pioneering and revelatory. As an intellectual exploit I place it next to such phenomena as Freud or Proust. He has written to me that he is sending you a copy of his book. I feel sure it is going to overwhelm you, too. I want to write about this book but have constant trouble gathering my thoughts, regardless of the fact that it undermines and perturbs me. I am loaded down with it. Gombrowicz himself, strangely enough, is very dispirited and worried about his book's fate. It is a strange experience—here you've been associating with a person on such intimate terms and suddenly genius erupts from him. Gombrowicz is a genius.

I have had a letter from Kuncewicz about this book—couched in the highest terms.

My book still hasn't come out, but Gombr. reports that it will appear in a matter of days. I am not doing any writing. My German novella (thirty pages of typescript) is finished. I gave it to Berman,[22] the translator of Wittlin into German, for appraisal.

Otherwise no news here. I wait for word from you with some unease. Kind regards,

Sincerely
Bruno Schulz

November 16, 1937

REVIEW OF WITOLD GOMBROWICZ'S *FERDYDURKE*

The publication of Ferdydurke *caused a stir that winter, and in January Schulz gave a lecture on Gombrowicz's book in the Warsaw quarters of the Polish Writers Society. The event was mentioned in* Apel, *the literary and artistic supplement to* Kurier Poranny, *no. 16, 1938, and the paper reproduced below was published under the title "Ferdydurke" in* Skamander, *August/September, 1938.*

FERDYDURKE

We have not been accustomed for some time in our literature to debuts so impressive, explosions of ideas on such a scale as Gombrowicz's novel *Ferdydurke.* We have here the unusual emergence of a writerly talent; a new, revolutionary novelistic form and method; a fundamental discovery at last; the conquest of a new realm of intellectual phenomena, a realm that is still ownerless, where until now only the irresponsible joke, the pun, nonsense held sway.

Let us stake off the terrain, locate the district in which Gombrowicz's unveiling takes place. Curiously, the district whose extent this unusual discovery first reveals to us had, up to now, no name; had not even managed to provide itself with a bona fide existence; went unmarked by so much as a white dot on the map of the spiritual world.

Until now a man looked at himself—and wanted to keep on looking at himself—exclusively from the official side of things. What happened inside him that was not contained in official meanings he disallowed, refused entry to the forum of intellect, simply did not recognize. Thus it led, so to speak, an orphaned life outside being, outside reality, a doleful life of unaccepted and unrecorded meaning. An oath of excommunication against stupidity, nullity, and nonsense barred its way, and its all too close proximity blinded anyone who approached it. Consciousness always demands a certain distance and the sanction of reason; what lies too near at hand and lacks this sanction escapes its bounds.

While the human shadow acted out an official plot, mature and acceptable, on the stage of consciousness, its true reality dealt hopelessly with stupidity and idiocy, bumped up helplessly against chimerae and shabby things in a region with no name and no location. The shadow illegally usurped all prerogatives of existence while the homeless reality of man led the secret life of an unacknowledged tenant. Gombrowicz showed that the mature and clear forms of our spiritual existence are rather a *pium desiderium* and live in us more as eternally strained intention than as reality. As reality we live permanently below this plateau in a completely honorless and inglorious domain that is so flimsy that we also hesitate to grant it even the semblance of existence. Gombrowicz's considerable achievement is simply that he did not hesitate to recognize this realm as the actual and quintessentially human domain of the true man, that he adopted it, disinherited and homeless, for consciousness, identified it and gave it a name: the first step down the path of a splendid career that this manager of immaturity has paved for it in literature.*

As every mature aspect of man has its corresponding counterparts in the forms and contents of higher culture, this clandestine and unofficial aspect of existence also possesses a world of corresponding counterparts in which it develops and functions. From the standpoint of culture these are specific subsidiary and waste products of the cultural processes, a zone of subcultural contents, misshapen and crude, a gigantic scrapheap littering the periphery of culture. Yet this world of sewers and gutters, this monstrous drain of culture, forms a basic substance, a compost, a life-giving pap out of which every value and every culture grows. Here is a reservoir of powerful emotional tensions that these subcultural contents have the ability to concentrate and gather. Our immaturity (and at heart perhaps our life force), tied with a thousand knots, with a thousand atavisms, with these secondary forms, with second-class culture, resides squarely in it by virtue of obsolete alliance and bonds. While under the shield of adult and official forms we pay homage to more elevated and

* The analogy to Freudianism arises here of its own accord, but while Freud, after he had discovered the domain of the subconscious, made a psychological curiosity out of it, an isolated island whose incomprehensible manifestations and distinct paradoxical logic he clearly delineated, so likewise, behind the bars of pathology, isolated from the background of normal acts, Gombrowicz directed his speculum at these allegedly normal and mature processes, pointed out that their legitimacy and regularity are an optical illusion of our consciousness that—itself a product of a certain training—accepts only meanings that are adequate to it, but does not recognize the element of immaturity that flows around the tiny lagoon of official meanings. The area under discussion does not fall under any category of official recognition: We have no organ at all at our disposal with which to grasp it. Here Gombrowicz has brought off an ingenious trick: He made use of the psychic apparatus that normally functions as a safety valve, as protective insulation, with which the weak structure of officialdom protects itself against the pressure of subterranean chaos: Namely, he has used the comic, the convulsion of laughter that shakes off the usurpations and temptations of this diffuse element, the subconscious—and in it, since it communicates with these problematical areas, a new visual and cognitive organ. Gombrowicz's grotesqueness is nothing more than a vehicle of defiance and repugnance, adopted for the purpose of recognition. Freud showed a small sector of this subterranean world accessible only to the psychologist's methods, methods with which he neutralized the destructive influence of ridiculousness and nonsense. And so he stays fundamentally on the level of scientific seriousness. A general assault on this position could nonetheless only succeed in total liquidation and sacrifice of the position of seriousness, and an opening up of the front line to the element of laughter for a boundless invasion of the comic. It became evident that the biggest obstacle to a radical unmasking of the mechanisms of thinking lay solely in scientific seriousness and in the dignified pose of the investigator. Driven from their unmasked position, officialdom and hypocrisy took flight in the seriousness of investigative behavior. This was blind man's bluff, and Gombrowicz blew it to bits by breaking through the barrier of seriousness with unheard-of audacity. He was successful in making a constructive tool out of the instrument of destruction. Thanks to this he directed a ray of humanizing humor into an area that did not previously wish to be submitted to any analysis through the power of the human mind. [B.S.]

refined values, our actual life runs secretly and without more elevated sanctions in this dirty indigenous region, and the emotional energies concentrated in it are a hundred times stronger than those given over to the thin stratum of the official. Gombrowicz showed that just here, in this scorned and inglorious region, exuberant and abundant life proliferates, that life can also manage very well without higher sanctions, that it is better to develop under the hundredfold pressure of disgrace and shame than on the plateau of sublimation.

Gombrowicz repealed the unusual position of content in the psychic world, destroyed the myth of its godly origin and shows that its zoological pedigree comes out of those lower regions from which it has proudly distanced itself. Gombrowicz demonstrates the homogeneity of the cultural and subcultural realms; moreover, one may asume that he considers the model and prototype of all values to reside in the subcultural realm, in the realm of the immature, and he perceives, in that mechanism of their functionings he ingeniously reveals, a key to the understanding of culture. Up till now man saw himself through the prism of finished and completed form, saw himself from the side of the official facade. He did not notice that while in his ambitions he had reached for the ideal, in his reality he was eternally unfinished, botched, patched up, and fragmented. The miserable tailoring of his form, sewn with big, clumsy stitches, escapes his notice. Gombrowicz presents us with the backyard inventory of things, the rear building of the self. Amazing inventory: in the front parlor everything goes on formally, according to etiquette, while in the kitchen of our self, behind the scenes of official business, the worst kind of household is run. No form is so trashy and filthy that it wouldn't still be quoted at a high rate of exchange and do a brisk trade. Here the structure of mythology, the violence hidden in the form of linguistic syntax, the terror and predatoriness of the platitude, the omnipotence of symmetry and analogy, shows itself in all its misery. Here the mechanism of our ideals is revealed to be based on the dominance of naive literalness, metaphors, and primitive imitation of linguistic forms. Gombrowicz is a master of this ridiculous and grotesque psychic machinery; he knows it will blow all the fuses, lead to splendid explosions in a wonderful and grotesque condensation of substance.

How Gombrowicz achieves the granulation of the plasmalike entities of this nebulous realm, how he tangibly and visibly calls them onto the stage of his theater, is a mystery of his talent. The instrument of his grotesqueness, which he constructs for this purpose, a grotesqueness that plays the role of a magnifying glass under which these imponderables become flesh and blood, should be the subject of special study.

But the chain of Gombrowicz's discoveries does not end here. They still contain a profound diagnosis of the very essence of culture. Gombrowicz's scalpel lays bare the primary motivation of culture, its nerve and root, and liberates it from the plexus of secondary motives that obscure it. Gombrowicz discovered and fully appreciates the magnificent meaning of the problem of form. One can say along with him that human culture in its entirety is a system of forms in which man is reflected and appears to man. Man cannot endure his nakedness and cannot make contact with himself nor with his fellow man by any other means but forms, styles, and masks. The whole of human attention was always captured so, by the use of forms and hierarchies, by the manipulation and shift of values away from the essence of the matter so that the hierarchialization and production of forms was located seemingly outside all problems. Gombrowicz's gain was that this matter, which until now was always considered only from the absolute and essential perspective, from the perspective of content, he shows from the perspective of genetics and evolutionary development. He shows the embryology of form. He identifies its multiplicity, reduces the whole scope of human ideologies to a single denominator, and beyond all their shapes he shows a human substance. The primeval womb of this form-fabric he locates in a dominion previously inaccessible to the eyes, so dubious, devalued, and trashy that to make an association of these matters at first glance so distant from one another must seem like a real flash of clairvoyance. We already know the place where this laboratory of form lies, this factory of sublimations and hierarchies. It is the sewer drain of immaturity, a region of disgrace and shame, site of coarseness and defects, a sad trash heap of culture, full of fragments, wretched rag-and-straw ideologies for which there is no name in any cultured language.

Such discoveries are not made on the smooth, safe path of pure speculation and cold cognition. Gombrowicz comes to them by way of pathology, his own pathology. With greater or lesser difficulty we must all suffer through the crisis of maturation, the painful processes of deficiency and defects, with greater or lesser difficulty bearing wounds, injuries; deformity and deviations grow out of these troubles. For Gombrowicz the agonies of maturation with all their defeats and hindrances do not end in this or that form of equilibrium, are not silenced in this or that compromise, but rather become for themselves a problem, ripe for self-recognition, ready to become word and expression.

Gombrowicz's attitude is not that of a passionless investigator; his book is permeated from beginning to end with ardent apostleship, with feverish, militant confession, with the reformer's zeal. This apostleship is perhaps the heart and starting point of the book, out of which other components and branches grow as from a trunk. It is not easy to explain the merit of such an apostleship and certainly because it doesn't have to do here only with a single viewpoint, doctrine, or catchword, but rather with the remodeling of the whole style of life and reformer's spirit *in capite et membris,* as fundamental now as it ever has been. And again he errs who assumes that the author proceeds from generalizations and abstractions. The book's point of departure is as concrete, personal, keen and fiery as one can imagine, and Gombrowicz according to his own lights underscores the origin of his work from the perspective of his personal situation. He shows that all "fundamental" and "universal" motives underlying our behavior, each sailing under the flag of ideals and slogans, do not express us fully and truly but always only a small and, in the bargain, accidental and insignificant portion of us. Gombrowicz opposes the fundamental tendency of culture, which is founded on the circumstance that man always finds an outlet through whatever fragments, ideologies, phrases, and forms suddenly appear from within him instead of living with himself, with his integral wholeness and his living heart. Man has always seen himself as an incomplete, unimportant appendage of his cultural substance. Gombrowicz wants to restore this relationship to its true proportions; he turns it upside down. He shows that as immature, ridiculous greenhorns fighting for our expression on the plain of concreteness and dealing with our meaninglessness, we are closer to the truth than if we were solemn, sublime, mature, and completed. He thus calls us back to the lower forms, orders us once more to reshape, refight, and remodel our entire cultural childhood: to become a child, not to find salvation in these ideologies that are ever baser, ever more primitive, ever trashier, but because in developing out of the phase of his primitive naiveté, the same man has wasted, squandered, and lost the treasure of his living concreteness. All these forms, gestures, and masks have been fleshed out with what is human and contain the rudiments of the wretched but concrete and sole true human condition—and Gombrowicz revindicates them, recovers them, calls them back from their long exile. The more these masks denounce and compromise forms and ideas, the more they reveal their mechanism as still more rough, clear, perspicuous, and scandalous, the faster man liberates himself from the forms that bind him. Yet Gombrowicz's relationship to form is not so straight-forward and explicit as it might seem from this presentation.

This demonologist of culture, this obstinate bloodhound of cultural lies, is at the same time strangely given over to them, is enamored of their trashy, shoddy charm via a pathological, incurable love. It is the love for the ridiculous, awkward human creature, moving in its helplessness, unable to cope with insatiable, demanding form. Both the troubles, the misfortunes, and the puns of form, and the torture of man on form's Procrustean bed, excite and move him passionately.

But how meager and dry, how poor is the skeleton of these problems lifted out of the living organism of the novel *Ferdydurke*. It is scarcely one cross-section of the living, whirling bulk of its body, hardly one of the thousands of aspects of this thousand-faceted creature. Here we finally encounter a natural, first-hand mind that has not been stuffed full of readymade ideas. Wherever we lay our hand on the flesh of this work we feel a powerful musculature of thought, muscles, and sinews of an athletic anatomy that needs no artificial padding. This book bursts from an abundance of ideas, overflows with creative and destructive energy.

What consequences for the practice of life and literature does Gombrowicz derive from his insights? He despises individual form, scoffs at its breakneck efforts to anchor itself in reality. No pedigree, no alibi before a material and absolute forum can rescue it, in his eyes. But this positivist and worshiper of the fact looks on all of it indulgently if it proves itself to him through its efficiency and success, if it succeeds in surviving and preserves itself in every intermonad medium we call public opinion. Then form momentarily attains its beatification. Success is the highest court of appeal, the irrevocable criterion of every human deed. Gombrowicz greatly respects this court, although he knows its composition and substance, and even though he knows that it is the crude average opinion of person X or Y, the common pulp of the narrow-minded estimations of the hoi polloi. And still—Gombrowicz shows—there is no other or higher court of appeal; still it illegally judges the worth of our personal goals; to it all our most secret longings aspire; and still our ardent aspirations founder on it. By virtue of all its flimsiness it is the prototype of a force of assessment, and it means in the end all absolute criteria and standards. It limits us and presses upon us; our form forces its way into it; every shape we try to give ourselves clings to it.

With all its positivistic cult of the fact, however, the foreword to "Philidor" points to the upset of this ideology, to disloyalty, because Gombrowicz restricts it, takes some problems out of its sphere of jurisdiction. Gombrowicz should not have been so frightened about his one-sidedness. Every great system of thought is one-sided and has the boldness of this one-sidedness as well. The concession that Gombrowicz makes to "first-rate writers" is purely formal; a double standard should not be introduced here. The exceptions, again, that Gombrowicz makes also weaken the believability of his theory with regard to every fact that he places under its jurisdiction. Gombrowicz, in fact, demands that the personal motives that move a writer to write—and, according to his daring assertion, these are always problems of carrying a writer's individual qualities through the forum of public opinion—should no longer be an underground, shameful, secret functioning mainspring of his activities that transposes its energy into totally strange and distant subjects, but should become simply the open subject of his creative work. Gombrowicz aims to bare the whole machinery of a work of art, its connection to the author, and he actually provides—along with the claim—the confirmation of this possibility as well, for *Ferdydurke* is nothing else than the great example of such a work. He believes this to be the single way out of the common, hopeless hypocrisy that literature will be restored to health by a powerful injection of reality. But what does "second-rate writer" mean? A master of relativity and worshiper of the concrete like Gombrowicz should not have had to operate within such limited categories nor condemn second-rateness only on the strength of the definition. Gombrowicz knows the strange, capricious path of the careers of great ideas and great works; he knows that greatness can be the experience of a lucky trend and the course of internal and external circumstances. Thus one should also not take Gombrowicz's loyalty to the great minds of mankind too seriously. Here, in this regard, it is worth remembering, without disadvantage to the undoubted originality of the novel *Ferdydurke,* that this book has a predecessor perhaps unknown to its author—the premature and therefore heirless *Pałuba,* by Karol Irzykowski. Perhaps the situation in this literary sector is now ripe for a general offensive.

The critic is doomed to translate the artistic prose of *Ferdydurke* into a conventional and popular vernacular. Yet how much must the work, through this sort of stripping and medical prepping of the bare skeleton, suffer damage to its unlimited perspective, ambiguity, metaphorical expansiveness that bestows on Gombrowicz's ideas the value of a microcosmos, the value of a universal model of the world and life!

1938

64

Dear Roma:

I have just come home, am in my bed at last, and want to thank you so very much for your kindness and friendship. In that press of people I could not show you the attention you deserve—if it were only as the sponsor of this evening. I suspected you felt a little orphaned. I apologize most humbly if you didn't feel as happy as you should have. I don't know why, but I came out of this evening a little dejected by the splendid speeches of the discutants and filled with distaste for my own lecture, but the feeling is slowly fading.

I only wanted to write these few words so you would not lose faith in our friendship, which is going to be a very enduring one.

How did the evening continue? Was there much more talk? Did you recognize Kuncewicz? Did you hear that Brochwicz, that tall, fair-haired fellow, offered to use his influence in the matter of a German translation of *Cinnamon Shops*? Let me thank you most warmly for everything and promise that in the future I will be less absentminded and scatterbrained.

Greeting you very fondly, with a kiss of the hand,
Bruno Schulz

January 12, 1938

Be so kind and thank Madame Kragen[23] warmly for the enthusiasm she has shown for me and beg her pardon for my inability to go up to her and express my gratitude directly.

Did you give *The Comet* back to Grydz?[24]

Many thanks! Excuse me for using this paper—I don't have any other. I will send the book tomorrow!

From Schulz's letter below it's clear that Romana knew something of that "tall, fair-haired fellow" Brochwicz whom Schulz met at the lecture. Stanislaw Brochwicz (Kozłowski), author of pulp novels, was an agent of the Gestapo and Nazi counterintelligence. During the Nazi occupation he was sentenced to die by the underground court of the Polish resistance movement, and was stabbed to death in Warsaw.

65

Dear, kind Roma:

Your letter moved me strongly, dear Roma. You undervalue yourself and you underrate the importance of your friendship to me. I keep reproaching myself for having neglected you during the reading, but in my defense I cite the fact that I am ill equipped to deal with people who throw themselves at me, and a mass of people were doing that there, neatly cutting me off from you. I was sorry, too, that I couldn't spend the last few minutes before our departure with you, but my nephew is a bit difficult and rough-hewn; I was afraid there might be some unpleasantness or discord if we rode together. You overestimate my vulnerability and my explosive reaction to Eiger's speech. I don't care a bit about that, and it never entered my head to feel offended with you for having arranged that evening. Gombrowicz writes me that we have rendered him a tremendous service, that the effect was excellent—so he is informed everywhere—and that he feels immensely obliged to us. "In one way or another, this makes an enormous difference to the book; it startles people, creates a sensation, emboldens kindred spirits and stirs things up"—these are Gombrowicz's words. I expect, too, that Gombrowicz will be awarded the Young Writer's Prize, which has great moral significance.[25]

What has me worried, on the other hand, is the news of your illness. You mustn't fool around with this but should treat it conscientiously. I am afraid it will last longer than a week. Please don't take it lightly but consult a good doctor; you mustn't neglect it if you want to avoid nasty complications. Please promise me you will follow the doctor's orders religiously.

Of course I don't resent your opening Gombrowicz's letter; I have no secrets. I too have been in bed since Friday with a light flu; I plan to be back in school tomorrow, though. I had a letter from Professor Chwistek[26] in which he offers me his help for a move to Lwów, but to the public school system. Somehow that doesn't exactly thrill me. I have put down roots in Drohobycz, and besides I'm afraid that working in the very crowded public schools will wear me out even more. What do you advise?

Thank you for your warning where Brochwicz is concerned. I am not writing to him but am waiting to hear from him. He gave me the address of a translator, a woman, in Vienna, whom I have known for some time. I have written to her.

Gombrowicz took a great liking to Egga Haardt;[27] he intends to keep up the acquaintance in Warsaw. She made a strong impression on him.

I am deeply moved by the proofs of your attachment and your great readiness to help me. My wish for you is that you could rent a large apartment where you could host me too during stays in Warsaw. I accept your friendly "thou" but, unlike you, prefer to begin it orally. I am more self-concious writing than speaking. Oh, well, you start, and I'll give it a try.

Thank you for delivering my manuscript to *Wiadomości.* Did you put it in an envelope and address it? Perhaps you wouldn't mind telephoning them one of these days between 4 and 6 P.M. to have them confirm receipt.

I received 50 zloty for the lecture, and afterward Wanda Melcer[28] reproached me for making it so short.

I enclose a letter to Wanda Kragen and request you kindly to hand it to her. I don't have her address. I couldn't even greet her and thank her for the high opinion she holds of me; not to mention the trouble she took for me in various matters.

I wish you a speedy recovery and all the best of things; once more, heartfelt thanks for everything and warm greetings—

Bruno Schulz

January 18, 1938

66

Dear Roma:

I'm afraid you overrate me; you are falling into a state of exaltation, unhealthy for both subject and object. It is a kind of emotional binge that is very pleasant for me, but I fear the "morning after." I don't see any reason why Wanda Kragen shouldn't have some compensation for the unpleasantness she experienced as a result of her enthusiastic championship of me. Apart from that, it wouldn't hurt to cultivate her, as a reviewer, for the future. I feel you might as well turn that letter over to her.

I am glad to know you're better. It must have been only an irritation of the gall bladder, but watch out for your diet!

As for Eggi Haardt—no involvement there for me, and anyway, the risk of involvement is never acute in my case. The only thing that holds a threat for me is a strong emotional involvement on the part of the woman. I am a reactive creature, by and large, and that hooks me, but it is a rare thing. Just the same I am going to write to Gombrowicz not to spoil my pitch. It is decent of him to have put things so fairly.

Self-portraits.

What you said about my book gives me great pleasure. It is so good that you like it, I was close to losing faith in it. No one besides you has had one good thing to say about it.

I sent money to Poznań and—odd business—received neither confirmation nor thanks. As a matter of tact, it won't do to ask about this. Only now do I understand the way you headed your letters. So this is the transition to "thou"? All right, then, no more petty scruples, let's be on "thou" terms together, dear Roma.

So . . . you may do as you like with the letter to W. Kragen. As for placing the lecture on Gombrowicz, Grydzewski had already accepted it for *Skamander;* I only need to send it in. Thank you for delivering *The Comet.*

That Sandauer[29] who wrote about Gombrowicz in *Pion* is a good acquaintance of mine, a boy of 23, highly intelligent. I have known that article for some time in manuscript. He lives in Kraków.

Don't be angry that it's only a short little screed today.

Stay healthy, and warm good wishes.

Your
Bruno Schulz

Drohobycz, January 23, 1938

67

Dear and beloved friend:

Your silence worries me. Have I hurt you in some way or has something saddened or disheartened you? How is the gall bladder —properly subdued and behaving itself? How is your mood?

I spent three days in Lwów—needlessly. I wasted free time I had better use for and came back sick. I have been in bed since Wednesday with laryngitis, but am free of fever now and almost without discomfort. I might do something, but I prefer to think. I rather enjoy thinking and scheming. Maybe something will come of it.

In Lwów I got together with Józefina. She still doesn't have a job and is in an awful mood, but is very smartly and fetchingly dressed. I was at the Chwisteks[30] with her, where their 19-year-old daughter, a splendid young woman of unusual gifts, fell in love with her. Have you an idea perhaps how one could find her (Józefina) a position?

Do you attach any weight to my candidacy for the *Wiadomości* award? Do you know any details? I assume that my name was put forward only by Wittlin.[31] It is possible that someone seconded it?

Brochwicz has sent me his book with the request that I review it. I replied that I had given up reviewing and that he should not take offense. My impression is that it is a graphomaniac's book, although Gombrowicz supposedly was delighted with it—whether sincerely or not, I don't know.

In *Chochoł*[32] [literally, *Mulch*], the new satirical magazine, Korabiowski (Stronc) has published a dreadful, though accurate parody of my prose. *Pion* published a review article by Sandauer: "The Literature of the Mythologists: About Gombrowicz and Schulz."[33] Those are all the reviews I am aware of, since I don't subscribe to a press-scanning service.

Have you seen anything of Witkacy? What's your life like? Do you see people? I had a letter from Wanda Kragen, reporting some hostile articles by Skiwski and Piasecki[34] about *Ferdydurke*. I just hope that the *Ferdydurke* affair will not turn into some psychic trauma to her.

Egga[35] has already done the illustrations for *The Comet*. I think it will come out shortly.

I still haven't written to Thomas Mann.[36] I have very cold feet about this.

If I don't hear signs of life from you soon I'll be very uneasy.

Fond greetings, and please write.

Bruno Schulz

Drohobycz, February 6, 1938

68

Dear Roma:

I am worried by what you tell me about your illness. I hope the X ray will show your fears were groundless. You have certainly had your fill of illnesses in your life, and it somehow doesn't fit your personality. I am up but don't go out yet, I have a bad cough; I am off work until Monday.

All the news and gossip you gather for me greatly interest me. Do I really stand some chance for the *Wiadomości* award? I'm not allowing this conjecture to rise to the foreground of consciousness for fear of later disappointment. For that matter, it seems to me that a certain role is played in the awarding by considerations and influences that are not at my disposal here in my remote corner of the country. My judgment is that Gombrowicz will get it.[37] Thank you for your kind willingness to inform me of the result, but there is no need since the radio will broadcast it promptly.

I have stopped writing reviews for *Wiadomości.* It is no fun; on the contrary, it always cost me great inner struggles.[38] I am greatly surprised to see that Gombrowski wrote such a favorable review of Brochwicz. I couldn't read that book, but please don't tell anybody because I wrote to him that I liked it, of course. If you can, please send me the articles by Skiwski and Piasecki by periodical post.

Thank you for your suggestion in the matter of Józefina; I may take advantage of it. But Witkacy is singularly ill suited for such missions. He is incapable of doing anything of practical use for anyone. I don't hold that against him. I am grateful to him for my acquaintance with Szturm.

Egga has already finished the illustration for *The Comet I,* and it is to come out shortly.

Some two weeks ago I asked Kister of *Rój* to send me a copy of *Cinnamon Shops,* which I need for the translator in Vienna. Both

Bruno Schulz

— 1 —

Druga jesień.

Wśród wielu prac naukowych podejmowanych przez mego ojca w rzadkich chwilach spokoju i wytchnienia wewnętrznego, pomiędzy ciosami klęsk i katastrof, w jakie obfitowało to życie burzliwe – najbliższe jego sercu były studja nad meteorologją porównawczą, a zwłaszcza nad specyficznym klimatem naszej prowincji pełnym jedynych w swoim rodzaju osobliwości. On to właśnie, mój ojciec, położył podstawy pod umiejętną analizę formacyj klimatycznych, jego „Zarys ogólnej systematyki jesieni" wyjaśnił raz na zawsze istotę tej pory roku, która w naszym klimacie prowincjonalnym przybiera tę przewlekłą, rozgałęzioną, pasożytniczo rozrosłą formę, która pod nazwą „chińskiego lata" przeciąga się daleko w głąb naszych zim kolorowych. Cóż powiedzieć? On pierwszy wyjaśnił wtórny, pochodny charakter tej późnej formacji, nie będącej niczem innem, jak pewnego rodzaju zatruciem klimatu miazmatami przejrzałej i wyradzającej się sztuki barokowej, stłoczonej w naszych muzeach. Ta rozkładająca się w nudzie i zapomnieniu sztuka muzealna przecukrza się, zamknięta bez odpływu, jak stare konfitury, przesładza nasz klimat i jest przyczyną tej pięknej, malarycznej febry, tych kolorowych deliriów, któremi agonizuje ta przewlekła jesień. Piękno jest bowiem chorobą, uczył mój ojciec, jest pewnego rodzaju dreszczem tajemniczej infekcji, ciemną zapowiedzią rozkładu, wstającą z głębi doskonałości i witaną przez doskonałość westchnieniem najgłębszego szczęścia.

First page of "Second Fall," from *Sanatorium Under the Sign of the Hourglass*, in Schulz's hand. The only extant manuscript of a work of his fiction.

this request and, probably, the addresses I sent them of critics who asked for *Sanatorium,* have been ignored. Their treatment of me is scandalously slighting. I wouldn't like to expose you to an unpleasant answer, but perhaps you could inquire by phone?

Why haven't you written for so long? Do you see anyone we know? Szturm, Lieberwerth?

Please let me know the diagnosis based on the X-ray pictures. Thanks for your news, and fond regards,

Bruno

I have read part I of Montherlant's novel *The Young Girls.*[39] Brilliant. You must read it!

[about the middle of February 1938]

69

Dear Roma:

I am sad and worried to hear that you are ill and in the hospital. Why was it necessary to hospitalize you? Is it for observation, or for treatments that can't be given at home? I know that gall bladder attacks (colics) are terribly painful and impossible to bear without narcotics. Are you well looked after? Are they nice to you? Do you get vistors? Have you things to think about? What is that hospital world like? Are you in a double room or a private one? Write to me often and report about everything, especially all that concerns your health. How can you write that you bore me with your letters?!

How sweet of you to remember my affairs even while you are

India-ink drawing from the first edition of *Sanatorium.*

India-ink illustration of "The Old Pensioner."

in the hospital, to escape from medical care to run an errand I hadn't even asked you to do, knowing how busy you are. I am truly grateful.

I'd very much like to capture that prize [the *Wiadomości* award], chiefly because it is the stepping-stone by which to break through the boundaries of the Polish language. And then, the money means something, too! In spite of everything, your earlier letter kindled some hope in me, though I knew that considerations of literary politics, favors allotted to secure the support of those honored, are decisive in this matter.

I have received Piasecki's article, many thanks. It is vulgar and stupid. A long review appeared in Pomirowski's[40] *Tygodnik Ilustrowany,* but it was unenthusiastic. In *Pion,* issue 5 I think, there was a handsome article about myself (mainly) and Gombrowicz by A. Sandauer, a young critic who has earned his literary spurs by his very intelligent discussion of my work (and Gombrowicz's). I have sent a second article[41] by this critic about *Sanatorium* to *Skamander* along with mine about *Ferdydurke.*

I am in constant contact with Gombrowicz. He is about to leave for Italy, as you know, but is perhaps waiting for the outcome of the literary award. From Eggi Haardt and her friend I keep hearing enthusiastic echoes of my book, which they are reading together. They see a kinship between this book and T. Mann's *Tales of Jacob,*[42] a juxtaposition I find very flattering. My friend's mother wants to take *Heimkehr* to T. Mann when she goes to Zurich.[43] Apart from this, I wonder about the silence reigning on the subject

Draft in pencil of an illustration for *Sanatorium*.

of *Sanatorium.* What could it spring from? One journal in Lwów carried a very laudatory review by I. Berman, who was severely beaten up by NDK[44] students a few days later. I. Berman is the publisher of the satirical journal *Chochoł,* which is modeled on *Szpilki,*[45] brought out by the same team.

I'd feel tolerably good now if I weren't surrounded by people who depress me by the remoteness of our respective intellectual interests. Drawing interests me at this point. I'd like to have someone from my own sphere here. I've repeatedly invited a painter from Lwów, a very bright fellow, but he doesn't answer.

I don't know if these matters interest you now that you belong to that second world of which you write. In response to my book Nałkowska has sent me four or five of hers. One is inscribed: "To B. S.—with wide-ranging approval of his book."

I haven't answered Wanda Kragen yet.

I wish you a speedy return to health with all my heart and meanwhile lots of peace and quiet and pleasant musings. Waiting for news, I am, with fond greetings,

Bruno Schulz

February 21, 1938

70

Dear Roma:

Why no answer, no sign of life from you? I'm worried. Are you still ill, still in the hospital? Does my handwriting give you trouble? Or is it just low spirits? After several pretty fair months I too have had a downturn. I feel so knocked out of kilter, so unhinged, that I can't make myself write even the most urgent letter. I regret my lost, my foolishly wasted youth; some fever and restlessness has taken hold of me, and "that panic before the gate closes."[46] But I don't want to write about myself as long as I haven't had any word from you. Aren't you getting better yet? How much longer are you going to be under treatment? Write me a few words at least, or dictate them to Stefan. Maybe you had better give me the hospital address?

For the moment my trip to Paris is not coming off. Kister[47] isn't sending me any money. I finally wrote to him today. Out of the press responses I received a very enthusiastic review by Berman in the *Opinia*[48] of Lwów and a positive one in Promiński's *Sygnały*[49]. I don't read the Warsaw papers. Otherwise complete monotony. I have had a visit from one of the outstanding Jewish painters, N. Spiegel,[50] who was delighted with my drawings and advised a trip to Paris to arrange an exhibition.

I wait impatiently for news from you and send fond greetings.

Bruno Schulz

March 3, 1938
Drohobycz, 10 Floriańska

Pencil draft of an illustration for "Spring."

71

Dear Roma:

I had a premonition that your silence had to have a serious cause, and so it turned out, poor brave Roma. Was this a major operation? Where was it located? Was it very painful? Was there anyone with you, your family, friends? What is the connection between that "cyst" and a liver disease? Was it causing any ill effects; did it have to be removed? Why is your morale rotten? Wouldn't you like to have someone from the family around to look after you for the duration of your stay? Why do your people leave you alone in such a situation? Don't sink into despair. All will be well. Spring is coming. After all you have been through, you need to go away somewhere and recuperate. A few miles from Drohobycz there is a very beautiful sanatorium for convalescents where some visionary has set up a retreat for "ailing souls." That was his goal. Its realization changed the concept somewhat, but it is a beautiful mountain slope, utterly secluded, covered with a park full of umpty-thousand roses and acres and acres of carnations. The inn is furnished with a mixture of Hutsulian mountaineer touches and Empire or Biedermeier: a very handsome lobby and dining hall, something between a forester's lodge and an old Polish manor. Add to this that it isn't expensive, the innkeeper is nice, and in the spring season there are only a few guests. I would be able to come and see you, for it isn't far, and I know the proprietor: Reitman,[51] at Korostow [now Korostov, U.S.S.R.] near Skole. Somehow you must get the money to go there. The place has its own power station, its own post office; in a word, it is an isolated mountain keep. Think of a way to make it possible for you to go there for four weeks in April. Let your family see to it.

I'd be so glad if you'd come; with your responsiveness to beauty, your imagination, and your ability to master unusual situations, it would be as if you were in your own true country there.

About myself I really have nothing to write. I would like a bit of serenity, a change of environment, company—yours, for instance. I thirst for silence, nature, receptive minds one wouldn't have to shut oneself off from or translate into a foreign tongue for. Maybe I could plan on taking off for Korostow myself for two weeks in April. I am setting aside a separate room in our house, but

Two versions of an illustration for the story "The Book." India-ink drawing at top from the collection of the Museum of Literature, Warsaw.

the expenses terrify me: a couch-bed, etc. I have a large light room and some of the furniture, but no couch, curtains, or any kind of rug.

Is it all right if I ask you to write oftener? I'll be worried about you now if you don't write. Please write me in detail about your medical condition. Do you have any painful symptoms? Are you by yourself?

It's clear from the report that Wittlin did not plead very hard for my book; Kuncewicz and Dąbrowska[52] did more.

Warm regards and greetings, please stay in touch.

Yours
Bruno Schulz

Drohobycz, March 10, 1938

Pencil sketch illustrating "Eddie." Collection of the Museum of Literature, Warsaw.

The "shattering historical events" referred to in the following letter (March 20) were the invasion of Austria five days earlier and the immediate brutalization of Austrian Jews by indigenous Nazi mobs.[53] At the same time "ideological currents" (Letter 73) in Poland came in the form of increasingly brazen anti-Semitic propaganda, which the government did little to counter, from pro-Fascists of the extreme right who advocated the barring of Jewish Poles from university study and ultimately from public life and citizenship.

72

Dear Roma:

Don't be angry that I didn't reply at once. Spatial remoteness causes the written word to seem too weak, ineffective, powerless to hit its target. And the target itself, the person who gets our words at the end of that road through space, seems only half-real, of uncertain existence, like a character in a novel. This discourages writing, robs it of topical timeliness, makes it seem—in the face of the onrush of nearby reality—a questionable activity, a sleight of hand, a gesture of dubious impact. One probably shouldn't say such things, but fight instead that weakness of imagination which refuses to believe in the reality of remote objects. I am greatly touched to think that weakened and exhausted as you are, you make yourself think of me, even write letters and take an interest in my business. It really is wonderful that such women exist, that such disinterested feelings exists, and such close connection. Can you read, at least? Do you have any side effects to contend with? I hope those stones will dissolve and vanish from your body. A good place for this is Truskawiec (fifteen minutes from Drohobycz), but you are still too weak for that. I hope you can come to Truskawiec in May, when it is beautiful there. You will get a place tucked under the white blossom of sour-cherry trees, which grow all over Truskawiec. It's my favorite place; one day I am going to write a novel about it. In May it is wonderfully wistful and solemn there. The nightingales sing, and all the trees are white. Korostow is not indicated for you in this situation. I would think we could come to terms with Reitman at a rate of 5–6 zloty a day for very good room and board.

Such shattering historical events have taken place in the meantime. The course ahead is worse and worse. It depresses me intensely. At certain moments I have come close to despair, as before an imminent catastrophe. It is such a beautiful spring—one should live and soak up the light. And here I spend days and nights without woman or Muse and go to seed, fruitless. One time here I jumped up from sleep in sudden deep despair over life winging away without my catching hold of any of it. If such a despair were to last for long, one might go insane. And what if some day that despair were to come and settle down for good, when it will already have been too late to live? Get well soon and live, for the worst unhappiness consists of not living out one's life. Are you at Śródborowa[54] already? Is it beautiful there? Are you a little stronger and healthier by now? I take it yours was an internal operation, leaving no external scar? I have just read Huxley's magnificent book, *Eyeless in Gaza*.[55] I read it with genuine admiration for the bestial cleverness of that man. I can't read anything else. Nothing interests me. I believe it is because I miss a woman.

Please write me all about yourself. Whom have you met at Śródborowa? Does anyone come to see you? Does Wanda Kragen visit you? Do you think I ought to thank Wittlin, Kuncewicz, and Dąbrowska for supporting me with the jury?

Gombrowicz is not in Warsaw. He doesn't write me. I'm getting no letters at all these days.

Fond greetings and warm wishes for good health and a good rest,

Bruno Schulz

Drohobycz, March 20, 1938

73

Dear Roma:

It's been so long since I last heard from you. Did you get my letter? Has something occurred that disinclines you to write or are you possibly still too weak? Are you at Śródborowa? Does Stefan come to see you? It is hard to write when I don't know anything about your state of health, mind, or mood. I don't know what might interest you now, what would get to you. Don't the doctors recommend a cure at Truskawiec? How fine it would be if you could come to Truskawiec (fifteen minutes from Drohobycz).

I am almost completely alone now. From Józefina I've heard nothing for several months. Gombrowicz came to Warsaw recently and wrote me after a long interval. I am not in touch with anyone else. Egga Haardt has fallen silent, too.

I am busier in school now than before. I try not to give my superiors any pretext for getting rid of me, but it may be useless, since pretexts will no longer be needed if the ideological currents now agitating this country lead to legislation. Very much at the wrong time, I am arranging my apartment. I have a very handsome room measuring 6 x 6 meters and another smaller one. I have ordered a couch. I am doing this with neither confidence nor zest. I should have made myself independent of the school years ago and taken up journalism. That was possible then, and I would have grown accustomed to work-to-order and might even have found in this discipline a certain incentive to write and some more accessible, everyday form of writing.

What do you think? Should I thank Kuncewicz and Wittlin for their willingness to promote my cause on the prize committee?

Write me at least a few words about yourself, what condition you're in, what you're doing. Do you feel a little better, may I write to you, are you interested right now? Do you have any social life over there in Śródborowa? Do friends from Warsaw come to see you? I am worried by the lack of news from you. I reason that, if you leave my letters unanswered, you must feel bad. Can't you set my mind at rest with a few words?

Warm greetings and every good wish for health and well-being!

Bruno Schulz

Drohobycz, March 31, 1938

74

Dear Roma:

I apologize for giving you cause for uneasiness because of my silence. I did receive one letter from you and, as is apt to happen when one puts off the reply, the freshness of the contact was lost, and I didn't answer. The second letter you write about never reached me. I am very happy about the possibility of seeing you. Come to Truskawiec. It would be most convenient for me because it is very near, and lovely. I suspect, however, that the doctors will direct you to Morsztyn [now Morshin, U.S.S.R.], which is farther away. Truskawiec, though, is milder in its effect, and larger, and prettier. From your intimate experiences, "of the heart and others," I conclude that your recovery is progressing, and that makes me very happy. The gap in my writing was caused—besides that

Schulz with Dr. Władysław Balicki at Truskawiec, 1939.

school inspector's visit—by my trip to Lwów, where I sojourned a week in the company of Debora Vogel, Promiński, and the painter Janisch. Nothing noteworthy happened, however. Gombrowicz has written an article about me, which he sent to *Kurier Poranny.*[56] He reports, furthermore, that Otwinowski[57] is going to write about me in *Czas [Time]*—and Laszowski, hitherto an adversary, was to write a laudatory review for *Prosto z Mostu [Off the Bat]*.[58] Breza is also working on something about me. Gombrowicz sends me many compliments on my book. I'm joyously anticipating the meeting with you. I like such meetings in spring. I have rearranged my room, involving myself in a great deal of expense—needlessly, since at bottom I don't care much for luxury and comfort. I am going to have a number of guests besides yourself now: the painter Janisch, Sandauer, a Madame Herman—but I look forward most to you.

Don't be angry if I don't write much, I have to work up arrears of correspondence; drop me a note soon with your news. Fond greetings—

Bruno Schulz

April 17, 1938

75

Dear Roma:

I was annoyed at you for not reacting to my alarm signal at all for such a long time, I thought something bad must have happened. But that's all bygones now since you haven't forgotten me. For the last few days I have been feeling better. I definitely want to go to Paris for two or three weeks at the end of June. *Czas* will supply a press card for me as their correspondent. What I don't know is how to obtain a passport at reduced fee. I have an idea that you have some connections in the Foreign Office. Could you possibly find out what I would have to do to secure, the fast way, a reduced-fee passport for foreign travel? I wonder if some sort of permit is needed for the drawings I'm going to have with me. I can get a 66 percent reduction on Polish railway travel through the Professional Society of Letters. One can also apply at the French Embassy for a discount fare on the French railways, but I don't know how that's done. It looks as if I'll have to come to Warsaw on June 25 (after the end of the school year). I count very much on your talent and goodwill to help, on your always faithful and kindly readiness. I want to join the PEN Club and have already asked Gombrowicz about this.

Could you try to line up some recommendations for me to eminent people in Paris, painters, writers? Forgive me for writing about nothing but technicalities, but I'm in something like a fever, assailed by the fear that I might fall behind the various things to do and not be ready by the end of June. I would have answered right away but you didn't give me your new address. Will you have a little time to spare for me? I have decided in my mind, of course, that this trip will not yield me anything tangible, but I want to try. I will write you about my other plans, or maybe I should wait till I can tell you personally; I'm superstitious about committing them to paper before they are realized. I plan on taking about 100 drawings to Paris. I may have an exhibition. A woman wants to introduce me to Jules Romains.[59]

What's new at your end, my dear? To what experiences do you allude when you say they are more terrifying than the trials of everyday life? Are you struggling with bouts of depression? Why aren't you more specific about this? Has it to do with some love? Do let me know!

Any day now *The Comet* will be coming out. Mar. Eile[60] is to set up a display case for that week under the auspices of *Cinnamon Shops.* No reviews of my work are reaching me. I have asked Gombrowicz to send me his.

Forgive my writing telegraph-style. There will be more and better shortly. Warm good wishes,

Bruno Schulz

Drohobycz, May 19, 1938

76

Dear Roma:

Thank you so much for all the efforts you're making on my behalf. Gombrowicz also advised me to get a passport right away. I wouldn't like to travel through Germany, that would depress me. In spite of the higher cost I'd rather go via Italy and possibly spend two days in Venice. I can't come to Warsaw for Whitsun. I'd have only two days, and those are holidays. I would be very grateful to Stas W. [Witkiewicz] for addresses and recommendations. What's he up to, and how does he feel? Has he regained some ground?

I take it you have read Breiter's review[61] of me. It has a passage at the end about Gombrowicz that forced me to write a letter to Grydzewski in which I quash as tactfully as possible the assertion that Gombrowicz and I may be linked together. Gombrowicz published his first book, the fruit of a fully formed and mature talent, in May 1933. *Cinnamon Shops* appeared in 1934. How can there be any talk of my "school"? I felt sorry about this on account of Breiter, but considered it a duty of loyalty to Gombrowicz. Did I do the wrong thing? My letter[62] will probably be published by Grydzewski in *Wiadomości,* but don't tell anyone about it.

In connection with that review, Grydzewski has devoted a showcase to me at the journal's office that Eile, the author of *Gryps,*[63] a very nice boy, has decorated with my drawings. How does it look? Nice of Grydzewski.

I have written to Natanson,[64] who is to send me an ID as a correspondent of *Czas.* That, too, serves to smooth one's path somewhat. I'd like to ask one more thing of you: Could you inquire at the Professional Society of Letters what one has to do to get the 66 percent reduction on the Polish Railways (though in case I choose the Italian route the Polish section is short: Lawoczne–

Budapest)? In which case it isn't worth asking about.

I've had a letter from Maria Chasin, the pianist, from which it appears that she too will be in Paris in June; this could very important to me since she knows many French writers and intellectuals, among them very eminent people.

How are you feeling now? Is your health back to normal? You're not working too hard, I hope? Do you have a comfortable apartment? My bachelor flat doesn't look bad, but I don't have a couch yet; I am saving that expenditure for afterward, or I might run out of money for Paris.

Write often, if your time allows. Are you preoccupied with someone? Why don't you write to me about it? What is your relationship with Stas W.?

With very warm regards,

Bruno Schulz

Drohobycz, May 28, 1938

77

Dear Roma:

I am very depressed again. My trip to Paris is going up in smoke over the difficulties that are piling up. Let me explain them; maybe you can find a way out.

1. A tourist passport is issued on the basis of foreign exchange purchased. This year the Foreign Exchange Bureau has placed the allocation of foreign exchange to individuals under its own direct authority, not allotting any to banks. I sent an application, No. 1175, dated June 4, for a foreign exchange allotment through the General Union Bank in Drohobycz. The Foreign Exchange Bureau is at 11 Zgoda Street. The section chief is one Mikucki. Perhaps you have someone who could push this matter.

2. Alternatively, one may obtain a tourist passport via purchase of a steamer ticket from Gdynia to Cherbourg. No foreign exchange is needed for this, but one can take no more than 200 zloty along.

3. One may, as a literary man, obtain a passport at a reduced fee through the Ministry of the Interior; it is valid for two months, but one has to have certain vouchers from the Society of Letters or the express support of the Society.

4. One may join a charter tour, where the arranging agency takes care of passport and foreign exchange. There are charters that consist only of a round trip.

Please, please, do anything you can in this matter, time is running short, and the second half of July is already dead season in Paris. Advise me what to do. Perhaps you can find out at Orbis[65] or Cook's what excursions to France may be available and have them send me prospectuses. The simplest solution for me would be a charter that covers only the passage; to be tied up with some group makes no sense for me.

Perhaps you know somebody who could put in a word with the Foreign Exchange Bureau, where I am sure I am unknown. Maybe the Society of Letters could do it.

Gombrowicz is to arrange the PEN Club membership for me and a press card from one of the journals. Or could you perhaps take steps to get such a card?

Have you read Breiter's piece and seen the showcase at *Wiadomości* devoted to me? Why don't you write at all? Are you preoccupied with something? What is Witkacy doing? How is he?

May I ask you for an early reply about what you advise me to do, what is the most sensible thing to do? Don't be angry at me for loading you up like this.

Warm regards and greetings,

Bruno

June 8, 1938

78

Dear Roma:

Thank you so much for the information and your efforts. I have written to the Society of Letters, asking for their support with the Foreign Exchange Bureau, and they informed me how to secure a passport for abroad. I have the feeling I am not properly prepared for the trip. I have no plan and no proper recommendations, but I think I'll get hold of them over there. I have heard that L. [Lieberwerth][66] is in Warsaw. That's an awkward thing to happen, I had counted on him.

Kazimiera Rychter[67] was here and brought me a photograph from the display case at *Wiadomości;* she is an aunt of Marian Eile, who arranged the display. M. Eile is taking steps with [illegible] to have them arrange an exhibition of my drawings and graphics, with the idea of my making some sales against my journey. Menasze Seidenbeutel [a painter] is here; he says that such an exhibition could prove a financial success. Both the Seidenbeutels[68] are settling at [illegible] for a few months.

Prosto z Mostu carried an unfavorable review of my book.

What news at your end? Why such short notes? Where are you off to for the summer? Are we going to meet?

Once more, many thanks and warm regards—

Bruno

Can you give me any recommendations for Paris?
[after June 12, 1938]

The review of Sanatorium *that Schulz mentions above appeared in* Prosto z Mostu, *no. 27, 1938. Under the title "Ivy on Ruins," the reviewer, Włodzimierz Pietrzak, said, among other things: "There is something childish in that old man's ruinous gaze. . . ." "That morbid solitude is not substantiated, it calls for explanation by diagnosis. . . ." "It is Schulz, no one else, who impoverishes the world . . . how poor this nabob is!"*

79

Dear Roma:

Thank you so much for thinking of me. I did receive *Łąka* by Leśmian,[69] but so miserably packaged the cover was broken in several places. No point in sending in a claim, though. Thomas Mann, they added, is unavailable.

My efforts to obtain foreign exchange look as if they will be crowned with success, just when in fact it doesn't suit me. The dead season is on in Paris, everybody is leaving town. If I go, it will be for the sake of consistency, I suppose, and in order not to waste all this effort.

I have started to write. The work is very tough and sluggish. If I had four months of free time, I would finish the book.[70] That is another reason I don't feel like taking the trip.

Have you seen anything of Stronc [Wilhelm Korabiowski]? I am really sorry we couldn't get together anymore. I wrote to him right after his arrival, but he didn't answer. I would like his essay about me to be placed in *Tygodnik Ilustr.*, which is his vehicle. Have you seen any more of those people? Eile? What are you doing? When do you leave town?

Szturm wrote to me that Witkacy departed quite broken up. You should have propped up his morale a little, since you have some influence over him. Aren't you going to Zakopane?

Very warm greetings to you and the best possible wishes;

Your Bruno

Drohobycz, July 12, 1938

80

Dear Roma:

I feel guilty not having written for such a long time. I count on your much-tried indulgence and kindness. Several times I meant to write but didn't know where you were and suspected that the card (I wrote only cards from over there) might not reach you. Nor do I know now if you are back in Warsaw or if perhaps Stefanek is there, taking in your mail.

I hung on in Paris over three weeks, though even after the first week I realized that I wouldn't put my program into effect. It was naive of me to rush out the way I did with the intent of conquering Paris, which is the most exclusive, self-sufficient, standoffish city in the world. With my sort of language preparation, I could not dream of initiating any contact with Frenchmen. The Embassy took no interest in me at all; I cannot count on it for anything even for the future. Apart from this, Paris was empty—all the better art salons were closed. I did actually form an acquaintance with a certain merchant on rue Faub. St. Honoré, who wanted to sponsor an exhibition for me; but in the end I withdrew from it myself. For all that, I am glad to have been to Paris, to have seen so many amazing things, to have looked for once at close range and not via reproductions at the art of the great epochs; and, finally, to have rid myself of certain delusions concerning an international career.

I have seen beautiful, shocking, terrible sights. The lovely women of Paris impressed me greatly, both ladies of society and of the night; the ease of manners, the pace of life.[71] I don't like to write more just now when I don't know where you are and how you are. Did you go to Krynica? How are you feeling? How is Stefan? I look forward to word from you and meanwhile greet you affectionately.

Bruno

August 29, 1938

81

Dear Roma:

I'm sure you're angry with me for my silence and for not visiting you when I was in Warsaw recently. Please don't feel offended, I was there very briefly (a day and a half) and didn't see anybody else either. I had been asked up by *Wiadomości* to write up a certain story.[72] And why didn't I write afterward? I really don't know. I have cut down my correspondence quite a bit. I don't get letters from anyone except Gombrowicz; I have been utterly abandoned. What are you doing? How is your health? How is Stefan? It would make me very happy if you wrote me a letter. I had a very unpleasant experience lately with Eggi Haardt, who turned out to be a common swindler, blackmailer, and cheat. You doubtless had your attention called to my article about her in *Tygodnik Ilustrowany,* no. 40. Half of that article is a fabrication by her. At the time I had given her the manuscript to look over, with permission to omit certain passages as too private. That creature then decided to exploit my name by inserting paragraphs of her own manufacture that were extremely tasteless and scandalous in form. I am wrestling with the decision to publish a correction, since I can't achieve the purpose without destroying her, and I am afraid of her, because she is a person who is capable of anything. Let me know what people are saying about this, and whether they know that a falsification is involved.[73]

I am sending this letter by Zygfryd Bienstock,[74] a talented young musician, who took first prize recently in a music contest for his jazz compositions.

Bienstock will be in Warsaw for the first time and is looking for contacts. I would be glad if you took him up and were able to show him around a bit in Warsaw society. B. is a very nice and likable young man of a fine freshness of spirit and a certain ingenuous nature that promises a very good development to come.

Sending fond greetings and looking forward to news from you,

Bruno

Drohobycz, October 13, 1938

82

Dear Roma:

I have written two letters to you in the meantime that I sent by young men about to leave for Warsaw. Probably they have fallen down on their assignments. The reduction in my correspondence is general, and I am in touch with nobody but Gombrowicz. I lead a life much below my level. Beyond the books, which trickle in slowly (I have to read what I can get, not what I have a mind to read), I have nothing to sustain my inner life; and everything around me exudes an indescribable prosiness, which presses down on me too with its brutal weight. Nothing on the order of a stroll with a dear person, not one hour of quiet and serene contemplation—all is tainted by mundane worry and staleness. I take it that productive creators fence themselves off from their environment by a certain regimen of living, a certain organization of their daily routine that does not allow the workaday banality, humdrum job, and the rest of it to get to them. I badly feel the lack of such a regimen, my incapacity to subject myself to such a discipline. One must, for instance, fence off one's inner life, not permit the vermin of ordinary cares to infest it. Some blindness used to protect me from this truth; I wore blinkers like a horse in harness. Now reality has won and penetrated my interior.

I will clearly have to think in earnest about safeguarding my private inner life and erecting fortifications in the shape of regular mental work.

I am not going anywhere for the four-day holiday. It appears I am going to spend them, very drearily, at home.

What about you? How is your health? What do you do for a good time? Do you maintain many contacts with literati? Do you know that Witkacy has made up with his girlfriend?[75]

Have you heard anything about the scandal Egga Haardt hung on my neck by placing an article almost half fabricated by herself under my name? When we have a chance I'll tell you what prompted me to overlook this fraud and not have it spread by tattling.

Please write me about yourself and all those around you. With very warm greetings,

Bruno

October 29, 1938

83

Dear Roma:

I have long felt pangs of conscience over not answering your letter. This had nothing to do with the kinds of reasons you mentioned. Why should your reaction to circumstances wound me? Don't I feel the same, and is anybody above this sort of thing? You mustn't make some kind of little ivory tower out of me or ascribe to me the need for a cult of my person or my "artistry"—these are alien to me. You regard artists as peculiar creatures who take offense over who knows what and with whom one can't be careful enough how one behaves. It's not like that at all. In everyday life I am a perfectly normal person.

For your gracious and generous offer of hospitality I thank you very warmly. I won't take advantage of it right now because I have come to the conviction that travel yields me nothing but fatigue. I have not been well lately—heart trouble. I believe it's over now, but it left an awful nervousness and depression behind—especially in the morning. What can one do?

Lieberwerth leaves for Paris in a few days for an extended stay. Do you see him sometimes?

How is life treating you? How is your love life? Doesn't it involve you in excessive complications? Whom do you get to see often?

Fond greetings and all good wishes for a Happy New Year!!

Bruno Schulz

Drohobycz, December 26, 1938

84

Dear Roma:

Your letter worried and disheartened me. I could not answer at once since I am in a deep depression myself, this time not even just a crisis of morale, but something like a collapse of my whole personality. I have been ill for six weeks, that is, felt ill, while the doctors can't find any grounds for such a poor subjective state. I am convinced, though, that some mischief is going on in my body that the doctors are not yet able to detect. I am afraid of some serious illness. In spite of this continual state of anxiety and low spirits I find myself in, your letter had a very disheartening impact on me.

You must have written it, I feel, in a moment of deep discouragement. At those times all one's life seems a failure, a string of mistakes and errors. My notion is that everyone has had his very own life, just the one that should have been his and to which he alone had a right. We could have lived no differently than we did. It's only that the balance of a whole life, when we add it up at a given juncture, is always zero. However this may be, the act of adding up such a balance is a sign of profound depression.

As for your job, the situation is sad, all right. This might just prove a turning point in your life, though; could you perhaps be reconciled with your husband and return to him? Is that impossible? You could have your Stefan always with you and would be happy.

I have no advice for you, of course, in the matter of a position. You yourself know better where to turn and what to try. Please God your morale should rise and your vital force restore your equilibrium.

You have a fairly well connected family, after all; they ought to do something for you. I hope shortly to get a letter from you with better news.

Despite my illness, depression, and work at school, which torments and exhausts me, I am fairly active intellectually and feel greatly stimulated. I am not writing now, I am drawing. Two weeks ago I wrote to Mortkowicz[76] to ask if some monograph about the German painter Karl Hofer[77] had appeared, in which case I wanted to order a copy. I got no answer. Perhaps you would be good enough to ask at your convenience if they could supply this book, and at what price. I am mainly interested in the illustrative material (how many illustrations?). I really need that.

I won't go on, writing is an effort. Let me hear from you soon. Fond greetings and all the best,

Bruno

Drohobycz, January 21, 1939

I understand that *Pióro* [*Quill*] has published an article by Fryde in which he attacks me.[78] Is it very vicious? If so, I don't want to read it. Basically I feel this hardly has the power to affect me now.

85

Dear Roma:

It really seemed to me you had forgotten about me. Somehow it came about that the teeming swarm of my friends has thinned out considerably, contacts have grown feebler, and it looks as if I am once again headed for those territories and zones where loneliness reigns. As before. Sometimes this prospect fills me with sorrow and the terror of emptiness; then again it lures me with an intimate, all too familiar temptation.

What made you write again after such a long time? I am reluctant somehow to come to Warsaw, afraid of contacts and people. If I had my way I would take myself, with some one person, into the heart of stillness and, like Proust, take up the definitive formulation of my universe. For a time I found support in the thought that year afer next I would retire (at 40 percent of salary). Now I have abandoned that idea for the sake of my family, whom I wouldn't be able to support.

I have trouble deciding on a place to spend the vacation. I possess very limited means—no money so far, I'll borrow some. I would like quiet and isolation, though not totally: one or two people who don't get in the way.

What do you plan to do for the holidays?

Gombrowicz has asked me to apologize to you on his behalf for not saying hello to you. It happened because of his terrible visual memory, which often betrays him.

Do you know a good neurologist in Warsaw who might agree to treat me free of charge? I am definitely ill—completely distraught, onset of melancholia, despondency, sadness, a sense of inevitable disaster, irreparable loss . . . I ought to seek help. Yet I don't believe in doctors.

About my plans and projects I won't write, can't write. It makes me too angry, and I can't discuss it calmly.

Don't neglect me like this anymore. Let me hear from you sometime!

Warm greetings—

Bruno Schulz

[June 1939]

TO MARIAN JACHIMOWICZ

Marian Jachimowicz (1906–), poet, painter, and translator of Hungarian verse. Jachimowicz became acquainted with Schulz the year before the German invasion, and their friendly contact lasted almost to the end of Schulz's life.

86

Dear and Esteemed Sir:

I am writing upon the suggestion of a Miss Laura,[1] who is endeavoring to enlist the interest of certain influential people on your behalf and is generally full of benevolence and appreciation toward you. For these plans of hers and other still more extensive ones, you would have to submit without delay a brief curriculum vitae showing your qualifications as a tutor[2] (naming the institution in Budapest where you worked) and generally. In this context you should also mention your literary aspirations and their directions. For the time being this represents no more than a certain opportunity, but I hope that if not by this avenue and through these persons, then through others something may be done. It would be good, too, if you could be in Drohobycz next week. We speak of you often and plan on coming over. Whenever it works out for you to come here, I will be very glad to have you visit and I look forward to it. Please don't forget my request for your manuscripts. Warm greetings to you and best regards from Laura.

Yours sincerely
Bruno Schulz

[November 27, 1938]

87

My dear Marian:

Please forgive my long silence. I was ill for four weeks, straight through the Christmas holidays. We haven't forgotten about you, however. Laura had the idea of interesting some people from Polmin [an oil refinery near Drohobycz][3] in you; through them she got through to Dr. Jakobowska, the secretary of the ranking director, Biluchowski. I duly took my turn as well, impressing upon Dr. Jakobowska your qualities and gifts, as well as the potential that in favorable conditions might be realized in you; and I received a very favorable answer. Dr. Jakobowska promised to use her great influence with Polmin to do something for you that would set you up in new living conditions. The affair is getting delayed somewhat by

Borysław, August 1938. From left: Schulz, Laura Wurzberg, Marian Jachimowicz, Anna Płockier. Collection of Marian Jachimowicz.

the fact that Dr. Jakobowska left town for treatment after her illness, but she will take up your case immediately upon her return, and I hope something decisive will be done to extricate you from your situation and open up an opportunity for development. Laura and I speak of you often and work on plans to visit you. We wonder how you are and whether you and the family are in good health. Laura too is in very bad condition, vegetating miserably. We will have to do something for her, too. Be in good spirits. This matter had to undergo some delay because Dr. Jakobowska was seriously ill and could deal with nothing. Accept my warm regards and let me hear a few words from you.

Bruno Schulz

[undated]

88

Dear Marian:

Many thanks for your letter, which I truly haven't deserved. Please don't be angry that I didn't answer at once. I thought I might have something tangible to report about your situation, but the matter rather drags along. Dr. Jakobowska has already returned from her vacation, and your concern is being examined by sympathetic parties. Great obstacles exist, though, which is why I have no favorable news to convey yet. A certain idea was advanced that I hardly dare report to you because it seems inappropriate for you. There are 600 unprocessed job applications in the personnel office at Polmin, so that one more stands little chance without very influential backing. Be that as it may, the people taking an interest in you proposed your being taken on as a seasonal employee at a modest wage, with the idea that after a certain time, thanks to the benevolent interests watching over you, you would be transferred to the regular force and a place would be located consonant with your aspirations. The proponents of this scheme themselves feel that it is not really fit for you and brought it forward with great hesitancy; but I decided to seek your opinion of it. Independently of this, we will be looking for other solutions.

We much regretted that you were not with us last week because Zegadłowicz was here,[4] a very nice person whom no doubt you would have enjoyed meeting. It may be that next Sunday Laura and I will visit you. It would have given me great pleasure to invite you here, but I don't know beforehand when I may be free, nor whether you will be free when I am. Please write me something about yourself and indicate when you might be free for an afternoon with us. Warm greetings to you and best regards from Laura.

Bruno Schulz

March 5, 1939

89

Dear Marian:

You cause has progressed (at Polmin) to the extent that they want to meet you there. I have been instructed to have you report to Polmin on Friday at 2 P.M. Kindly call first on Madame Pitakow, wife of Major Pitak, at the Polmin colony; she will furnish you all needed information and pass you on to some director. This person is the one who took charge of your case. Try to see that she takes a liking to you, which will give you no trouble at all if you rely on your nature and your inborn charm. This is only the beginning, and I have to ask you not to get your hopes up because nothing is certain yet.

When you get back from Polmin, please come to me; I am very eager to hear about the outcome. Laura will probably come here, too. Don't lose your temper or your peace of mind. Madame Pitakow will give you the warmest possible recommendation, so you may be sure of good treatment during that visit.

With affectionate greetings and a handshake,

Bruno Schulz

March 22, 1939

90

Dear Marian:

Wit[5] came back from you dazzled, as by a revelation, by your poetry. He was deeply aroused by the thought that great poetry could be brought to full term in such a backwater. The sincerity of his emotion is beyond doubt. I myself was deeply moved and elated, though saddened as well to have to receive the joyful message from others, like a blind man. What heartens me is the hope that my eyes will be opened yet. For I am having a receptive spell, a period of a certain objectivity and clarity. Less absorbed by myself, less buried in my own world, I begin to understand others. I have a desire to see you and submit once more to your poetry. Marek S.[6] told me that you will come up to see me. I am pained to confess that your visit would give me redoubled pleasure if you came alone; Wit's presence, I don't know why, depresses and paralyzes me. Ania [Anna Płockier] can testify how stricken I have lately been by his presence. I tell you this in confidence, of course. Perhaps you could arrange things so as to see me separately or on another day, or be at my place first and then at Wit's.

I hope that such a powerful echo from one who is a good poet and not in the habit of overrating others will strengthen your faith and self-confidence. I am glad that a poet like you is a devotee of my work. I expect a certain freshening and fortifying effect from the meeting with you. With a warm handshake,

Bruno Schulz

May 28, 1939

Witkiewicz's growing depression ended with his suicide less than four months later.

TO ANNA PŁOCKIER

Anna Płockier (1915–1941) graduated from the Warsaw Academy of Fine Arts as a painter. At the age of twenty-six she died at the hands of the Ukrainian militia in Borysław.

91

Dear Ania:

I am glad we've arrived at an understanding, as I had expected to, knowing your great forbearance. It is necessary, notwithstanding the slight disappointment this renunciation occasions me—for this is a renunciation on my part. I have no fears that we might lack the intellectual and human substratum upon which to continue our relationship. As long as I myself am mentally alert and absorbed, the opportunity to share with you the objects of my interest is always welcome. During the voids of inner stagnation I can count on impulses flowing from your person and your feeling of friendship for me. Regardless of what I once flung out in anger, you occupy an important place in my mind.

In spite of this, and in spite of my frequent need to talk with you, I cannot bring myself to take the trip. My inner equilibrium, reinstated with difficulty, is still highly precarious and always on the verge of collapse. I can't foresee two days or even one day ahead that I won't be in the most defeatist and melancholy mood, which might spoil the afternoon for you and me both. Maybe you would be good enough to take this into account and, without being angry with me, plan on all the more frequent visits to me here; they could be alternately by yourself alone and with your entourage, to which one might enlist Jachimowicz[1] from the library. Does that sound good? If you insist on my visiting you, please write.

My very best to you,

Bruno Schulz

Many thanks for the information about S. Gottlieb;[2] I will write to him.

[July 10, 1940]

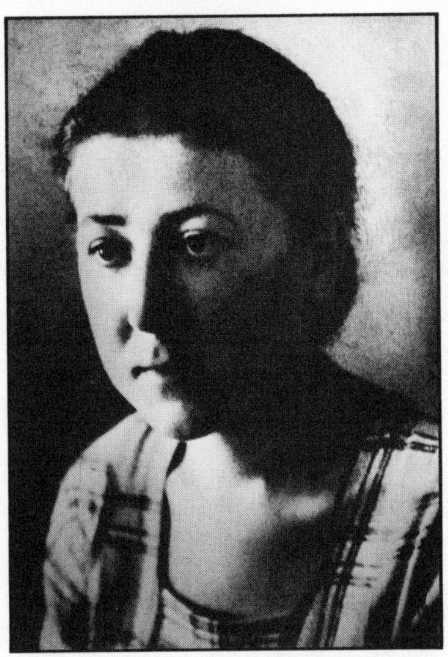

Anna Płockier, 1937. Collection of Marian Jachimowicz.

92

My dear Lady:

I am very glad you proved accessible to Rilke. In time, as you familiarize yourself with his poetry, worlds of still more concentrated beauty will open up to you. May you often experience such revelations, and may you always preserve sufficient flexibility to revise your views and corrections. As for myself, after a period of reckless enthusiasm for *Malte*[3] I am now capable of discerning his borders and the point where I consciously distance myself from his prose. In his poetry Rilke passed through an evolution of several (three or four) stages, each of which demands a reader's reorientation.

I spent four days at Lwów. I saw lots of people in the Writers' Association, but a closer contact developed only with D. Vogel and with Weber,[4] who is truly a genius. Maybe I'll be able to have him come to Drohobycz for a while. Please come, we'll talk of *Malte*. With warm regards,

Bruno Schulz

August 23 [1940]

93

Dear Ania:

Thank you for your card; I thought you had grown disillusioned with me. I am glad it isn't so. Unfortunately I don't see how I could come on Sunday because I am to undergo another operation [for kidney stones] that day. The prospect makes me glum and uneasy, though no risk is involved. I am having it done in the local hospital. Tomorrow they will decide if it will be Sunday or later. I'm free Saturday afternoon; I'd be very glad if you would come then. Greetings and best regards,

Bruno Schulz

[undated]

Schulz underwent two operations in 1940 for the removal of kidney stones. His reluctance to leave Drohobycz wasn't a simple matter of inertia: Drohobycz was in the eastern third of what was then Poland, annexed by the U.S.S.R. in 1939, not in the core region of Warsaw and Kraków, where the Jewish and Polish populations were quickly "pacified" by the Germans and where the extermination of the Jews began with the construction of the Warsaw ghetto in August 1940. Under Soviet occupation life remained relatively normal for the Jews, and medical care was still available to them until June 1941, when the Nazi assault on the U.S.S.R. began.

In the letter below Schulz mentions making drawings for the school for September 17 (1940): the first anniversary of the 1939 partition. The date was observed as a Soviet holiday marking the "liberation of the western Ukraine from Polish oppression." "Painting as a craft" (Letter 98) was Schulz's term for the kinds of pictures commissioned by local authorities in connection with such official festivities; among these were portraits of Stalin and scenes symbolizing the joys of annexation, painted in the obligatory manner of Socialist Realism.

94

Dear Ania:

Thank you so much for your sincere concern and compassion for me, which does my heart good. I am much better by now; the fever is down to 37° [normal]. I am already up and about indoors, making drawings for the school for September 17. If Marek[5] has time and is so inclined, he could offer his services to the main hospital, but I believe this is a short-term opening. Would Marek by any chance be willing to take my place in the school for about a month? I'm asking an academic question; I know he won't say yes.

I'd really like to persuade you to come, but no earlier than the seventeenth, since I'd like to be finished with drawing by then. I think I'll have a day off on that date. Once more, thanks and greetings.

Bruno

[undated]

95

Dear Ania:

I sincerely apologize for the atmosphere that developed around me and that I was unable to fence off from you. Think of it, if you like, as the Lares and Penates of the poet, the underbred wife and the rude children who spoil his real friends' pleasure in being with him. Please don't judge me by that atmosphere, and be persuaded that it was only my illness that lured this procession of specters, which will presently disperse. I can't reward the good intentions of these people with discourtesy; I count on your understanding that I pay in quite a different coin here. I have thought a great deal about your goodness and unselfishness and can only hope you won't come to regret it. In the presence of other people I couldn't tell you how much your drawings and pictures impressed me. You are truly a personality. The shortest phrase in your letter evokes in my soul an image of your entire being; the same is true of your drawings. I promise you that next time you will find me alone. I don't know if it was a good thing that you got to know me so well from behind the bedroom scenery. . . .

Warm greetings and hot apologies,

Bruno

[September 17, 1940]

Graduating Class of Drohobycz Gymnasium, 1940. Schulz is on the left.

96

Dear Ania:

I have been in Truskawiec since yesterday; I am staying at the Aida and spending long hours in discussions with Artur[6] that sometimes seem to me vibrant with meaning. The weather and landscape are on our side. On one early autumn evening we wandered through the park in the rain and behind our backs the traffic of families, the most intimate family history, unfolded in lighted windows. We miss you, who would bring some connection to our searchings, act as the germ of a synthesis. Some day, we beg you, appear at the park's edge, a lightfooted wanderer crossing from the groves of Borysław to the lanes of Truskawiec. Will you keep your promise? Warm regards,

Bruno Schulz

Which greetings, awaiting you, are wholly shared by

Artur Rzeczyca*

October 7, 1940]

* Hand-written addition by Rzeczyca.

97

Dear Ania:

Following up your words, which were memorable for me, I repeat my invitation to Truskawiec, and it will be your decision whether we are to be alone or if you care to widen the circle of participants. Nature is lovely now. There are certain exotic trees that look like birds of paradise in the splendor of their gorgeous purple trailers. I understand you have a fair number of lessons and am afraid this might stand in the way. I am disquieted also by a certain disappointment and reserve you have shown lately. But I hope this is over. I am staying in the Aida boardinghouse on the way to the railway station, room 8. But I may be in the park near the music.

Waiting for you with longing, I am with affectionate greetings

Bruno Schulz

[October 10, 1940]

98

Dear Ania:

Here I am bitterly reproaching myself that I left you without a word of explanation, giving the impression that my silence is connected with the scene you made. To tell the truth, that scene was not without the poetic charm that emanates from your whole being and all your caprices. I experienced it as a gusty blast of wind and rain—in April, when those bursts of rain slapping one's face can't help smelling like spring.

I didn't come on Saturday because I was called to an urgent family council at Stryj [now Stryy, U.S.S.R.], where I spent almost the whole day. Very nasty of me not to have explained my dereliction. Please don't ever think that I have become de-interested or have cooled toward you. I think of you always with tender emotion and gratitude. All you do is dear and poetic. And I think our friendship has a long history before it yet, carries within it the possibility of many occasions and adventures. It is up to our courage and enterprise to determine whether that possible tale knitted between us will find tangible expression.

I am busy working for money, painting as a craft. I still haven't got the money for the paintings done while you were here. I was invited by personal letter to associate myself with *Nowe Widnokręgi* [*New Horizons*],[7] a journal in Polish edited by Wasilewska.[8] But what could I write for them? I grow more and more conscious of how remote I stand from real life and how little idea I have of the mood of the times. Somehow everybody else has found an assignment; I got left out in the cold. It comes from a lack of elasticity and a refusal to compromise, which I deplore. Perhaps you would come over sometime? I am busy only on Tuesday and Thursday afternoons; otherwise I am free. Affectionate greetings,

Bruno Schulz

November 15, 1940

A warm invitation to Madame Chwistek.

99

Dear Ania:

Please forgive my long silence. You would not find the explanation for it convincing. Please take it from me that nothing has changed in my relationship to you. I have various worries, which I'll tell you about in person sometime. That's why I couldn't take off for Borysław. Something was always getting in the way. Do come, I'm looking forward to you. Tuesdays and Thursdays I'm busy in the afternoon. I have a nervous ailment, feel incapable of any work not in line with my preferences. There are times when I have a real breakdown, other times I can still pull myself out of the slough. Affectionate greetings,

Bruno Schulz

January 13, 1941

100

Dear Ania:

Your silence has been like a thorn dully festering in my consciousness. I thought you were hurt and disappointed by my obtuseness of spirit (the last time), whereas I am very animated and mentally active, only physically unwell to the point that I didn't feel up to the trip to you (the sidewalk off 30 Mościckiego Street). I have a dilation of the aorta, but lately it has improved a little.

Come on Sunday, it will give me great pleasure. Maybe we'll finally have good weather so we can take off into the landscape, as we did last year. So you are definitely moving to Lwów? It's a pity my own moving plans have gone awry. Ważyk[9] has rejected my novella. I will read it to you. I look forward to your coming. The Jewish poet Ben Horowitz[10] is with me now. Warm regards

Bruno Schulz

[May 10, 1941]

101

Dear Ania:

Last Sunday Sandauer came to see me; that is why I could not live up to my promise. He found me in very low spirits. My complex about "life gone to seed" and "zero future" revived under his influence. He arrived in excellent form and with the full ruthlessness of the younger generation demanding that the arena be cleared for themselves. All this only seeped through, of course; it wasn't stated outright. You will take pleasure in this experience of mine—which may only have been spawned by my hypochondria, after all. You have quite a different effect on me.

Do please come to see me some time (before Sunday). Independently of this, I am coming up on Sunday, possibly before noon. We're having such lovely days now, even when it rains, that one must spend them with a close and sensitive person if one is too destitute and dried up to nourish hope and joy anymore. More and more I have occasion to realize that delight with the world, spasms of disinterested joy, are only forms of personal hope, generalized pictures of vitality projected onto the artist's sensitivity. I'll be expecting you every day until 6 P.M. Fond regards,

Bruno Schulz

June 4 [1941]

102

Dear Ania:

I was mortified when I found we had missed each other. I had caught a cold on Sunday and decided to stay at home. That evening J. Wit dragged me out and made me lose a meeting with you. Please don't get discouraged with me, but come as soon as possible. I feel very dismal now and deep in a pit. Perhaps you can give me a little lift. I have never felt quite this bad. Give me some advice. Should I consult Dr. Reinhold in Truskawiec after all? Do you know him? Perhaps you could intercede with him in this matter?

I look forward impatiently to your coming. With warm regards,

Bruno Schulz

June 9, 1941

103

Dear Ania:

Please don't lose any sleep over inequality of privilege. My diminished mobility, my age, my complexes compensate for that. I am glad that you sometimes think of me and remember me. I'm inviting you warmly and joyfully. I intend to wait every day until 6 P.M., assuming that you won't come any later. I am a little better and very much feel like a stroll with you and a talk. Thank you for your card. Warm regards,

Bruno Schulz

Do you think you could bring me *Die Heimkehr?*[11] Please give the Friend [Hilda Berger][12] my regards.

June 13, 1941

104

Dear Ania:

I am still under the spell of your charming metamorphoses. I believe the reason they are so touching is that they exist so independent of your will, so automatic and unconscious. It's as though somebody substituted another person to take your place on the sly, and you, as it were, accepted this new person, took her for your own, and continued playing your part on the new instrument, unaware that someone else was acting onstage. Of course I am exaggerating the situation toward the paradoxical. Do not take me for naive. I know what happens is not altogether unconscious, but you don't realize how much of it is the action of more profound forces, how much is the doing of a metaphysical puppetry in you. Add to this the fact that you are incredibly reactive, transforming yourself instantly into a complementary form, a wondrous accompaniment. . . . All this goes on outside the intellect, as it were, by some shorter and simpler circuit than thought, simply like a physical reflex. It is the first time in my experience that I have come across such natural riches that don't have enough space, you might say, within the dimensions of a single person and therefore mobilize ancillary personae, improvising pseudopersonalities ad hoc for the duration of a brief role you are compelled to play. This is how I explain your protean nature to myself. You may think that I'm allowing myself to be taken in, that I'm pinning a deep interpretation on the playfulness of ordinary coquetry. Let me assure you that coquetry is something very profound and mysterious, and incomprehensible even to you. It is plain that you cannot see this mystery and that to you it must present itself as something ordinary and uncomplicated. But this is a delusion. You underestimate your possibilities and spoil the magnificient demonism of your nature by the ingenuous snobbery of saintliness. It isn't enough for you to be a demon; you want to be—in addition and on the side—a saint, as if it were all that easy to combine these traits. You, with your fine nose for kitsch in art, lose your taste and instinct when it comes to the moral sphere and cultivate an unconscious dilettantism of holiness with a clear conscience. No—holiness is a thing of toil and blood that cannot be grafted onto a full and rich life like some pretty ornament. This dilettantism, by the way, is very charming and touching on the part of a soul who communicates with the pit from a yard away. With the Pit, capital P. I don't know how it happens, but you are playing with the keys to the Pit. I don't know if you are familiar with everyone's abyss of perdition or only with mine. In any case, you are moving with light, somnambulist ease on that cliff's edge I avoid in myself with fear and trembling, where the gravel shifts underfoot. I have to assume that you yourself are probably safe. You detach yourself lightly and delicately from the one who has lost his footing and let him slide into the abyss by himself. For a few steps you may actually pretend you are losing the ground under your feet, confident that at a certain point the parachute will open and carry you off to safety. With all this, you remain genuinely innocent and, as it were, unconscious of what you are doing. You are truly the victim, and truly all the guilt falls upon him who bears within him that abyss whose rim you carelessly set foot on. I know all the guilt is on my side, because the abyss is mine and you are only a sylph who has strayed into my garden, where it becomes my duty to keep your foot from sliding. That is why you should feel no self-reproach. You are always innocent whatever you do, and here a new perspective opens on your holiness. Your holiness in fact costs you nothing, for you are a sylph, and we are dealing not with dilettantism but with the superhuman elfin virtuosity of an entity that is not subject to moral categories.

Please come, secure and unthreatened as always, and don't spare me. Whatever happens, I endorse you in all your metamorphoses. If you are Circe, I will be Ulysses and I know the herb that will make you powerless. Of course, I may be just bragging, just being provocative.

Every day I wait till 6 P.M. I have a project for Sunday: let's meet in Truskawiec. I have a morning train there and an evening one back; we could spend the whole day there.

Are you game?

Fond greetings, and thank you for coming.

Bruno Schulz

[June 19, 1941]

The Sunday meeting Schulz suggested in the letter above fell on the day of Hitler's assault on the U.S.S.R., June 22. The next letter, written in September, is the first of Schulz's surviving letters written after the Nazi occupation of Drohobycz.

105

Dear Ania:

The thought of you is real sunlight for me, I fence it off from everyday thoughts and save it for the best moments, evenings. You are the partner of my interior dialogues about things that matter to me. I am longing for a time when we may be able to enter into frequent and intensive contact, and am fearful that in the meantime you may leave. I didn't answer right away for the comic reason that I lacked the few groszy for a postcard. I cannot make up my mind to come myself. It is too great an undertaking for me and seems foolhardy and dangerous. I am glad you sometimes think of me, and I dream of your coming someday. I greatly enjoyed your Friend's short visit. Are you writing something? Is your mind active? Fond greetings to you and everybody.

Bruno Schulz

September 23, 1941

106

Dear Ania:

Thank you for a kind and undeserved letter. I feel shamed and touched by the friendship you lavish on me. I think of you often and devotedly, waiting for you to come. We're having such lovely days, they seem to cry out for you to make them perfect. The only pity is that I can't keep you longer; the curfew imposes early departure. It also bothers me not to be able to host you as I should. But please come anyway. I'm not doing anything now, just contemplating my "inner riches," the stockpiles and caches of goods I've accumulated in life. Is that all right?

What are you working on? Please bring the fruits of your work. With fond regards,

Bruno

[October 4, 1941]

107

Dear Ania:

I don't know how to justify the delay I have let mount up between your letter and my reply. I seem to have felt incapable of untying the knot of misapprehension in which you—so it seemed to me—had become entangled, and so I put off that job. To my mind, realism, as the exclusive urge to copy reality, is a fiction. No such thing has ever existed. Realism became the incubus and scarecrow of the nonrealists, a veritable medieval Satan daubed in lurid

Cottage on Stolarska Street in the Drohobycz ghetto, Schulz's last location. Photo taken by Jerzy Ficowski in 1964.

colors on every wall. I would suggest a purely negative term to designate realism: It is a method that endeavors to keep all its means within the confines of certain conventions, is determined not to break a certain convention we call reality, or common sense, or plausibility. Within these limits a very broad range of means remains at its disposal; how broad is perfectly demonstrated by Mann, who exhausts all spheres and hells without violating the realistic convention. Mann or Dostoevsky (read *The Double* or *Brothers Karamazov*) prove how little depends on overstepping or observing the line of realism—which is simply a matter of manner, attitude, style. If by realism we intend a certain down-to-earthness, a mundane quality of the reality being described, then these authors are a striking denial of such a definition. On the other hand, the battle is not won simply by breaching the realistic convention. The mere contravention of realism confers no merit—all depends on what was achieved by this contravention. The conscious and deliberate violation of realism opened up certain new possibilities, but one mustn't delude oneself that possessing this trick frees one from the duty to offer opulence of content and access to one's world. No method, however touched by genius, can replace the effort of producing one's own content. I am saying this because I am afraid you are launched on the road of opposition, of negation; that instead of doing work of your own, you are keeping track of that foul fiend's every move; and that maintaining this vigil over the sins and errors of realism keeps you from any positive output of your own. You well know I have a high opinion of your writing and believe in your gift, and that is exactly why I fear you may be replacing your own creative talent and your own writing with a critique of realism. Nonrealistic modes have already won their citizenship and don't need to fight for their existence or recognition. All they need to do is achieve in there sphere what realism did in its. This will be their best justification. I liked the samples you read to me very much. I would like to see you take heart and muster the élan to tackle broader subjects, to process larger chunks of your inner world this way. Merely being right does not redeem you in the realm of works of the imagination. I am afraid the achievement of a genuine and accurate insight into a matter gives you such a large dose of satisfaction that it puts the need to produce to sleep.

As for your analysis of Mann, you may be partly right. Mann may not offer the same density of impression, but he makes up for it many times over by the breadth and opulence of his world.

I wouldn't depress you for the world, but I can't leave you in what I consider a state of error. The very fact I dispute you should be your proof of how seriously I treat you. My great respect for your competence as a painter is coupled with my insight into my own incompetence. In literary questions I arrogate a certain competence to myself, which you, after all, do grant me—by turning to me with these questions.

I am very eager to learn what you've written. When will I be able to read it? When are you going to come? Affectionate greetings to you and Marek. Warm regards, too, to Hilda [Berger][13] and Marek S.

Bruno Schulz

November 6, 1941

Schulz writes the following letter after learning that Anna, with her fiancé, has decided to leave for Warsaw without delay.

108

Dear Ania:

Just today I felt sharp pangs of conscience at the thought of my letter to you, in which I allowed myself to indulge an urge to play mentor and moral tutor instead of being happy about the successes and public notice of a near and dear person. It also occurred to me that you are probably off to Warsaw carrying away with you a tainted and spoiled memory of me. From your letter I see I was right, but I gather also that you are not angry, for which I am deeply grateful to you. Your leaving is a sad blow to me. I wasn't able to make the most of your presence, I didn't exploit you fully, but your mere presence so close to me was to some degree a thing to lean on and cling to. Actually, we never talked about the things that matter most. We popularized the results of our respective experiences to each other not like initiates of the same secret society, but like profane outsiders. Now I see we should have had more confidence in our closeness, should have reached for the matters of direct topical concern to us and talked them through while they were hot, as we do in soliloquies for our own benefit. The distance between us was artificial and conventional, it existed only in the terminologies and lexica of different schools that are really identical in spirit and intent.

Schulz's last letter to Anna Płockier, November 19, 1941. Collection of Marian Jachimowicz.

I hope that our close contact will not break off with your departure, but that we will communicate frequently and in a meaningful way. It is even conceivable that such contact at a distance will prove productive for us and bear a crop of minor writings. I have a premonition that we shall meet again soon and that the annals of our friendship are not closed. They are only beginning, objectively speaking, whereas up to now they've stayed within the boundaries of the subjective.

Would you think it a hopeless venture to take me on as an adept of painting under your tutelage? To put me through, perhaps with Marek's aid, a course in painting purged of the academic? In return I would share with you my experience as a writer.

I now have the feeling I would have a lot more to tell you, unexhausted supplies of matters that vividly concern us. Now that, in mundane terms, I am losing you. Do write to me still if you are ready to respond to my propositions with equal fervor, and if our contact will be maintained. May we be granted the opportunity to continue our exchange, which is important and real, peacefully and without surprises. Maybe you'll manage to write a note while you're still here. Otherwise, I look forward to having word from you shortly from there. Most affectionate greetings,

Bruno

November 19, 1941

How sad to think that at 30 Mazeppa Street, where I spent so many lovely hours, no one will be left, all of it will become mere legend. I don't know why I feel guilty toward myself, as if I had lost something and it was my own fault.

30 Mazeppa Street, formerly Szczorsa Street, was Anna's and Marek's address in Borysław. Anna's plan to make her way to Warsaw ended in failure when both she and Marek were killed by Ukrainian militia on November 27, 1941, a few days after she received Schulz's last letter.

Bruno Schulz was killed by a Nazi officer a year later, on November 19.[14]

Bruno Schulz, about 1936.

NARRATIVE PROSE

THE REPUBLIC OF DREAMS

Here on the Warsaw pavement in these days of tumult, heat and dazzle I retreat in my mind to the remote city of my dreams, I let my vision rise to command that low, sprawling, polymorphic countryside, that greatcoat of God flung down at the sills of heaven like a mottled sheet. For that country submits utterly to heaven, holds heaven over itself in vaulted colors, variform, intricate with cloisters, triforia, stained-glass roses, windows opening onto eternity. Year after year that country grows up into the sky, merges with the dawn redness, turns angelic in the reflected light of the greater atmosphere.

A good way to the south, where the mapped land shifts—fallow from the sun, bronzed and singed by the glow of summer like a ripe pear—there it stretches like a cat in the sun, that chosen land, that peculiar province, the town unique in all the world. There is no point in speaking of this place to the profane—no point in explaining it is from that long tongue of rolling land over there lapping up breath for the countryside in the summer conflagrations, that boiling island of land facing south, that lone spur sticking up among swarthy Hungarian vineyards, that this one particle of earth detaches itself out of the collective landscape and, tramping alone down an untried path, attempts to be a world in itself. Sealed in a self-sufficient microcosm, that town and its countryside have boldly installed themselves at the very brink of eternity.

The garden plots at the outskirts of town are planted as if at the world's edge and look across their fences into the infinity of the anonymous plain. Just beyond the tollgates the map of the region turns nameless and cosmic like Canaan. Above that thin forlorn snippet of land a sky deeper and broader than anywhere else, a sky like a vast gaping dome many stories high, full of unfinished frescos and improvisations, swirling draperies and violent ascensions, opens up once again.

How to express this in words? Where other towns developed into economies, evolved into statistics, quantified themselves—ours regressed into essence. Nothing happens here by chance, nothing results without deep motive and premeditation. Here events are not ephemeral surface phantoms; they have roots sunk into the deep of things and penetrate the essence. Here decisions take place every moment, laying down precedents once and for all. Everything that happens here happens only once and is irrevocable. This is why such weightiness, such heavy emphasis, such sadness inheres in what takes place.

Just now, for example, the yards are drowning in nettles and weeds, tumbledown moss-grown sheds and outbuildings are up to their armpits in enormous bristly burdocks that grow right to the eaves of the shingled roofs. The town lives under the sign of the Weed, of wild, avid, fanatical plant life bursting out in cheap, coarse greenery—toxic, rank, parasitic. That greenery glows under the sun's conjury, the maws of the leaves suck in seething chlorophyll; armies of nettles, rampant, voracious, devour the flower plantings, break into the gardens, spread over the unguarded back walls of houses and barns overnight, run wild in the roadside ditches. It is amazing what insane vitality, feckless and unproductive, lives in this fervid dab of green, this distillate of sun and ground water. From a pinch of chlorophyll it draws out and extrapolates under the blaze of these summer days that luxuriant texture of emptiness, a green pith replicated a hundred times onto millions of leaf surfaces, downy or furred, of veined translucent verdure pulsing with watery plant blood, giving off the pungent herbal smell of the open fields.

In that season the rear window of the shop's storage room overlooking the yard was blinded by a diaphragm of green glitter from leaf reflections, gauzy flutterings, wavy foliated greenery, all the monstrous excesses of this hideous backyard fecundity. Sunk in deep shade, the storeroom riffled through all shades of virescence, green reflections spread in undulating paths through its vaulted length like the sibilant murmur of a forest.

The town had fallen into that wild luxuriance as into a sleep raised to the hundredth power, supine in a daze from the summer's heat and glare, in a thick maze of cobwebs and greenery, empty and shallow of breath. In rooms greenly lit to underwater opacity by the morning glory over the windows, platoons of flies struggled on their last wings, imprisoned forever as in the bottom of a forgotten bottle and locked in a dolorous agony that they proclaimed by drawn-out monotonous lamentations or trumpetings of fury and grief. In time, the window became the gathering place of all that lacework of scattered insectdom for one last premortal sojourn: huge crane-flies, which had long bumped against the walls with a subdued drumming of misdirected flight and made a final torpid landing on a pane; whole genealogies of flies and moths, rooted and branching out from this window and spread by slow migration across the glass; pullulating generations of meager winglings, sky-blue, metallic, glassy.

Over the shop displays, great bright opaque awnings flap lazily in the hot breeze, wavy stripes baking in the blaze. The dead season lords it over the empty squares, the wind-scoured streets. Distant prospects gathered up and shirred by gardens lie in a dazzled faint in the heat-glazed sky, as if they had only just fluttered down, a vast garish cloth, from the hollows of heaven, bright, glowing, rumpled from the flight, and were waiting, already spent, for a new charge of brilliance in which to renew themselves.

What to do on those days, where to flee from the conflagration, from the incubus lying heavy on the chest in a torrid noontime nightmare? On such days, Mother might hire a cab and, jammed together in its black body, the shop assistants up on the box with the bundles or clutching onto the springs, we would all ride out of town to Little Hill. We rode into the rolling, hill-studded landscape. The vehicle toiled its long, lonesome way among humped fields, rooting through the hot golden dust of the highway.

The convex necks of the horses bulged tensely, their glistening hindquarters knotted with honest toil, swept every so often by bushy slaps of the tail. The wheels turned slowly, squeaking on their axles. The old hack passed flat pastures dotted with molehills and broadly humped with reclining cattle, forked and horned, prodigious shapeless lumps of bones, knots, and ridges. There they lay, monumental as barrows, their quiet gaze mirroring remote and shifting horizons.

We came to a halt at last on Little Hill, next to the squat masonwork tavern. It stood alone, its roof spread out against the sky, on the watershed, the high spine between two opposed territories. The horses strained to struggle up the high edge, then stopped on their own, as if in bemusement, at the pike-gate dividing two worlds. This gate commanded a wide sweep of landscape seamed by highways, pale and opalescent like faded tapestry, breathed on by a vast afflatus of air, sky–blue and vacant. From that distant rolling plain a breeze rose, lifting the horses' manes and floating past under a high clear sky.

Here we might stop for the night, or Father might make a sign for us to forge on into that landscape, capacious as a map and webbed with highways. Barely visible in the distance before us on the winding roads crawled the vehicles that had come before us, making their way on the bright macadam lined by cherry trees straight to what was then a small inn, wedged in a narrow glen full of the chatter of springs and tumbling waters and muttering leaves.

In those far-off days our gang of boys first hit on the outlandish and impossible notion of straying even farther, beyond that inn, into no-man's or God's land, of patrolling borders both neutral and disputed, where boundary lines petered out and the compass rose of the winds skittered erratically under a high-arching sky. There we meant to dig in, raise ramparts around us, make ourselves independent of the grownups, pass completely out of the realm of their authority, proclaim the Republic of the Young. Here we would form a new and autonomous legislature, erect a new hierarchy of standards and values. It was to be a life under the aegis of poetry and adventure, neverending signs and portents. All we needed to do, or so it seemed to us, was push apart the barriers and limits of convention, the old markers imprisoning the course of human affairs, for our lives to be invaded by an elemental power, a great inundation of the unforeseen, a flood of romantic adventures and fabulous happenings. We wanted to surrender our lives to this torrent of the fabulating element, this inspired onrush of historical events, be carried away by its surging waves without a will of our own. The spirit of nature was by its very essence a great storyteller. Out of its core the honeyed discourse of fables and novels, romances and epics, flowed in an irresistible stream. The whole atmosphere was absolutely stuffed full of stories. You only needed to lay a trap under this sky full of ghosts to catch one, set a wooden post upright in the wind for strips of narrative to be caught fluttering on its tip.

We resolved to become self-sufficient, create a new life principle, establish a new age, reconstitute the world—on a small scale, to be sure, for ourselves alone, but after our own tastes and pleasures.

This was going to be a stronghold, a blockhouse, a fortified base ruling the neighborhood; part fortress, part theater, part laboratory of visions. All nature would be yoked to its purpose. As in Shakespeare, this unleashed theater spilled over into nature, expanding into reality, soaking up impulses and inspiration from all elements, undulating with the great tidal ebb and flow of natural currents. Here we were going to locate the node of all processes that course through the body of nature, the point of entry to all story threads and fables shimmering in her great misty soul. Like Don Quixote, we wanted to divert the channel of all those histories and romances into our lives, throw open the frontiers to all those intrigues, convolutions, and intricate ventures that are spun in the great ether when it overreaches itself in the fantastical.

We dreamed the region was being threatened by an unknown danger, was permeated by a mysterious menace. Against this peril and hazard we would find safe refuge and shelter in our fortress. The countryside was crisscrossed by packs of wolves, bands of highwaymen infested the forest. We constructed shelters and bulwarks and, shaken by not unpleasant forebodings and delicious shudders, made ready for sieges. Our gates drew fugitives out from under the knives of brigands, and they found haven and sanctuary with us. Carriages chased by wild beasts flew up to our gates at a dead gallop. We played host to mysterious distinguished strangers and lost ourselves in conjectures in our desire to penetrate their disguises. In the evenings everyone gathered in the great hall, where, by flickering candlelight, we listened to one tale or revelation after another. There were times when the plot spun through these stories jumped out of the narrative frame and stepped among us, live and hungry for prey, and tangled us up in its perilous whorl. Sudden recognitions, unexpected disclosures, an improbable encounter pushed their way into our private lives. We lost the ground beneath our feet, placed in jeopardy by contingencies we ourselves had unleashed. From far away the howling of wolves was carried on the air, we brooded over romantic entanglements, ourselves halfway caught up in their coils, while an inscrutable night rustled on the other side of the window, fraught with shapeless aspirations, ardent, incomprehensible confidences, unplumbed, inexhaustible, itself knotted into labyrinthine convolutions.

Today those remote dreams come back, and not without reason. The possibility suggests itself that no dreams, however absurd or senseless, are wasted in the universe. Embedded in the dream is a hunger for its own reification, a demand that imposes an obligation on reality and that grows imperceptibly into a bona fide claim, an I.O.U. clamoring for payment. We have long since abandoned our dreams of that fortress, but here, years later, someone turns up who picks them up and takes them seriously, someone ingenuous and true of heart who understood them literally, took them for coin of the realm, and treated them as things that were plain, unproblematic. I have seen this person, I have spoken with him. His eyes were an improbably vivid sky-blue, not made for looking

Untitled pencil sketch, 1930s.

outward but for steeping themselves in the cerulean essence of dreams. He told me that when he came to the neighborhood I am referring to, that anonymous, virginal no-man's-land, he caught the scent of poetry and adventure at once, perceived the ready contours of myth suspended over the site. He discovered in the atmosphere the preformed outlines of this concept, the planes, elevations, and stone tablets of data. He heard a summons, an inner voice, like Noah did when he received his orders and instructions.

He was visited by the spirit of this design, which wandered at large in the atmosphere. He proclaimed a Republic of Dreams, a sovereign realm of poetry. On so many acres of land, on a surface sheet of landscape flung down in the woods, he established the exclusive domain of the fictive. He staked out its borders, laid down the foundations for a fortress, converted the realm into a single great rose garden. Guest apartments took shape, cells for solitary contemplation, refectories, dormitories, libraries, cabins tucked away in the park, arbors, pavilions and scenic vistas . . .

That man who drags himself to the gates of this fortress, wolves or brigands hot on his trail, is saved. In triumphant procession they usher him in, relieve him of his dusty clothing. Festive, joyous, exhilarated, he enters the Elysian ambience and breathes in the rose-laden sweetness of the air. Off behind him cities and worldly affairs, the days and their fevers, dwindle. He has entered a radiant new holiday regularity, has cast off his own body like a bony carapace, has shed the grimacing mask that had grown onto his face, has completed the liberating metamorphosis.

The man with the sky-blue eyes is no architect. He is, rather, a director, a director of cosmic landscapes and sceneries. His art consists in catching nature's intentions in midair, knowing how to read her arcane ambitions. For nature is full of potential architecture, rife with plans and construction. Did the master builders of the great ages behave any differently? They eavesdropped on the immense pathos of great squares, the dynamic perspectives of distance, the silent pantomime of symmetrical lanes. Long before Versailles, clouds in the immense skies of summer evenings arranged themselves into the kinds of spacious compounds that religious orders live and worship in, ethereal megalomaniacal residences; had tried their hand at stage-setting, piling up towering structures, oversized and world-scale layouts. The grand theater of uncircumscribed airspace is inexhaustible in its ideas, its projects, its aerial preliminaries; it hallucinates an architecture of grandiose inspiration, an ethereal, transcendental brand of urbanistics.

Human works have the peculiarity that, once completed, they become hermetic, cut off from nature, consolidated on a base of their own. The work of the Blue-eyed One, in contrast, has not cut itself off from the great cosmic contexts; it is immersed in them half-humanized like a centaur, harnessed to the sublime processes of nature, still unfinished and growing. The man with the sky-blue eyes invites everyone to keep on working, fabricating, jointly creating: We are all of us dreamers by nature, after all, brothers under the sign of the trowel, destined to be master builders . . .

Tygodnik Ilustrowany, no. 29, 1936

AUTUMN

You know that moment when summer, so recently buoyant and vigorous, universal summer hugging to itself all things imaginable—people, events, objects—one day sustains a barely perceptible injury. The sun still blazes dense and copious, the landscape still wields the classic magisterial flourish bequeathed to this season by the genius of Poussin, but, strange to report, we return from a morning stroll oddly wearied and jejune: Was there something to be ashamed of? We feel a bit out of sorts, avoid looking at each other—why? And we know that at dusk someone or other will take himself with a worried smile to a remote corner of summer and knock, knock at the wall to check if, in fact, the sound is still full and genuine. This testing carries with it a perverse relish in treacherous unmasking, a small frisson of scandal. But officially we are still full of respect and loyalty: We are dealing with a solid firm, an enterprise with sound financial backing . . . And yet, if the next day brings tidings of summer's bankruptcy, it seems like day-before-yesterday's news and no longer has the explosive impact of a scandal. And as the auction of assets takes its sober and revitalizing course, and the desecrated apartments, stripped and empty, fill with luminous sober echoes, this rouses no regret or sentiment: All this liquidating of summer displays the same languor, irrelevance, casual spirit of a belated carnival that has run on into Ash Wednesday.

On the other hand, indulging in pessimism is perhaps premature. Negotiations are still going on, the summer's reserves not yet exhausted, full rehabilitation is yet in the cards . . . But deliberation and cool heads are not what summer people are known for. Even the hotelkeepers, who

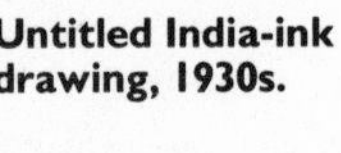

Untitled India-ink drawing, 1930s.

have invested over their heads in the stock market of summer, are capitulating. Really—such lack of loyalty and proper feeling toward a faithful ally shows little trace of the royal merchant! They are shopkeepers—petty, craven souls incapable of taking the long view. One and all, they hug to their bellies what they have scraped together. Cynically they take off the mask of courtesy and the cutaway suit to reveal . . . the cashier.

And we, too, pack our luggage. I am fifteen years old and quite unburdened by mundane duties. Since an hour remains before our departure, I run outdoors once more to say good-bye to the summer place, check out the season's yield, decide what may be taken along and what will have to be relinquished for good in these doomed surroundings. But at the little round plaza in the park, empty now and bright in the afternoon sun, next to the Mickiewicz monument, the truth about the crisis of summer dawns in my soul. In the euphoria of this revelation I climb up the two steps of the pedestal and, drawing an impassioned arc with my eyes and outspread arms as if addressing the entire resort, I say: "Farewell, Season! You were very beautiful and rich. No other summer can compare with you. Today I recognize this even though there have been times when you made me terribly unhappy and sad. As something to remember me by, I leave you my adventures, littered all over the park and the lanes and gardens. I can't take my age fifteen back with me, that will have to stay behind here for good. I've slipped a drawing I did for you into a crack between two beams on the porch of the bungalow where I stayed as another souvenir. Now you're sinking among the shades, and down to the underworld along with you goes all this town full of cottages and gardens, too. You have no offspring. You and this town are dying, the last of your kind.

"But you're not guiltless, O Season! Let me tell you wherein your guilt lies. You did not want to stay, O Season, within the bounds of the given. No reality satisfied you; you broke out beyond the realm of what can be realized. Finding no surcease in reality, you created a superstructure out of the figurative stuff of metaphor, you moved among associations and allusions, the imponderables between things. All things referred to other things, which in turn called further things to witness, and so on ad infinitum. In the end your honeyed words grew cloying. People wearied of rocking on the billows of an unending rhetoric. Yes, rhetoric—pardon the expression. This became clear when, in many imaginations, in one place and another, a longing for the genuine and essential welled up. That moment already spelled your defeat. The borders of your universality became visible; your grand style, your splendid baroque, which satisfied the needs of reality when you were in your prime, now turned out to be a mannered trick. You dulcitudes and reveries bore the stamp of childish inflation. Your nights were vast and boundless like the megalomanic aspirations of lovers, or they were swirling spectacles like the hallucinations of feverish patients. Your perfumes were extravagant, beyond the ability of human delight to absorb them. Under the magic of your touch everything dematerialized, grew toward ever further, higher forms. Eating your apples one dreamed of fruit from the territory of Paradise, your peaches brought up the image of ethereal fruit that is consumed by smell alone. Your palette held only the highest registers of color, you didn't know the saturation and pith of the dark, earthy, greasy browns. Autumn is the human soul's yearning for matter, essence, boundary. When for unexplored reasons human metaphors, projects, dreams begin to hanker for realization, the time of autumn is at hand. Those phantoms that, formerly spread out over the farthest reaches of the human cosmos, lent its high vaults the colors of their spectra now return to man, seeking the warmth of his breath, the cozy narrow shelter of his home, the niche that holds his bed. Man's house becomes like the little stable of Bethlehem, the core around which all demons, all spirits of the upper and lower spheres, condense. The time of beautiful classical gestures, latinate rhetoric, the histrionic roundedness of the south, is over. Autumn looks for herself in the sap and primitive vigor of the Dürers and Breughels. That form bursts from the overflow of material, hardens into whorls and knots, seizes matter in its jaws and talons, squeezes, ravishes, deforms, and dismisses it from its clutches imprinted with the marks of this struggle as half-formed hunks, with the brand of uncanny life stamped in the grimaces extruded from their wooden faces."

All this and more I said to the empty half-circle of the park, which seemed to recede before me. Only some fragments of this soliloquy issued from my mouth, partly because I couldn't find the proper words, partly because I was only miming my oration, eking out words with gesticulation. I made reference to nuts, the classic fruits of autumn, kindred to house furnishings, nourishing, tasty, and durable. I mentioned chestnuts, those polished models of fruit, cup-and-ball toys made for children to play with; I spoke of fall apples on windowsills flushed an honest, homey, prosaic red.

Dusk was fumigating the air by the time I returned to the boarding-house. Two large carriages were already drawn up in the courtyard against our leavetaking. The horses, not yet harnessed, snorted with their heads buried in feedbags. The doors all stood wide open, the candles burning on the table in our room flickered in the draft. The fast-descending gloom, the people grown faceless in the dusk who were hurrying out with luggage, the disorder in the ravished opened room, all this held a dismal suggestion of haste and belated panic, intimations of terror and disaster. Finally we took our places in the deep caverns of the carriages and started off. The dark, dense, deep air of the fields blew over us. The coachmen drew vigorous cracks from this intoxicating ether with their long whips and took pains to steady the gaits of the horses, whose powerful, splendidly sculptured withers rocked in the darkness between bushy slaps of their tails. Thus the two masses of horseflesh, rattling trunks, and creaking leather shells shifted through the dark, starless, solitary landscape of night. At times they seemed to disintegrate, come apart like crabs separating and scuttling away. Then the coachmen would take the reins more firmly in hand, reassemble the scattered hoofbeats and gather them into regular disciplined patterns. The lighted carriage lanterns sent long shafts into the deep of the night that telescoped out, broke off, and fled in great leaps into wild vague voids. They slunk off on their long legs just to be able to mock the coachmen with derisive gestures far off somewhere at the edge of the woods. Unperturbed, the coachmen swept them with broadsides of whip-cracking. The town lay sleeping when we drove in among its houses. Streetlights shone here and there in empty streets, as if created simply for the purpose of illuminating a low-slung house or balcony, or to rivet to one's memory a number over a closed gate. Caught by surprise at this late hour, heavy-lidded padlocked shops, gates with prolapsed sills, signs jerked by the night wind displayed the hopeless desolation, the profound orphanhood of objects left to themselves, objects forgotten by people. My sister's carriage turned into a side street while we drove on to the marketplace. The horses changed their gait when we entered the deep shade of the square. On the threshold of his open hallway the barefoot baker stabbed us with a glance of dark eyes, the apothecary window, still wide awake, proferred and withdrew raspberry balsam from a great jar. The pavement thickened under the horses' feet, single and paired clinks of iron separated out of the clatter of hoofbeats more and more slowly and distinctly, and the scored facade of our house gradually drew out of the darkness and stopped beside the carriage. A maid opened the gate for us, a kerosene lamp with a reflector in her hand. Our enormous shadows grew up over the stairs and skewed off at the arches of the stairway. The apartment was lit by a single candle, which dipped its flame to the draft from the open window. The dark wallpaper was mildewed with the sorrows and afflictions of many ailing generations. Roused from its slumber and released from long solitude, the old furniture seemed to gaze at the returning family with wry knowingness and patient wisdom. You can't escape from us, they seemed to be saying; in the end you have to reenter the realm of our magic, because we've long since divided up among ourselves

Self-portrait.

all your movements and gestures, risings up and settlings down, all your future days and nights. We can wait, we know . . . The vast cavernous beds, piled high with chilly layers of sheets and blankets, waited for our bodies. The night's floodgates groaned under the rising pressure of dark masses of slumber, a dense lava that was just about to erupt and pour over its dams, over the doors, the old wardrobes, the stoves where the wind sighed.

Sygnały, no. 17, 1936

FATHERLAND

After a great many of fate's capricious ups and downs, which I have no intention of going into here, I found myself abroad at last, in that realm of my youthful dreams I once ardently yearned for. Fulfillment came too late, though, and in circumstances vastly different from those I had fondly imagined. I made my return not as a conqueror but as one of life's derelicts. The intended domain of my triumphs was now the scene of wretched, inglorious, petty defeats in which I lost, one after the next, my proud and lofty aspirations. By now I was fighting for mere survival; battered, trying as best I could to save my flimsy shell from shipwreck, blown here and there by the whims of fate, I finally came upon that middle-sized provincial town where, in the dreams of my youth, a certain countryhouse was to stand, the famous old master's refuge from the world's turmoil. Unconscious even of the irony involved in the coincidence, I now intended to hunker down and stay there some little time, hibernate maybe, until the next windy burst of events. I didn't care where chance might carry me. The glamour of the landscape had faded irrevocably for me; now, harassed, worn out, I wanted only peace.

But things took a different turn. Evidently I had reached some fork in my road, a peculiar twist of my personal fate, for unexpectedly my existence began to stabilize. I had a sense of having passed into a favoring current. Wherever I turned I met a situation that seemed tailored for me, people dropped everything as if they had been waiting for me, I spotted that spontaneous glint of attention in their eyes, that instant decision to put themselves at my service, as though at the dictate of some higher authority. This was illusion, of course, produced by the deft interaction of circumstances, the dexterous meshing of the gears of my destiny by the clever hands of chance, which led me from event to event in what seemed like a sleepwalker's trance. There was scarcely time for astonishment: the happy turn in my fortunes went hand in hand with a complaisant fatalism, a blithe passivity and trust that bade me submit to the gravitational pull of events with no resistance. I had barely registered all this as the fulfillment of a long unsatisfied need, the profound gratification of the unrecognized and rejected artist's perennial hunger, when my gifts found appreciation at long last. From a café fiddler eager for any kind of job, I rapidly advanced to concertmaster of the local opera; the exclusive circles of amateurs of the arts opened before me and I entered the best society by what seemed like long-standing privilege—I, who had been halfway domiciled in the underworld of the *declassé,* the between-decks stowaways and freeloaders of society's ship. Aspirations that had led a tormenting subconscious existence in the depth of my soul as smothered, mutinous pretensions swiftly gained legitimacy and embarked on a life of their own. The mark of usurper and vain pretender faded from my brow.

I recount all this in abridged form, in the context of a general outline of my fortunes, not permitting myself to delve into details of this odd career, since all those events really belong to the prehistory of occurrences already reported. No—my happiness had absolutely no element of excess or unbridled abandon in it, as might have been suspected. I was utterly possessed by a feeling of deep calm and certainty—a sign by which (sensitized by life to every tremor of its countenance, seasoned physiognomist of destiny) I recognized with profound relief that this time it hid no malign intent. The quality of my happiness was enduring and genuine.

My whole past of homeless wandering, the submerged misery of my former existence, separated itself from me and floated back like a stretch of country positioned crosswise against the rays of the setting sun, rising one more time over distant horizons, while the train that bore me away rounded the last curve and headed straight into the night, full-breasted with the future that thrust against its face, a swelling, intoxicating, future slightly seasoned with smoke. This is the place for me to introduce the cardinal fact, the fact closing and crowning that age of prosperity and happiness: Eliza, whom I met at that stage of my pilgrimage, and whom after a brief rapturous engagement I made my wife.

The measure of my good fortune is ample and full. My position with the opera is unassailable. The conductor of the philharmonic orchestra, Maestro Pellegrini, values me and seeks my opinion on all decisions of importance. He is a dear old man on the verge of retirement, and there is a tacit three-way understanding among him, the opera management, and the town's Philharmonic Society that on his departure the conductor's baton will devolve upon me with no further ado. I have already held it in my hand more than once, conducting the monthly philharmonic concerts or in the orchestra pit of the opera, standing in for the maestro when he was ill or did not feel up to the demands of a modern piece of music alien to his spirit.

The opera is among the best endowed in the country. My salary is ample to sustain a comfortable style of life, even a certain gilding of luxury. Our lodgings have been furnished and arranged by Eliza in accordance with her taste, since I am quite without ambitions or enterprise in that direction. By contrast, Eliza has very decided (though constantly changing) ideas, which she puts into practice with an energy worthy of a better cause. She is forever embroiled with suppliers, battling vigorously over quality and price and bringing off exploits on these lines in which she takes no little pride. I watch her bustling with a tender indulgence tinged with some apprehension, as one might witness a child playing carelessly near the brink of an abyss. What innocence to imagine that we shape our destiny by struggling with a thousand mundane trifles!

Happily come to anchor in this calm bay, I want no more now than to cheat fate's vigilance, not to thrust myself upon its attention, to cling unobserved to my good fortune and be unnoticeable.

The city where fate has granted me to find such quiet and serene refuge is famous for its venerable cathedral, situated on a high bluff some way distant from the boundary of the residential quarters. Here the town comes to an abrupt stop, the terrain breaks off into steep battlements and promontories covered with stands of mulberry and walnut and commands a sweeping view. This is the last outcropping of a high cretaceous *massif* that stands guard over the broad clear plain of the province, which is open all along its width to the warm breath of the west. Under the caress of these mild currents the town has wrapped itself in a calm, sweet climatic zone, creating as it were a miniature meteorological orbit of its own within the larger one containing it. All the year round, mild and barely perceptible breezes wander through, gradually fusing toward autumn into one steady harmonious current that resembles a bright gulf stream of the air, a universal monotone of wind that is gentle to the point of oblivion and blissful dissolution.

The cathedral, chiseled and chased over the centuries in the precious twilight of its endlessly swelling hoard of stained glass, jewel grafted on jewel over the generations, now draws throngs of tourists from all over the world. During any season one can find them roaming our streets, clutching guidebooks. They take up the lion's share of our hotel space, comb our shops and antique stores for curios, fill up our places of amusement. From the far-off outer world they bring the smell of the sea, sometimes the zest and verve of great projects, the broad élan of big business. Some, charmed by the climate, the cathedral, the pace of life, have been known to settle down for a longer stay, adjust to the environment, and remain for good. Others carry off wives when they leave, the fair daughters of our merchants, manufacturers, and restaurateurs. Thanks to these ties, outside capital is often invested in our enterprises and strengthens our industrial plant.

The town's economic life, for that matter, has been running a placid course for years, free of shocks and crises. The highly developed sugar industry feeds three quarters of the population at its sweet artery; the town boasts as well a celebrated porcelain factory that carries on a fine old tradition. It produces for export, but every Briton returning to his country makes a point of ordering a set of so many pieces of ivory-colored china featuring views of the cathedral and town as created by the young ladies of our art academy.

Generally speaking, this is a liberally and efficiently managed town, like many others in this country—moderately bustling and business minded, moderately fond of its comfort and civic well-being, also moderately given to snobbish ambition and social climbing. The ladies display an almost metropolitan sartorial extravagance, the gentlemen emulate the lifestyle of the capital, laboring with the help of a few cabarets and clubs to keep a marginal sort of nightlife alive. Card playing is very popular, even the ladies indulge in it; and for us too hardly a day goes by that does not end, sometimes deep into the night, over cards at the elegant quarters of one of our friends. The initiative in this matter lies once again with Eliza, who in justifying her fervor to me cites her concern for our social standing, which she claims makes it necessary for us to go out more in order to remain part of the scene. But in fact she is simply addicted to the charm of this mindless and lightly stimulating waste of time.

Sometimes I watch her excitement as she gives herself over heart and soul to the mutable nature of gaming, eyes shining, a hectic flush spreading over her cheeks. The shaded lamp casts mild light on the table around which a group of deeply absorbed people, cards fanning out from their hands, run their imaginary race on the trail of treacherous fortune. I catch glimpses of her, an elusive figure tense with the challenge of the seance, fleetingly revealed behind the back of this player or that. Into the reigning silence remarks are dropped in undertones that mark the varied and winding itinerary of luck. For my part, I wait for the moment when the silent fervid trance has enveloped all their senses, when, oblivious of all else, they are stooped in a cataleptic crouch over a whirling disk, to withdraw unnoticed from that realm of magic arts to the solitude of my thoughts. Sometimes, dropping out of the game, I manage to leave the table without attracting notice and move quietly into another room. The space is dark, lit only by a distant streetlight. With my head resting against a windowpane I stand there for a long time, meditating.

Above the autumnal opacity of the park the night is flushed by a vague reddish glow. In the ravaged upholstery of the treetops crows wake with caws of mindless alarm and, deceived by the false dawn, take off in noisy squads; their yawping, wheeling disarray throws tumult and vibrations into the murky redness tartly redolent of herbage and fallen leaves. Eventually the great flurry of loops and turns all over the sky subsides; calming gradually, it descends, lighting in the combed-out tangle of trees in a ragged, provisional file that still shows signs of unrest, rife with misgivings, chatter falling silent, plaintive queries. At last the swarm settles down for good and becomes part of the sibilant stillness of the surrounding languor. And night, deep and late, resumes its sway. Hours pass. Hot forehead pressed against the pane, I sense and know: from now on no harm may come to me, I have found a peaceful haven. A long succession of years heavy with happiness and fulfillment now lies ahead, an unending mathematical progression of joyful good times. The last few sighs, shallow and sweet, fill my breast utterly with happiness. I stop breathing. I know one day death will take me into her open arms, as she does all life, bountiful and benign. I will lie, entirely sated, among the green undergrowth of the beautifully manicured local cemetery. My wife—how beautiful she'll look in her widow's veil—will bring me flowers on those bright, calm mid-mornings we enjoy here. Out of the depth of this boundless plenitude a ponderous full-throated music, the solemn, mournful, resonant bars of a majestic overture, seems to rise. I sense the powerful pulsing of its rhythms as it thrusts upward from the deep. Eyebrows rising, my gaze riveted on a distant point, I feel the hair stand up on my head. I freeze, listening . . .

A louder babble of conversation wakes me from my torpor. People are asking about me and laughing. I hear my wife's voice. From my place of retreat I come back into the bright room, rubbing eyes still steeped in darkness. By now the party is breaking up. The host and hostess are standing in the doorway, chatting with their departing guests and exchanging valedictory courtesies. Finally we are alone in the dark street. My wife adjusts her free, buoyant steps to mine. We walk well together; going up a hill with her head slightly bent, she kicks at the whispering carpet of dead leaves that covers the pavement. Still keyed up by the gambling, the luck that favored her, the wine she has drunk, she is full of little feminine schemes. By a tacit covenant between us, she exacts absolute tolerance on my part for this sort of noncommittal fantasizing and takes sharp offense at any sober critical comments. A green smudge of dawn already shows above the dark horizon as we enter our apartment. The good smell of a heated and well-groomed interior envelopes us. We don't turn on the light. A distant lantern traces the silvery pattern of the curtains onto the opposite wall. Still dressed, sitting on the bed, I silently take Eliza's hand and hold it a while in mine.

Sygnały, no. 59, 1938

Drohobycz.

NOTES

EDITOR'S INTRODUCTION

1. Debora Vogel's place in Polish literature rests on a single book, a volume of avant-garde philosophic-lyric prose called *Akacje Kwitną (The Acacias Are Blooming,* 1935*)*. She was probably the most nourishing and influential among Schulz's correspondents in the all-important matters of intellectual kinship, informed interest in his mind and his writing, sustained literary dialogue, unflagging sympathy. Important literary motifs or symbols they share include mannequins (cf. "The Hollow Men" of Eliot), trash and artifice, and the "haggishness of matter" (cf. *die Tücke des Objekts,* the malice of inanimate things, made famous by Theodor Vischer and the great German cartoonist-poet Wilhelm Busch).

Debora Vogel exemplified those among the Jewish intelligentsia in Poland who were literate and active both in Polish and in Yiddish, whereas Schulz, whose roots and home environment were equally Jewish, was linguistically at home in Polish and German, but knew almost no Yiddish. Debora's father was an officer of the Jewish community and a Hebraist who administered a Jewish orphanage in Lwów. She took a degree in philosophy and thereafter started intensive private study of Yiddish literature—against the inclinations of her father, who, like many educated European Jews of the time, had a strong distaste for "the jargon." Debora earned a doctorate and traveled in Europe—Stockholm, Berlin, Prague.

In 1930 a Polish-Jewish magazine of literature and the arts was founded by a group of distinguished artists: the poet and painter Ben Horowitz; the outstanding Yiddish poet Rachela Korn; Debora Vogel; Rachela Auerbach; the poet, artist, and critic Hersz Weber; and others. The name of the journal, which lasted only one year, was *Cusztajer* (Polish spelling for Yiddish *Zuschtajer,* "contribution"). Debora Vogel had some work accepted by this magazine, and later privately published two small volumes of Yiddish verse, in addition to the aforementioned prose work. She showed her doctoral thesis on Hegel's aesthetics to Witkiewicz, discussed with him her manuscript critique of his literary theory, corresponded with him, and had her portrait drawn by him. It was through Witkiewicz that she made Schulz's acquaintance.

TO OSTAP ORTWIN

Letters 1 and 2

1. About contemporary literature and its emerging writers and works, Ostap Ortwin wrote rarely and sparsely: We have essays or sketches by him only on Tuwim, Pawlikowska, Wierzyński, and Choromański, and these did not always display adequate appreciation of the significance and weight of what was then "young" poetry. Ortwin died in 1942, in the course of the Germans' liquidation of the Lwów ghetto. Both the letters by Schulz to Ortwin in this volume were preserved in the holdings of the Ossolineum Institute in Lwów, and are now kept in the State Academic Library of Lwów in folder no. 10 of the Ortwin Papers.

2. The MS shows only the initial of the square's name, presumably Plac Grzybowski. No number given.

3. Wilam Horzyca (1889–1959), critic, playwright, director, translator, poet.

4. Władysław Skoczylas (1883–1934), graphic artist, painter, and sculptor, cocreator of the contemporary art of the woodcut.

5. Roman Kramsztyk (1885–1942), graphic artist and painter (landscapes, nudes, portraits, still lifes). His last work, partly preserved, is a cycle of drawings from the Warsaw ghetto, where he himself perished in September 1942, murdered by Nazi liquidation squads.

6. *Cliché-verre* prints by Schulz from the cycle *Xsięga Bałwochwałcza.* This technique was used by Schulz in the twenties.

7. Since Schulz's last letter to Ortwin fourteen years have passed.

8. Ludwik Lille (1897–1957), painter, member of the Lwów association of sculptural artists, *Artes.* He died in Paris.

9. Herman Sternbach, Germanist, literary critic, essayist, editor, and translator of Goethe, Grillparzer, Novalis, and others.

10. Roman Alexandrowicz (proper spelling), doctor of law, prominent Lwów attorney in the interwar period, art lover, childhood friend of Ostap Ortwin's.

11. Karol Irzykowski (1873–1944), literary critic, writer.

TO STEFAN SZUMAN

Letters 3–5

1. Schulz took part, in July 1932, in a voluntary vacation course offered by the Ministry of Education at Żywiec for craft teachers and others, where Stefan Szuman gave a series of lectures.

2. Schulz read Rilke only in the original German and regarded him as his patron saint in aesthetics and art.

3. The title of one of the poems by Szuman discussed in the letter.

4. Quoted from a Szuman poem.

5. Title of a Szuman poem.

6., 7., 8. Titles of Szuman poems.

9. *"Ptaki"* ("Birds") is a tale by Schulz which was his debut as a writer. It was published under the name of Bronisław Schulz in *Wiadomości Literackie* no. 52, 1933. It later went into the making of *Cinnamon Shops* (1934).

10. Title of a Szuman poem.

11. *Neue Sachlichkeit* (roughly "The New Objectivity," sober and purpose-oriented style) was a movement in German art (important at first chiefly in architecture and associated with the *Bauhaus* group) which originated in 1923. It decried imitative ornamentation, decorative kitsch, and conspicuous consumption of space.

12. Title of a Szuman poem.

13. Bruno's elder brother, Izydor Schulz, occupied a high position in the Polish oil industry. Izydor died suddenly on January 20, 1935, after returning from a conference in Warsaw. Henceforth Bruno's semi-invalid sister, her son, and a cousin depended entirely on him for their livelihood.

14. *Cinnamon Shops* appeared in the book jacket designed by Schulz; some other design sketches of his meant for the jacket have also been preserved. The book edition of *Shops* did not have illustrations in the text.

15. Theater and film director (1878–1953), who later worked in Hollywood and at the Metropolitan Opera in New York.

TO ARNOLD SPAET

Letters 6–8

1. The papers Spaet left behind were consigned to the Ossolineum archives at Wrocław (Breslau) by Dr. Krystyna Śreniowska, whose father had taken care of Arnold Spaet until his death. Schulz's letters to Spaet from Dr. Śreniowska's collections are now kept in the Manuscript Division of the National Ossolinsky Library at Wrocław.

2. Even before the start of his teaching career, Schulz had spent some time at Kudowa, a popular Sudeten spa.

3. Richard Dehmel, *Poezje,* translated and introduced by Arnold Spaet, Lwów, 1933. Dehmel (1863–1920) was a prominent German poet, friend of S. Przybyszewski's, author of the verse collection *Erlösungen* ("Redemptions"), 1891, among other works.

4. Bernard Mantel, Doctor of Philosophy, Germanist, teacher of German, French, and elementary philosophy in the public high school at Drohobycz. Murdered by the Germans in 1942. "[Jakub] Blatt, principal of the [private] academy at Drohobycz, and the high school teacher [Bernard] Mantel spent the last moments of their lives during the November *Aktion* in 1942 at Drohobycz in discussion of the ideas of Plato." (*Ruch podziemny w ghettach i obozach: materiały i documenty,* Warszawa, Łódź, Kraków, 1946, p. 44). (*The Underground Movement in the Ghettos and Camps: Materials and Documentation*).

TO JULIAN TUWIM

Letter 9

1. Julian Tuwim (1894–1953), poet, cofounder of *Skamander.*

2. Schulz here gives thanks to Tuwim for a letter (not extant) in which, almost immediately after *Cinnamon Shops* appeared, Tuwin expressed to him his delight with the book. Important about this may be the discrepancy between the actual date of publication of *Cinnamon Shops* (December 1933) and that printed on the title page (1934).

3. This probably refers to a poetry reading held in the twenties at Drohobycz by Tuwim and Slonimski.

TO TADEUSZ AND ZOFIA BREZA

Letters 10–19

1. Tadeusz Breza (1905–1970), novelist and essayist.

2. Drohobycz and its surroundings were the scene of all the mythical adventures —based on the author's "spiritual autobiography"—experienced by the characters of *Cinnamon Shops;* see J. Ficowski, *Regiony wielkiej herezii* (*Regions of Great Heresy*), Kraków, 1967, chapter on *"Fantomy a realność"* ("Phantoms and Reality").

3. Schulz suffered from kidney-stone inflammations all his life.

4. The subject of this leave, which to Schulz was the essential condition of more intensive literary work, turns up in many letters. After a great deal of effort, and thanks to potent interests mobilized in his behalf, he was released from teaching duties for 1936.

5. *Rocznik Literatury* (properly: *Rocznik Literacki, Literary Yearbook*) started publication in 1932. It was chiefly made up of reviews of the literary output of the preceding year. Schulz's topic here is not the review of *Cinnamon Shops* in the *Yearbook* (written by Leon Piwiński) but a note by Tadeusz Breza on the subject, headlined "*At the Margin of* Literary Yearbook *for 1933.*" Another piece by Breza, titled "*Odprawa Pesymistom,*"

"Retort to the Pessimists," appeared in the daily *Kurier Poranny* of November 10, 1934, no. 312, signed "T.B-a."

6. Schulz was the teacher of drawing and handicrafts at the King Władysław Jagiełło State Classical High School at Drohobycz.

7. Breza's *Adam Grywald* was published in 1936.

8. Mieczysław Grydzewski (1894–1970), journalist and publisher of *Wiadomości Literackie*.

9. Schulz probably has in mind *Mesjasz* (*The Messiah*).

10. Works of Schulz's written before *Cinnamon Shops,* which along with some more recent ones were to be combined into a collection under the *Hourglass* title (1937).

11. "*Dziewictwo* ("Virginity") is a novella by Gombrowicz in the collection *Memoirs of the Time of Immaturity* (1933).

12. The novella "*Wiosna*" ("Spring"), first published in *Skamander,* nos. 74 and 75, 1936, later incorporated in the collection *Sanatorium.* The first version lacked Chapter 17, which Schulz added later for the *Skamander* book.

13. Schulz's review of Breza's *Adam Grywald* appeared in *Tygodnik Ilustrowany,* nos. 3 and 4, 1937, under the title *Książka o miłości.*

14. Wacław Czarski was the editor-in-chief of *Tygodnik Ilustrowany.* He died in exile after the war.

15. See Note 9.

16. The Young Writer's Prize was awarded annually by the Polish Academy of Literature between 1933 and 1939.

17. Zofia and Tadeusz Breza were married on June 3, 1937.

18. This passage refers to Breza's opinion of Schulz's second book, *Sanatorium,* conveyed to Schulz in the shape of remarks and observations in a letter to him. But no review of *Sanatorium* by Breza appeared in print.

TO ZENON WAŚNIEWSKI

Letters 20–27

1. Zenon Waśniewski (1891–1945), painter and graphic artist, cofounder and editor of *Kamena,* a literary monthly published in the years 1933–1939. In 1942 Waśniewski was arrested by the Gestapo, held first in the dungeons of Lublin Castle, then taken through Majdanek, Oświęcim (Auschwitz), and Oranienburg to Bergen-Belsen. He perished there in April 1945, having failed to survive Hitler by a few days.

2. Juliusz Flaszen, doctor of chemistry, owner of a medical laboratory in Cracow.

3. When he describes his prints inaccurately as "aquaforts," nitric acid etchings, he means his *cliché-verre,* etched-glass technique. See note 6 to Ortwin correspondence.

4. Kazimierz Andrzej Jaworski (1897–1973), poet, translator of Russian and Czech poetry. After spending the war in the Nazi camp of Sachsenhausen, in 1945 he returned to editorial work on the revived *Kamena.*

5. Aleksander Blok's "Garden of Nightingales," translated by K. A. Jaworski, with lino cuts by Z. Waśniewski. Series *Kamena,* no. 2, 1934.

6. The demonstration class in handicrafts took place on March 23, 1934, "in classroom 1B of the Classical High School 'King Władysław Jagiełło' in Drohobycz in the presence of Franciszek Madyda, director of the Center for Methodology in the Teaching of Workshop Skills at Public High School VIII in Lwów (Bruno Schulz reporting)." *Proceedings of the Classical High School at Drohobycz, 1934.*

7. The reference is to the locality of Zwiniacz (not Zwiniącz, as Schulz writes it several times), a village in Czortków county (now Chortkov, U.S.S.R.). It lies on the Zwiniacz, a creek of the same name, which empties into the Seret. Zenon Waśniewski's brother had a manor farm there, where Zenon was a frequent vacation guest.

8. Zenon Waśniewski also wrote poetry and published it in his magazine.

9. A print with the dedication: "To his fellow student Zenon Waśniewski with greetings from Bruno Schulz."

10. *"Nocy lipcowe"* ("July Nights") was the original title of the story that went into the makeup of the collection *Sanatorium* under the title "*Noc lipcowa* ("A Night in July"). Eventually Schulz changed his mind and had "A Night in July" published in *Sygnały,* no. 12, 1934.

11. *Rój* was a Warsaw publishing house devoted mainly to belles-lettres, Polish and translated, and to books of popular science. It was owned by Marian Kister and Melchior Wańkowicz.

12. Aleksander Wat, properly A. Chwat (1900–1967), poet, writer, translator. In the years 1920–1925 he was one of the exponents of Polish futurism.

Adam Ważyk (1905–), poet, writer, translator, literary scholar. After the Fourth Partition of Poland following the Nazi and Soviet invasions of 1939, he became coeditor of the journal *Nowe Widnokręgi* (*New Horizons*) in Russian-annexed Lwów. Schulz was invited to contribute in 1940, but his work was rejected by the editors.

Stanisław Brucz (1899–), journalist and translator.

Pola Gojawiczyńska (1896–1963), novelist and short-story writer, author of fiction descriptive of social groupings and manners.

13. Aleksander Leszczyc, active in Lwów theater life until 1931, became an art dealer who took in on commission the paintings and graphic works of major Polish artists, such as Lasocki and Norblin, as well as provincial artists of the Lwów and Kraków regions. He organized exhibitions in many places, most frequently at Truskawiec and other resorts during the tourist season.

14. See note 7.

15. Schulz was accorded a sick leave for the period from August 20 to September 15, 1934. (*Proceedings of the Classical High School at Drohobycz,* 1935.)

16. Wojtów, the ministerial inspector's name.

17. *Ilustrowany Kurier Codzienny* (*Illustrated Daily Mail*) (IKC), the influential Kraków daily of the period between 1910 and 1939, with its weekly supplement *Kurier Literacko-Naukowy* (*Courier of Literature and Science*). It eventually became a national medium, reaching a circulation of 250,000 in the interwar years.

18. The date of this letter seems to indicate that it was written one day before the end of Schulz's leave. His leave must have been prolonged to October 1, though, for it is not until his letter of October 6 that we read: "My medical leave has run out, and I am back at work in school."

19. "*Druga jesień*" ("A Second Fall") was first published in *Kamena*, no. 3, 1934. The story was subsequently added by Schulz to the collection *Sanatorium*. The manuscript remained with the papers left by Zenon Waśniewski on his death. It is the only extant manuscript of Schulz's literary works. A facsimile of it was prepared for publication in book form under the editorship of Jerzy Ficowski and published by *Wydawnictwo Literackie* (Literary Publishers) in Kraków in 1973.

20. Instead of the year's leave applied for, Schulz was granted six months from January 1 to June 30, but only in 1936. Added to the normal two months of school vacations, he thus had eight months to spend on writing. One of the products of this period was "*Wiosna*" ("Spring").

TO THE EDITORS OF *SYGNAŁY*

Letters 28–33

1. Tadeusz Hollender (1910–1943), poet, editor (1933–34) of the Lwów periodical *Sygnały* (Signals). Killed by the Germans.

2. Karol Kuryluk (1910–1967), writer active in social and cultural affairs, cofounder and editor of the Lwów journal *Sygnały*. Trained in Polish language and literature under distinguished scholars, Kuryluk founded his leftist journal when barely twenty-three years old and managed to keep it alive until the German-Russian invasions of 1939, despite lawsuits, confiscations, and bans against it by the authoritarian régime of the thirties. *Sygnały* was a monthly, from 1938 fortnightly, journal of a sociocultural orientation, which fought against the Fascist course advocated in the rightist student papers and (less openly) by sections of the government. It was these forces which caused Poland to participate in Hitler's outrageous dismembering of Czechoslovakia, her Slavic brother nation and ally, in 1938. We quote from Churchill's ominous remarks in Parliament in September: "It was no doubt very gratifying from the wreck of Czechoslovakia to acquire Teschen [Cieszyń], about which there was a long story. But after the feast comes the bill. The bill is presented by the German landlord. . . . There are many large items in the account; among these may be mentioned Danzig and the Polish Corridor [Gdansk and Polish Pomerania]." Kuryluk played a prominent role in Polish journalism under the Soviet occupation from 1940 to 1944 and later held high public offices, including that of Minister of Culture and Art, under the Moscow-dominated postwar régime.

3. "A Night in July." See note 10 to the Waśniewski correspondence.

4. Wilhelm Korabiowski, actor well-known from radio programs, literary critic, who contributed reviews to such media as *Nowe Czasy* (*New Times*) and *Pion* (*Plummet*), including a review of Schulz's *Cinnamon Shops* ("*Spóźniona Recenzja*" ["Belated Review"], *Nowe Czasy*, no. 23, 1935).

5. According to oral testimony from Anna Baranowska, who was Kuryluk's companion at the time, this visit took place in June 1934.

6. Korabiowski was a comedian on the Lwów radio program *Na wesołej lwowskiej fali* ("On the Merry Wave of Lwów"). His role was that of a comic elderly dignitary, Councillor Strońć.

7. Maria Kuncewicz (1899–   ), prominent writer, representative of sociopsychological realism in the Polish novel.

8. One of two sections of this translation of *The Trial*, with corrections by Schulz's hand, has been preserved in galley proof in the files of *Sygnały* in Lwów.

9. It is not clear whose prose Schulz refers to here. Schulz may have sent in a piece by Anna Płockier, whom he had met in Borysław in 1938. She was a painter who was also exploring a talent for writing.

10. The numbering of Schulz's house had been changed from 10 to 8.

11. *"Ojczyzna"* ("Fatherland"), a fragment from a work now lost, was published in *Sygnały*, no. 59, 1938.

TO WACŁAW CZARSKI

Letter 34

1. Wacław Czarski, chief editor of *Tygodnik Ilustrowany*, died in emigration after the war. Schulz's letter to Czarski is now the property of Jadwiga Sosińska.

2. *"Edzio"* ("Eddie"), a story with five drawings by Schulz, first published in *Tygodnik Ilustrowany*, no. 4, 1935.

3. *"Wywiad z Brunonem Schulzem"* ("Interview with Bruno Schulz") appeared in *Tygodnik Ilustrowany*, no. 17, 1935 (See p. 107).

TO WŁADYSŁAW ZAWISTOWSKI

Letters 35 and 36

1. Władysław Zawistowski (?–1944), theater and literary critic, public figure in the arts, at that time held the post of director, Department of Arts, Ministry of Religious Beliefs and Public Education. With Wierzyński he was a cofounder of the *Skamander* group and, beginning in 1918, editor of the journal *Pro Arte et Studio*. Deported from Warsaw after the Uprising, he died on December 31, 1944, at the Neuengamme concentration camp near Hamburg.
Schulz's letter to Zawistowski is presently owned by Jadwiga Sosińska.

2. Kazimierz Wierzyński (1894–1969), poet, cofounder of *Skamander*.

TO KAZIMIERZ TRUCHANOWSKI

Letters 37–39

1. Kazimierz Truchanowski (1904–), prose writer, translator. The letters to Truchanowski here published are in the possession of Truchanowski himself (or his assigns); more may still be found among his papers.

2. See note 1 to the letters to Czarski.

3. Two *cliché-verre* graphics preserved in the collection of Kazimierz Truchanowski (see note 6 to the Ortwin correspondence).

4. A section of Kafka's *Trial* titled "At the Attorney's" appeared in *Tygodnik Ilustrowany*, nos. 8–9, 1936.

5. "*Father and Adela*," a pencil drawing in K. Truchanowski's collection.

6. An episode from Chapter I of Truchanowski's novel *The Plot of the Demiurges*, begun several years before the war, completed and published in 1947.

7. *Gości* ("Guests"), a novella which formed part of Truchanowski's first book, *Ulica Wszystkich Swiętych* (*All Saints' Street*, 1936).

8. Emanuel Pilpel, born about 1893, the son of a well-known bookseller in town, died in Drohobycz of cancer in 1936. He had been Schulz's schoolmate and friend of long standing. In his father's bookshop Schulz used to meet with Emanuel (nicknamed Mundek), Stanisław Weingarten (murdered by the Germans in Łódź), and Michał Chajes. They carried on conversations on literature and art, and the rich book collection of the Pilpels became the source of young Bruno's wide erudition, in foreign literatures as well as in philosophy and psychology, aesthetics and art history.

9. The story "*Wiosna*" ("Spring"). See note 12 to the Breza correspondence.

TO STANISŁAW IGNACY WITKIEWICZ

An Interview

1. The text of this interview was composed during the winter of 1934–1935.

2. Goethe's ballad *Der Erlkönig.*

3. Schulz's admiration for Mann's *Joseph und seine Brüder* (1933–1943) knew no bounds, and tributes to it occurred frequently in his conversations and letters. Schulz regarded Mann as the greatest writer among his contemporaries and knew his works from many readings in the original. Next to the Joseph cycle he held *Buddenbrooks* (1900) and *The Magic Mountain* (1924) to be Mann's finest achievements.

TO ANDRZEJ PLEŚNIEWICZ

Letters 41–43

1. Andrzej Pleśniewicz (1909–1945), literary critic and essayist. Schulz had become acquainted with Andrzej Pleśniewicz in Warsaw at the start of his six months' leave, which began on January 1, 1936.

2. See note 8 to the Truchanowski correspondence.

3. The "dust-up with Witold" in *Studio* provoked a number of articles in various periodicals. Andrzej Pleśniewicz offered his commentary to the exchange between Gombrowicz and Schulz in *Kurier Poranny,* no. 329, November 26, 1936. In a piece titled "*Rozwichrzone problematy dyskusji literackiej—Spór o doktorową*" ("Tangled Problems of Literary Discussion: Quarrel over a Doctor's Wife"), Pleśniewicz defended Schulz's ideological and artistic theses. Other articles included J. E. Skiwski's "*Łańcuch szczęścia*" ("Chain of Happiness"), *Tygodnik Ilustrowany,* no. 42, 1936, which was answered by Gombrowicz in a guest column article called "*Łańcuch nieporozumień*" ("Chain of Misunderstandings"), *Studio,* no. 9, 1936. This was followed by W. Pietrzak in his article "*Swięte szukanie*" ("Sacred Search"), *Studio,* no. 9, 1936.

4. Schulz's story "*Wiosna*" ("Spring"), which was published in two successive issues of *Skamander* in 1936, was subjected by the editor to a number of peculiar unauthorized changes. They were quite characteristic of the spread of a native form of Nazism in Poland in the thirties, very similar also to the xenophobic, "cultural," anti-Semitism exploited with deadly effect by Stalin's "rootless cosmopolites" slogan in Russia. To the mind of the editor, Mieczysław Grydzewski, Schulz's reputation was evidently useful to his magazine, but his diction was not "native" or pithily Polish enough. The international —latinate and Gallic—vocabulary of aesthetics and criticism he used apparently was an embarrassment. Therefore he made the following kinds of replacements—not all absurd semantically—in Schulz's language (approximate English examples follow, inadequate because the language has not been "pure" in over a milennium, and American lexical snobbery tends to work the opposite way): "answerable" (responsible), "stamp collecting" (philately), "foreseeing" (anticipating), "pauses" (intervals), "guess" (conjecture), and so on.

A more insolent example of the same tendency came from the editor of *Wiadomości Literackie,* who in December 1933, just before *Cinnamon Shops* came out, published Schulz's story "*Ptaki*" ("Birds") under the Polishified name *Bronisław* Schulz. See note 9 to the Szuman correspondence.

5. Stefan Napierski, pseudonym for Marek Eiger (1899–1940), poet, critic, translator. It is not clear what Schulz is referring to here, but three years later, in a critical pronouncement in *Ateneum,* no. 1, 1939, he declared Schulz's work devoid of any artistic value.

TO MENDEL NEUGRÖSCHL

Letter 44

1. Mendel Neugröschl, born at Sącz, attorney, author of several poetry cycles, editor of an anthology of translations from Polish poetry into Yiddish. He belonged to the group of chiefly Yiddish Lwów writers called *Cusztajer* (in Polish transliteration of Yiddish), meaning *Zusteuer, Contributor,* in standard German. From Vienna, where he lived, he was deported to the Dachau concentration camp in 1938, but was released thanks to energetic representations by PEN International. He died after the war.

2. Debora Vogel (1902–1942), Ph.D., aestheticist, author of two poetry collections in Yiddish and a volume of Polish prose, *Akacje kwitną* (*The Acacias Are Blooming*), 1935. See Introduction.

TO MIECZYSŁAW GRYDZEWSKI

Letter 45

1. Mieczysław Grydzewski (1894–1970), publicist, founder, and editor-in-chief of the weekly *Wiadomości Literackie* and the monthly *Skamander*. He died as an emigré in London.

2. Emil Breiter (1886–1943), jurist, publicist, literary critic on the staff of *Wiadomości Literackie.* Arrested in the Warsaw area, where he lived in hiding, he was killed by the Gestapo in 1943.

3. This comment is slightly disingenuous, since *Shops* came out in December of 1933.

TO GEORGES ROSENBERG

Letter 46

1. Maria Chasin (also *Chazen*), friend of Schulz's, eminent pianist. She lived in Łódź until the German-Russian invasion, and eventually settled in New York City. See Introduction.

2. As previously noted, the numbering of Schulz's house had been changed from 10 to 8.

TO ROMANA HALPERN

Letters 47–85

1. Tadeusz Szturm de Sztrem (1892–1968), a friend of Witkiewicz's. He was a well-known social activist, from 1912 on a member of the revolutionary wing of the Polish Socialist Party (PPS). During World War II he was an active representative of the WRN. After the war he worked on a history of the PPS, and on an edition of the works of L. Krzywicki and L. Landau.

2. "*Emeryt*" ("The Old Age Pensioner") was among the stories gathered in *Sanatorium.* It was first published, with six illustrations, by Schulz in *Wiadomości Literackie,* nos. 51–52, 1935.

3. André Gide (1869–1951) was, like all the prominent French writers, much noted and discussed in Poland. Their leading observer and interpreter was the brilliant francophile critic, Tadeusz Boy-Żeleński, whose Polish version of *Les Caves du Vatican* appeared in 1937.

4. Stefanek, Stef, etc. was Romana Halpern's son. Now Stephen J. Howard, he lives in the United States. He made available copies of the letters written by Schulz to his mother, which he had preserved.

5. The death of Izydor Schulz had left Bruno the sole support of his family. See note 13 of the Szuman letters.

6. The letters to Debora Vogel, including all those from which *Cinnamon Shops* evolved, were located among Vogel's papers in her Lwów apartment in 1938, but later perished with Debora and her family.

7. Schulz's lecture on Thomas Mann. References in correspondence from Vogel (a few of her letters survived) indicate that it had been prepared, but never delivered.

8. Emil Zegadłowicz (1888–1941), poet, novelist, dramatist, author of the novel *Zmory* (*Nightmares*), 1935.

9. GUS, short for *Główny Urząd Statystyczny*. In this Central Bureau of Statistics Tadeusz Szturm de Sztrem occupied a position that allowed him to help many job seekers.

10. Samuel Lieberwerth (ca. 1915–1942), young painter, former pupil of Schulz's at the Drohobycz high school. He graduated from the Warsaw Academy of Fine Arts in 1938 and left for France on a fellowship. When France was overrun by Hitler's armies in 1940, Lieberwerth was serving as a driver in one of the divisions (Second Infantry Division, commanded by General Prugar-Kettling) of the Polish army salvaged from southern Poland via Romania in 1939–40; he was taken prisoner and killed by the Germans that year.

11. This was the final breach between Schulz and his fiancée, Józefina Szelińska, although they met a few times afterward under changed circumstances.

12. This review failed to appear in *Wiadomości Literackie*, but an article by Schulz about the work of the Danish novelist Karen Michaelis (1872–1950) and Maria Kuncewicz, *"U wspólnej mety"* ("At the Shared Goal"), was published by *Pion* in no. 35, 1937.

13. *si parva cum magnis*. Cf. Vergil's *si parva licet componere magnis* (if it is possible to compare small things with great).

14. Józefina Szelińska, Schulz's former fiancée, had been employed by Szturm at GUS.

15. Izaak Feuerberg, for whom Schulz intervened here, was rescued, survived the war, and lived in Warsaw during the seventies.

16. Wilhelm Schulz, one of Bruno's two nephews, was killed by the Germans in 1943.

17. Julian Ramberg, Slavic scholar, high school teacher, principal of the Leszno Street school in Warsaw; he was killed by the Germans in Lwów in July 1941, soon after they invaded Soviet Russia.

18. Wacław Berent (1873–1940), short-story writer and translator.

19. Edmund Husserl (1859–1938), the founder of modern phenomenology. The transcendental idealism he offered aroused Schulz's interest and seemed akin to his own views, leading Schulz to seek personal contact with the Polish disciple of Husserl, Roman Ingarden (1893–1970).

20. The novella *Die Heimkehr* (*Homecoming*), completed in 1937 but never published, has not survived. It was illustrated by the Poznań artist Egga van Haardt, who later falsified Schulz's judgment of her work.

21. Maria Kasprowicz née Bunina (1892–1968), Marusia to her friends, a talented Russian girl who at age eighteen married the celebrated Polish peasant-poet Jan Kasprowicz (1860–1926).

22. Izydor Berman, pseudonym "Iber," translator, journalist, and editor in Lwów, who translated J. Wittlin's *Sól Ziemi* (*Salt of the Earth*) into German. He edited the satirical magazine *Chochoł.*

23. Wanda Kragen (1893–), translator. Her first publication was a volume of poetry, *Poza Rzeczywistością* (*Beyond Reality*), 1931. This was followed by numerous translations, chiefly from German and Anglo-American literature.

24. Grydz, popular nickname of Mieczysław Grydzewski, editor of *Wiadomości Literackie.* Schulz's novella *The Comet* was published in his journal in 1938, no. 35.

25. See note 16 to the Breza correspondence.

26. Leon Chwistek (1884–1944), logician and mathematician, philosopher, painter. He was a member and leading theoretician of a Formalist group.

27. Egga van Haardt, painter and graphic artist of Poznań. She illustrated Schulz's story *Kometa* (*The Comet*) in *Wiadomości Literackie* no. 35, 1938, as well as the novella *Die Heimkehr.*

28. Wanda Melcer (1896–1972), writer, reporter.

29. Artur Sandauer (1913–), literary critic, writer, translator.

30. Leon Chwistek's family.

31. Schulz was mistaken. Józef Wittlin did not nominate Schulz's book for the *Wiadomości* award. It was Maria Dąbrowska among the jurors who did, but she supposedly had him third on her list. Only Maria Kuncewicz put *Sanatorium* first.

32. *Chochoł,* the satirical weekly published in Lwów by Izydor Berman in 1938. Its first issue contained a parody by W. Korabiowski titled *"A la manière de . . . Bruno Schulz."*

33. *Pion,* no. 5, 1938.

34. Jan Emil Skiwski (1894–), publicist, literary critic. During the occupation he collaborated with the Germans, editing a gutter sheet under the auspices of the Goebbels organization *(Reichspropagandaamt).* He emigrated to the West in 1945, and was subsequently sentenced in absentia to life in prison and loss of citizen's rights. His articles about Gombrowicz were *"Kurza pierś"* ("Chicken Breast"), *Kronika Polski i Świata,* no. 2, 1938, and *"Jeszcze kawałek kurzej piersi"* ("Another Piece of Chicken Breast"), no. 3, 1938.

Stanisław Piasecki (1900–1941), activist of the quasi-Fascist movement of the late thirties, *Obóz Narodowo-Radykalny* (Radical National Camp), known mainly for its pro-Nazi leanings and the anti-Semitic rioting its student members introduced into Polish universities. Piasecki edited the weekly *Prosto z Mostu.* His Polish nationalism had no use for the slavophobic racism of the invader, however, and he was executed by the Germans in Palmiry.

35. Egga van Haardt. See note 28 above.

36. The correspondence between Schulz and Thomas Mann (then living in self-imposed exile in Zurich) consisted of a few letters exchanged, beginning probably in 1938. It was broken off by the German invasion in 1939.

37. The recipient of the *Wiadomości* award in 1938 was Jeremi Wasiutyński for his novel *Kopernik (Copernicus)*, 1937.

38. Schulz wrote reviews of foreign fiction between April 1936 and September 1937. He had only a few items at a time to choose from, put before him by the publishers involved, hence the list of his reviews is no guide to his literary tastes.

39. Henri de Montherlant (1896–1972), the French novelist, three volumes of whose tetralogy *The Young Girls* (1936–39) appeared in Polish as *Dziewczęta* in 1937.

40. Leon Pomirowski (1891–1943), critic, literary theorist; the review by him to which Schulz alludes was *"Przezwyciężenie okresu dojrzewania"* ("Overcoming the Time of Immaturity") in *Tygodnik Ilustrowany*, no. 8, 1938.

41. No such article was published in *Skamander.*

42. *The Tales of Jacob,* the first volume of *Joseph and His Brothers.* See note 3 to Witkiewicz interview.

43. Schulz's German story *Die Heimkehr* was to be taken to Zurich by the mother of Jerzy Brodnicki, a friend of Egga van Haardt.

44. NDK

45. *Szpilki*

46. Panic

47. "Kister does not send me the money" refers to *Rój*'s delay in sending royalty payments for *Sanatorium*.

48. I. Berman's review appeared in *Nasza Opinia,* a Jewish weekly of politics, social questions, and literature, published in Polish in Lwów between 1931 and 1939. The year was 1938, but exact data are unavailable.

49. Marian Promiński (1908–1971), writer, dramatist, critic, on the staff of the Lwów *Sygnały,* where his review of Schulz appeared in no. 40, 1938.

50. Natan Spiegel (1902–1943?), painter, member of the *Start* group of Lwów artists, landscapist, water colorist, whose work was shown in London. He perished in the Łódź ghetto.

51. Jerzy Reitman, engineer, proprietor of the sanatorium at Korostow.

52. Maria Dąbrowska (1889–1965), eminent novelist and essayist, famous above all for a four-volume epic, *Noce i Anie* (*Nights and Days*), a quasi-Tolstoyan epic spanning most of Polish twentieth-century political and social history. See note 32.

53. The *Anschluss* (Union), the destruction of the Austrian republic by a Nazi invasion, took place on March 15, 1938. It was followed by the dismantling of Czechoslovakia that autumn and the following spring, and the attack on Poland on September 1, 1939.

54. A summer resort near Otwock, southeast of Warsaw.

55. A Polish edition of Aldous Huxley's *Eyeless in Gaza* (1936) appeared in 1938. Schulz was the author of the review of Huxley's *Music at Night* (which came out in Polish in *Rój* in 1936) in *Tygodnik Ilustrowany,* no. 6, 1936, under the title *"Wędrowki Sceptyka"* ("A Skeptic's Wanderings").

56. Witold Gombrowicz's article, *"Twórczość B. Schulza"* ("The Literary Work of B. Schulz"), appeared in *Kurier Poranny,* no. 112, 1938 (supplement).

57. Stefan Otwinowski (1910–1976), writer, dramatist, publicist. He did not publish anything about Schulz in *Czas* (*Time*).

58. Apparently a rumor only. *Prosto z Mostu* never published a favorable review of Schulz, either by Laszowski or by anyone else.

59. Jules Romains, properly Louis Farigoule (1885–1972), the French poet and writer, proponent of "unaninimism" in literature. The hoped-for meeting in Paris did not materialize.

60. Marian Eile (1910–1984), graphic artist, publicist, on the staff of *Wiadomości Literackie.* The magazine's current issue was on display in its show window.

61. E. Breiter's review appeared in *Wiadomości Literackie,* no. 23, 1938.

62. Schulz's letter to *Wiadomości* (see Letter 45) was printed in no. 26 of June 19, 1938.

63. "Pan Gryps" was the chief figure in a satirical comic strip carried in *Wiadomości.*

64. Wojciech Natanson (1904–   ), critic of literature and theater, translator of French literature.

65. Orbis is the official Polish tourist office.

66. Samuel Lieberwerth left for France on a fellowship shortly after this, in the closing days of December.

67. Kazimiera Rychter (1899–1963) was an actress specializing in recitation of poetry.

68. Menasze and Efraim Seidenbeutel (1903–1945), twin brothers, painters. Paintings on which they worked jointly were signed only with their surname. They did chiefly still lifes, townscapes, figure compositions. During the Nazi occupation they found themselves in the Białystok ghetto, where they witnessed the death of 60,000 of its inhabitants and were among the handful left alive in 1943, when the ghetto was liquidated. They were shunted among a number of Nazi camps, the last one being Flossenburg. In April 1945, just before the liberation by Allied troops, the Seidenbeutels and others were murdered by the German camp guards.

69. Bolesław Leśmian (1878–1937), poet. The bizarre quality of his imagination and the role of myth and mythologizing in his poetry made him a creative phenomenon as autonomous and original as Schulz, however disparate the worlds of *Napój cienisty* (*Shadowy Drink*), 1936, and *Cinnamon Shops.* Schulz had delighted in Leśmian's poetry for years, and *Napój* as well as *Łąka* (*Meadow*), 1920, were both in his library. He left his copy of *Łąka* with his fiancée, however, and he is here ordering a new one.

70. Some details concerning this new work are found in Schulz's reply to the *Wiadomości* questionnaire headed "From the Workshops of Polish Writers and Scholars," *Wiadomości Literackie,* no. 17, 1939.

71. See Letter 46.

72. This was to be an impressionistic report on archival collections in Warsaw. For unknown reasons it was never written.

73. The affair of Egga Haardt's forgery was never cleared up by explanations or corrections. Her acquaintance with Schulz was broken off.

74. Zygfryd Bienstock, winner of the Krynica jazz competition in 1938. Drafted into the Red Army during the war; after discharge went to the West, lived in Italy and later in Israel and the U.S., continuing his career in music.

75. This clearly refers to the person who accompanied Witkiewicz on his last journey and witnessed his suicide on September 18, 1939.

76. The publishing house of Jakub Mortkowicz, a distinguished firm founded in 1912.

77. Karl Hofer (1878–1955), German painter and graphic artist active in figure and landscape compositions, also in lithography. His work shows features of symbolism and a visionary expressionism.

78. The monthly *Pióro* in its issue no. 1, 1939, carried an article by Ludwik Fryde, titled "About Gombrowicz's *Ferdydurke*"; it contained three sentences averse to Schulz's work. Fryde (1912–1942), a literary critic and essayist, was killed by the Germans in Nowogródek (Nowogród).

TO MARIAN JACHIMOWICZ

Letters 86–90

1. Laura Wñrzberg (1913–ca. 1942), employed before the war in the library "Alfa" in Drohobycz, tried her skills in literature; was encouraged in this by Schulz. Killed by the Nazis.

2. Jachimowicz was a taxidermist who prepared zoological specimens, a skill which helped him to earn a livelihood during his long sojourn in Hungary.

3. Polmin—the acronym of the *Państwowa Fabryka Olejów Mineralnych* (State Mineral Oil Plant).

4. A writers' conference was organized at Drohobycz with Emil Zegadłowicz.

5. Juliusz Wit, properly Witkower (1902–1942), poet connected with the Kraków avant garde, murdered by the Germans in Lwów. Schulz published a review titled "A New Poet" about Wit's book *Lamps,* in *Sygnały,* no. 23, 1936.

6. Marek Holzmann, aka Singer (1919–1982), well-known contemporary photographer, who reproduced the Schulz drawings included in Jerzy Ficowski's *Regiony wielkiej herezji* (*Regions of Grand Heresy*), 1967, in Schulz's *Druga jesień* (*A Second Fall*), 1973, and in the present edition. Before the German invasion of the U.S.S.R. in 1941, he directed the library in Borysław.

TO ANNA PŁOCKIER

Letters 91–108

1. Jachimowicz, who was working at the time with Marek Holzmann in the Drohobycz library, was a friend of Anna Płockier's and her fiancé, Marek Zwillich.

2. Seweryn Gottlieb, jurist, patron of art, author of treatises on painting and exhibition notes. Killed by the Germans in Lwów in 1941.

3. Rilke's *Notebooks of Malte Laurids Brigge,* 1910.

4. Hersz (Henryk) Weber (1904–1942), innovative painter, art theorist, poet. Between 1939 and 1941 he was active in the work of the Lwów Societies of Writers

and of Sculptors. Upon the seizure of Lwów by the Germans in 1941, he took shelter with friends, then fled to Rzeszów in southern Poland, where he died when the Jewish population of the town was wiped out by the Germans.

5. Marek Zwillich (1912–1941), also called Fleischer by his father's name, painter, fiancé of Anna Płockier. He was murdered by the barbarous Ukrainian militia, operating under SS auspices.

6. Artur Rzeczyca, properly Buchsbaum or Buxbaum (1910–1942), poet of the Czechowicz circle, killed by the Germans in Drohobycz in 1942 after his attempt to escape across the Hungarian frontier.

7. *Nowe Widnokręgi* (*New Horizons*), a periodical published in Polish in the U.S.S.R. from 1941 to 1946. The flavor of its title (compare the titles *Red Newland, Neues Deutschland,* etc.) gave it away as a typical Soviet propaganda vehicle. In its maiden year it was published in Lwów as a socioliterary monthly, associated with the Union of Soviet Writers.

8. Wanda Wasilewska (1905–1964), pedagogue, editor, writer; politically active.

9. Adam Ważyk, then on the editorial board of *Nowe Widnokręgi* (*New Horizons*), rejected the contribution which had been sent in by Schulz on the naive assumption that literary criteria governed editorial policy. The manuscript is lost.

10. Ben Horowitz (1895–1941), Yiddish poet, graphic artist, painter, translator of Polish poetry. He perished in Stanisławów soon after the entry of Nazi troops in late June.

11. Schulz had lent Anna Płockier his unpublished novella, *Die Heimkehr,* to read.

12. Hilda Berger, a young woman in her early twenties who had fled from Nazi persecution in Berlin. She worked for a time as a secretary in a German institution at Borysław. Now Mrs. Hilda Ohlsen, she survived the war, emigrated to Sweden, and is now living in the United States.

13. See note 12.

14. We owe the sole eyewitness account of Schulz's murder in the ghetto of Drohobycz on November 19, 1942, to a fellow townsman, Izydor Friedman, who survived this particular butchery and the whole Occupation thanks to false papers in which he figured as Tadeusz Lubowiecki. He retained this identity after the war, when he settled as an attorney in Gliwice in Silesia. Dr. Lubowiecki responded to Jerzy Ficowski's appeals in the postwar press for information on Schulz by sending a personal account, the relevant portion of which follows.

> I was a friend of his before the war and remained in close contact with him to the day of his death in the Drohobycz ghetto.
>
> As a Jew, I was assigned by the Drohobycz *Judenrat* to work in a library under Gestapo authority, and so was Schulz. This was a depository made up of all public and the major private libraries. . . . Its core collection was that of the Jesuits of Chyrow. It comprised ca. 100,000 volumes, which were to be cataloged or committed to destruction by Schulz and myself. This assignment lasted several months, was congenial and full of interest to us, and was paradise by comparison with the assignments drawn by other Jews. We spent long hours in conversation. Schulz informed me at the time that he had deposited all his papers, notes, and correspondence files with a Catholic outside the ghetto. Unfortunately he did not give me the person's name, or possibly I forgot it. We also discussed the possibility of Schulz's escaping to Warsaw. Friends [Szturm de Sztrem?] had sent him a [false] identity card from Warsaw. I provided him with currency and dollars, but he kept putting

off the departure day. He could not summon up the courage and meant to wait until I received "Aryan" papers. On a day I don't recall in 1942, known as Black Thursday in Drohobycz, the Gestapo carried out a massacre in the ghetto. We happened to be in the ghetto to buy food [instead of at work outside]. When we heard shooting and saw Jews run for their lives we too took to flight. Schulz, physically the weaker, was caught by a Gestapo agent called Guenther, who stopped him, put a revolver to his head, and fired twice. During the night I found his body, searched his pockets, and gave his documents and some notes I found there to his nephew Hoffman—who lost his life a month later. Toward morning I buried him in the Jewish cemetery. I was unable to identify his grave site after the liberation of Drohobycz in 1944.

Over several months in 1944 and 1945, when I worked at Drohobycz, I searched for Schulz's papers, having realized that a monograph should be devoted to him. I had an announcement placed in a Ukrainian paper published in Drohobycz, requesting the depositary of Schulz's documents to come forward and give his whereabouts. This search, unfortunately, turned up nothing. . . .

All I have in my possession is a small portrait sketch by Schulz, done in the manner so characteristic of him. . . .

INDEX